Apprentice in a Changing Trade

Jean-François Perret and
Anne-Nelly Perret-Clermont

with the collaboration of
**Danièle Golay Schilter, Claude Kaiser &
Luc-Olivier Pochon**

Translated into English by
Nicholas Emler

INFORMATION AGE PUBLISHING, INC.
Charlotte, NC • www.infoagepub.com

Library of Congress Cataloging-in-Publication Data

Perret, Jean-Frangois.
 [Apprendre un mitier. English]
 Apprentice in a changing trade / Jean-Frangois Perret and Anne-Nelly
Perret-Clermont with the collaboration of Danihle Golay Schilter, Claude
Kaiser & Luc-Olivier Pochon ; translated into English by Nicholas Emler.
     p. cm. – (Advances in cultural psychology)
 Includes bibliographical references.
 ISBN 978-1-61735-411-3 (pbk.) – ISBN 978-1-61735-412-0 (hardcover) –
ISBN 978-1-61735-413-7 (e-book)
1. Occupational training. 2. Technological innovations. 3. Educational
anthropology. I. Perret-Clermont, Anne Nelly. II. Title.
 HD5715.P47 2011
 378'.014–dc22

                          2011005766

Printed in the United States of America

CONTENTS

LEARNING FROM THE TRADE SCHOOL—LEARNING FOR LIVING

How culture is embedded in education is a fascinating theme with profound practical ramifications. While most of the discourses in the social sciences have been dedicated to the obvious features of the cultures of schooling—pupils' successes or failures on exams, bullying in peer groups, and classroom group dynamics—the central question of education and culture remains, How is learning at school linked with living within the society where schools, pupils, and teachers are embedded? This is not a simple question—these links not just *are*, but they are constantly in the process of *becoming*. Inventing new technology breaks down the traditional boundaries of the classroom or school itself—a pupil sitting with his or her cell phone at a computer terminal in school may be mentally very far away, linked in with some happening on the other side of the globe. Such immediacy of "being elsewhere" can be turned into an educational advantage (Krikonis & Valsiner, 2009), even if the breakdown of traditional boundaries of the educational spaces undermines the core of traditional schooling—the separation of formal education from its informal counterpart. An "electronically

Apprentice in a Changing Trade, pages vii–xi
Copyright © 2011 by Information Age Publishing
All rights of reproduction in any form reserved.

wired" exam writer in a confined locus for individual knowledge "testing" can be assisted by others from any place in the world—making the notion of individual performance into a very idealistic notion still entertained by institutional administrators.

The whole structure of relations between formal and informal education is changing. The social order of education as institution is in tension. In the middle of such change stands the perennial question, What is education for? Of course we know the socially desirable answer—it is a *value in itself.* Yet our social practices do not stop in that recognition—the super-imposed upon learning a set of narrower representations of its value. Getting certified by degrees that are awarded in lavish graduation ceremonies? Finding a socially appropriate marriage partner? Feeling good among similarly educated peers? Or—more productively—leading to the creation of new technologies, and even of new forms of social living? Education leads to mastery—which in our present-day world equals readiness to cope with rapid changes in the technological environments of our life and work.

It is the latter that is covered in this book—how apprenticeship in a school leads not merely to success in school, but to productivity in life. The setting for such learning is an idyllic place in Switzerland—a vocational training school in the Jura Mountains where young men are about to master the skills of watchmaking. We—the readers—are not capable of such mastery—yet there is much to learn from how ordinary young Swiss men negotiate their entrance into watchmaking. Such negotiation brings the present—young men's aspiration toward mastery—together with the centuries-long traditions of apprenticeship in technological excellence. The quality of Swiss watches has become a legend all over the world—yet the simple question of how one becomes a watchmaker has been left without much attention. The authors of this book take the latter question and analyze it in detail– in the context of one particular vocational school.

What can be said about culture in education in general terms by studying "just one" school? The answer to this question depends on the perspective. As a microcosm of the dynamic processes of change, all general features of such change can be investigated in that single case. *Everything general is expressed in highly variable particulars*—is the credo of contemporary idiographic science (Lamiell, 2003, Molenaar, 2004; Salvatore, Valsiner, Strout-Yagodzinsky, & Clegg, 2009). Of course this perspective is countered by the hegemonic "belief in large numbers" that underscores our contemporary fashion for "evidence-based-anythings" (medicine, education, etc.). This opposite perspective considers generality reachable through dismissal of individual peculiarities in an act of inductive generalization from samples to populations—*anything general is what is left over after eliminating the nontypical cases.* What one is left with as an index of generality is then an average—or a prototype—of the class of phenomena.

However, learning—and living—is always concrete. It is taking place far from the equilibrium of any established prototype—in fact, it breaks the previously established order—to create a new one (Maruyama, 1963). When we get involved in a new adventure there is now preset prototype for it—nor has there been any accumulation of evidence to allow for finding any average. Columbus was not a regular captain of a ship crossing the Atlantic on a routine mission taking a prototypical route—he was a deeply confused explorer assuming that the riches of India can be reached traveling Westward. While being right in his general hypothesis, this right guidance led to the discovery of a new land that even now—as the West Indies—bears the mark of his utopian vision. Yet his exploration was *generative* in its nature—based on a general idea, he constructed the particular sequence of moves toward the goal. Never mind that the goal itself was obscure—the promised land somewhere in the West. Ever since his coincidental success has the land he discovered been promising for many who have settled there—exploring their own life futures, rather than fitting into a protoptype of any kind.

The teachers and learners in the small vocational school in Switzerland that has been the object of careful study in this book are—in their own ways—similar to Columbus. They face the goals of creating highly sophisticated technological devices—using new computer technologies that are yet to be mastered. The apprentices in this task are simultaneously emerging masters—the dialogue of creativity is between the novice watchmaker, the powerful equipment, and the desired goals. Yet it is a school where the techniques of creating the master work are being taught. The coverage of the teaching/learning context in the vocational school in Jura that we see in this book gives us a picture of real education—for life (as a watchmaker) rather than for a degree.

Two themes emerge from this book that are important to emphasize: (1) *all development is an inherently ambivalent process,* and (2) *competence is socially expressed only under specific circumstances.* These two themes make a crucial correction to popular images of education and development that present development as simple uncontested progression from one stage to the next, and that repeat the idealistic image of the usefulness of social interaction in the teaching/learning process. What is documented in this book is the inevitable ambivalence in the efforts to master new technology between what one already can do and what is not yet mastered. With each new solution to a problem the given ambivalence is resolved—only to be replaced by a next task—and next ambivalence.

In this process of moving from one ambivalent situation to the next the role of the "more experienced Other" (the teacher) as well as the "collaborating peers" (co-learners) is far from simple. The "help" of the other—peer or teacher—may be sought at some junctions of the problem-solving process, resisted or avoided at others, and merely tolerated most of the time. Social interaction is task focused—it is not a chat, but part of the wider system of ways to solve the given technical problem. Its value fluctuates with the current state of the solution process—a chatty peer can be a detriment at a crucial moment of problem solving, and the intervention of a highly didactic teacher can be a hindrance rather than help. It is therefore not surprising that the apparent paradox discovered by the authors of this book—that the most highly competent teachers rarely enter into explicit helping of the learners, but instead provide implicit "background support" by episodically hinting at the directions where solutions might be forthcoming—is no paradox at all. It is an indicator to the *modulation of intervention* that highly competent teachers have mastered in their learning of their (teaching) trade (Maciel, Branco, & Valsiner, 2004). The real help is the helper's smooth intuition of where assisting support is needed for the learner—and where it can be counterproductive. The mastery of the teaching profession is in the development of meta-communicative strategies that mostly entail silences—rather than highly vocal discursive interventions into the teaching/learning process.

The process of apprenticeship we can observe in Ecole Technique de Sainte-Croix is a perfect example of cultural construction of material realities. It is filled with ruptures (Zittoun, 2006) and their repairs; the negotiations between the value of vocational training and abstract educational practices become fitted in the context of making the cultural object. New technology here is a tool to be mastered—yet by internalized mental processes—to make something new. Novelty is what human beings create through culture, and by doing that, they construct their own life courses within the contexts of socially guided frames for competence (or ignorance) in different domains of expertise in society.

Jaan Valsiner

REFERENCES

Krikonis, M., & Valsiner, J. (2008). The instant of being everywhere: Options and obstacles in technology-mediated education. *Qwerty: Rivista italiana di tecnologia culture e formazione, 2,* 65–72.

Lamiell, J. T. (2003). *Beyond individual and group differences.* Thousand Oaks, CA: Sage.

Maciel, D., Branco, A. U., & Valsiner, J. (2004). Bidirectional process of knowledge construction in teacher–student transaction. In A. U. Branco & J. Valsiner (Eds.), *Communication and metacommunication in human development* (pp. 109–125). Greenwich, CT: Information Age.

Maruyama, M. (1963). The second cybernetics: Deviation amplifying mutual causal processes. *American Scientist, 51,* 164–179.

Molenaar, P. C. M. (2004), A manifesto on psychology as idiographic science: Bringing the person back into scientific psychology, this time forever. *Measurement: Interdisciplinary Research and Perspectives, 2,* 201–218.

Salvatore, S., Valsiner, J., Strout-Yagodzinsky, S., & Clegg, J. (Eds.). (2009). *YIS: Yearbook of Idiographic Science 2008* (Vol. 1). Rome: Fireira Publishing.

Zittoun, T. (2006). *Transitions.* Greenwich, CT: Information Age.

AUTHORS' INTRODUCTION TO THE INTERNATIONAL EDITION

This book is a result of a major research project in Switzerland that brings together the fields of Education and Socio-Cultural Psychology. It is focused on how culture is involved in very concrete educational practices. The reader is invited to follow the research group in a Swiss technical college that trains young people in precision mechanics during a period of major technological change: the arrival of automated manufacturing systems. This transition in the trade is an opportunity to explore the educational and psychological challenges of vocational training from a perspective inspired by activity theory and the consideration of social interactions and semiotic or other technical mediations as crucial to the formation of professional identities and competencies.

This technical college is situated in the Swiss Jura mountains, on a site which, at first glance, appears removed from the principal cities of the country, but that is located at the heart of a region with quite an exceptional industrial history. This history has for two centuries been distinguished by a passion for the creation of time pieces and automatons. Witness the Reuge works close to the technical college, an enterprise that has achieved

Apprentice in a Changing Trade, pages xiii–xxi
Copyright © 2011 by Information Age Publishing
All rights of reproduction in any form reserved.

world wide recognition for its music boxes since the 19th century. Despite several economic crises, which have left their mark on this region's traditional industrial activities, a close link has been sustained between the technical college and the economic fabric of the region. The international reputation of this Swiss watch-making tradition, together with related precision mechanics, is well-established.

This center for training in precision mechanics has been engaged in a major project: the installation of an entirely automated production workshop within the college walls. After the introduction of numerically controlled machines into its workshops, the next step for this technical college was to make this further technological advance so that its students could be initiated into the requirements of fully automated manufacture. The school project was also politically supported because it was going to allow the use of the same equipment to provide courses in continuing professional development for the region's manufacturing enterprises, which had embarked upon a restructuring of their production systems.

This ambitious project, and the numerous economic, organizational, technological and pedagogical questions that it did not fail to raise, was the inspiration for the present research. The school's management came to the University to invite us to set up a research team with the capacity to examine, in partnership with the school, the uncertainties surrounding the execution of this project. This provided us the opportunity, over a period of three years, to follow the progress of the introduction of this technological transformation in the school and to examine how the aspiration for change in existing training practices came to be (partly) reconciled.

In terms of the methodological and epistemological perspective that was the foundation for this research project, it should be acknowledged at the outset that this was not a conventional kind of research intended to test a hypothesis or to demonstrate the existence of a phenomenon or to validate a theoretical model. Nor, for us, was it a matter of comparing different approaches to training, let alone one of recommending a particular pedagogical model. Our ambition was first to help the staff of the college give meaning to the stress and growing anxiety that they were experiencing in this sudden confrontation with major changes; and also, in parallel, to examine a real life process of training that addresses the transition from school to the world of work, and to describe it in all its complexities. Our hope is that this "monographic" and "local" experience can contribute lessons learned that would be of interest to other "local" experiences facing similar challenges when professional activity, competencies and training have to adapt to technological changes. Drawing upon the resources of present theoretical advancements, our research efforts went into a description not only of what was happening in the college but also of the complex, multidimensional and changing reality of the wider environment surrounding this school project. Our objective was to try to make intelligible what was said, what was done and what was experienced in this professional setting during a period of transition and to allow for the partners a more conscious awareness of what was happening in their institution, which is committed to a reappraisal of the training it offers in order to respond to the expectations of professions that are themselves engaged in a technological restructuring of their activities.

We chose to focus our attention on three "layers" of reality: the representations that the participants had of the training process and the objectives aimed for; direct observation of pedagogical practices in the workshops; and the meaning that the participants in learning accorded to the facts observed. This necessitated analysis and interpretation of various sources of data, collected on the basis of interviews, questionnaires, direct and filmed observations and archival records.

This research is a form of idiographic study defined as:

> a systematic study of single cases as organized systems—and over time—that becomes the basis for psychological generalization. Indeed the idiographic analysis is of a single, unique case, but its results are generalized to the phenomenon as a whole. In this sense, idiographic science is the way of arriving at generalized knowledge through the study of single systems. (Valsiner, 2009, p. 15)

Looking into this training setting provided access to more general issues surrounding professional training, teaching situations, attitudes towards learning and transitions. At a deep level, the questions faced by the college studied, and the uncertainties and tensions it encountered in the context of technological changes, are present in other training settings and in other trades.

What are these questions? We have identified four main sets of partly interdependent issues corresponding to four questions (where, with what, how and why?): learning in different *settings* (school or work setting); *tools* for training or tools for work; *processes* of learning; and the *meanings* of training activities.

Where Should Professional Competences Be Acquired: In a School, in the Trade or Via a Dual System?

In Switzerland, around 70% of young people opt for professional training. Their choice is often (not always) voluntary and not as a result of failure in school: the reputation of Swiss vocational training is good and attracts students from abroad. Most of these young people carry out their apprenticeship in a company (dual system). Only 15% of them enroll full time in a professional school. These vocational schools (also named "technical colleges" or "trade schools" depending on whether students earn only initial degrees or also more advanced ones) imitate the dual system and provide, under the same roof, theoretical training in the classroom (courses on professional knowledge and general culture) and practical training in the school's workshops. The Ecole Technique de Sainte-Croix, the school under investigation here, is one such school.

For initial professional training, Switzerland has always favored a dual system, similar, to a large extent, to that of Germany and Austria. It is often now used as a benchmark in the context of international research on professional training (Hamilton, 1987, 1994). This dual system consists in organizing weekly education in two parts: three or four days are spent in the workplace, under the guidance and supervision of a professional expert (called *"maître d'apprentissage"*), and one or two days are spent in a technical school taking classes in professional knowledge and general culture.

The existence of trade schools, which provide such full-time training to young people under the same roof, is not a natural arrangement in a country like Switzerland, which has always valued the dual system (Gindroz, 2009). The situation is different, for instance, in France, where the general pattern is to provide professional training mostly in schools and more specifically in technical high schools (Brucy & Troger, 2000). In Switzerland, in the area of precision mechanics and watch making, trade schools date from the beginning of the 20th century. They were principally developed in the French speaking part of Switzerland in response to a crisis situation: at the turn of the last century, the forms of apprenticeship available within manufacturing enterprises no longer ensured achievement of the ever rising levels of competence demanded in watch making. It was therefore judged necessary to open trade schools that could offer training courses that were more systematic and more comprehensive than the training offered in work places, where the imperatives of production were not always compatible with the requirements of training.

Today these schools are being forced to reconsider the nature of their unique contributions in a new training landscape. To be sure, they want to emphasize the quality of their training programs, which they are proud of. But the staff is now greatly preoccupied with the lack of experience in the world of work among their students who are "protected" but also "isolated" from it in their full time schools. How can young people be socialized into the realities and demands of work while in a school that is by definition far removed from this world? Can this be mitigated through the development of more "authentic" learning activities that would mimic the organization of professional activities (Achtenhagen, 2003)? Or can it be done by scheduling more frequent placements in companies?

What are the most appropriate settings for learning? There is no simple answer to this question. What can lead a pupil to become engaged, even if this is within a school, with all the seriousness of a future professional?

Under which conditions is an internship in a company genuinely formative (Billet, 2002; Billett, Fenwick, & Somerville, 2006; Durand & Fabre, 2007; Fillietaz, de Saint-Georges, & Duc, 2008)?

Learning with What Tools: Machines for Training or Machines for Work?

In a technical college, pupils spend around half of their time in the college's workshops. A constant preoccupation of the school's management concerns the machine tools that it is appropriate to install and upgrade in these workshops. The questions posed by these equipment upgrades are various. To some extent, the schools feel obliged to follow the rapid changes of the industrial world so that the technical equipment in its workshops is always up to date, but sometimes they are insecure about whether the change is a momentary fashion and not worth the effort. In the Jura region, these technical colleges of precision mechanics and watch making have a long history of developing their own innovations and new tools that are then acquired by the firms. Will they manage to keep up with this reputation with computer-supported manufacturing systems? In the present case, the answer is no, as they have had to buy it from a firm because they could not develop it in the school. Moreover, is it necessary to possess the most recent technologies in order to offer high quality training?

The upgrading of equipment is not invariably a matter of *replacing* old technologies with new ones. Often, professionals need to be as familiar with older technologies as with the new. In precision mechanics, for example, systems of automated manufacture have not entirely supplanted conventional machine tools. A technical college, therefore, needs to retain several generations of tools, with the delicate task of defining the relative importance to be accorded to these different generations in the training programs.

Our study also drew our attention to another issue. Not all technologies can be mastered in the same fashion in a school. Certain tools readily find their place within the teaching environment; they are amenable to being "sent to school." Other systems, in contrast, are more difficult to integrate because they disrupt the educational order. This is the case, for example, when systems are nonresponsive (because of safety or cost) to trial and error, when they are hazardous to the expert user and not just to novices, or because they require teamwork to operate and carry high maintenance costs. For such technologies, the technological college is not a congenial ecological niche but is facing a major challenge. The challenge can be met by choosing proper simulation technologies. The simulation is not necessarily virtual; it can be physical, as in the case of a manufacturing system adapted for training purposes. Young people undergoing training are eager to learn to use "real machines" not "fake" ones. We will see that they do not take this training equipment seriously because they do not consider them true workplace machines.

Processes of Learning: Doing and Understanding

Another main issue in the book is the relation between doing and understanding. This is a key question in classical developmental psychology (Dewey, 1938; Piaget, 1974a, 1974b), and even more so in vocational education (Pastré, 2007; Samurçay & Pastré, 2004). To what extent is learning related to practice, and practice to context, and how can the boundaries between contexts or disciplines be made crossable (Ludvigsten, Havnes, & Lahn, 2003; Martin, 1995; Tuomi-Gröhn, 2007)? How do teachers and students understand the interdependence between doing and understanding (they call it "theory and practice") in a school setting inhabited by training practices relevant to different reference models, some close to an educational culture, others derived from the professional world?

We will see that the time spent on practice in the workshops is often conceived by teachers and students as mostly an opportunity to exercise already acquired knowledge, with a focus on the product to be realized. Even if the actors are not aware of this, it is clear to the observer that the activities in these workshops are also learning settings: they require reflection, discussion, planning, problem solving, and the invention of solutions. They are opportunities for the students to conceptualize a complex process, but all this seems to happen informally, which is paradoxical in some way, given that the setting is a formal school.

What do we know about the relation between doing and knowing in the construction of new competencies? Numerous researchers have sought to understand the conditions under which an activity can be the source of knowledge. They have sought to grasp how new knowledge and skills are born out of this articulation between action and reflection on action; between the activity and the conceptualization (Merri 2007; Vergnaud, 1996) between activity and learning (Pastré, 2007); between productive activities and constructive activities (Samurçay & Rabardel, 2004); or indeed between socio-cognitive activities and the development of thinking (Perret-Clermont, 2004). These works share the same agenda: it is not sufficient to be engaged in an action or interaction to learn from it. It is necessary that this approach be planned and informed, that it become an object of reflection and that it make sense in the eyes of the learner.

The Meaning of Training

Another issue that is addressed in this research bears on the meaning that the students attribute to learning activities. Our study has induced us into formulating new working hypotheses on the manner in which the young experience their training and on the significant role for them of professional specialization.

We have observed that young people continually pondered the meaning of the activities they were asked to undertake in school. To make sense of these, they assumed that a learning activity had to maintain a close link with the world of work such as they perceived or imagined it. The meaning accorded to learning activities seemed to be inseparable from their search for an identity and, more specifically, a professional identity. We have been surprised to observe how much importance these young people accorded to the specializations they had chosen, and also surprised to see the identity and symbolic functions fulfilled by their work tools: it mattered a lot to a young person to be able to describe himself[1] a specialist in this or that technical system. Indeed, each professional specialization is associated with specific tools. The students were invested in them, making them important points of reference through which to locate themselves in a changing technological landscape.

What is the value attached to these specialized tools and the skills they require? Young people's attachment to these tools could be a threat against innovation in the school: the students are not destined to become the defenders of professional identities derived from the guilds which have defined the trade sector from the Middle Ages right up to the present in Switzerland (Cassagnes-Brouquet, 2010; Dubar, 1995, 2000) Are they going to ignore the recent changes in the world of work and their new expectations with regard to professionals? The school authorities are aware of the need for greater versatility and more transferable skills.

We advance the hypothesis that professional specialization fulfills an important function in the dynamics of learning. Specialization effectively provides the opportunity to progressively master knowledge and skills, according the satisfaction of succeeding at something. Often these students have not known such satisfaction in the course of their previous educational experiences. They are strongly attracted to this sentiment when they do at last encounter it. Additionally, they fear that these goals of versatility and general competencies, which the training environment is concerned about promoting (such as industry does), will come to threaten what has begun to be an important reference point in the construction of their identities: the mastery of particular activities and tools.

The trade school is thus a particularly informative setting with respect to the current tension between two coexisting professional cultures. One, more traditional, is centered on the work station and is associated with a strong specialization of trades. The other, which is newer, places empha-

---

[1]We use the masculine form because the students were all male. This was not a decision of the school. But not a single girl signed up!

sis on general and transferable skills demanded in professional contexts that are constantly changing and rich in unforeseen events (Zarifian, 1999, 2003). But why regard versatility as contradictory to the mastery of particular procedures and tools? We believe that a priority task for researchers and trainers alike is to identify the conditions under which the acquisition of technical skills, even if particularly specialized, can become significant opportunities for supporting the development of more general knowledge and competence. To thoroughly master a particular task or a technology is no obstacle to this. On the contrary, it could furnish an occasion for the pupil to anchor his reflection in a practice which comes to serve as a springboard for trying others, examining them, comparing them, and understanding their relations, their limitations and the alternatives.

Interlinked Issues

The issues exposed above are interlinked with one another. Consequently, they are not the object of distinct chapters. They offer, instead, alternative readings of this book according to whether the reader wishes to pay particular attention to the settings for learning, the processes of learning, the tools of training and work, or instead the identity dynamics involved.

This work is addressed to all those who have an interest in professional training, whether as the designer or coordinator of professional training, or as teacher or trainer. It can also be of interest to researchers in human and social sciences, who will find within these pages an attempt to capture a complex educational reality undergoing a process of significant change.

ACKNOWLEDGMENTS

A number of people made this research possible. Great gratitude is here extended to Roland Bachmann, Director of the Ecole Technique de Sainte-Croix (Vaud), for his invitation to work together on the training problems created by the evolution of jobs and for the confidence he showed when welcoming us to his college. We also found an openness and availability among everyone responsible for training, as well as among the teachers who spoke freely with us ; we are very grateful. We would particularly like to thank Jean-Philippe Chavey, without whom we would never have gotten to know about the life of an automation laboratory. All the students of the Ecole Technique are thanked here, in particular the student-technicians, with whom we spoke with more than once. We are also grateful to our friends and readers of the first drafts.

This study received constant support from Professor Uri Trier, Director of National Research Program 33, which was devoted to "the effectiveness of Swiss training systems." At key stages of our work, he knew how to sustain us with his stimulating and constructive feedback; for this we heartily thank him.

This research was made possible thanks to a grant (to Anne-Nelly Perret-Clermont, Roland Bachmann, & Luc-Olivier Pochon) of the Swiss National Scientific Research Foundation (Project FNS 4033-35846).

Nicholas Emler has translated the book into English. In preparing this new edition, we have been helped by the useful comments and editorial help of Alexandra Bugnon, Lysandra Sinclaire Harding, and Athena Sargent, whom we all thank.

GENERAL INTRODUCTION

How should young people today be prepared for a world of work that is going through a process of change? In a rapidly evolving industrial context, how can one encourage development of the knowledge and skills that will not just allow them to cope with the transformations that are in process but to be proactive in them as players? Currently one certainly sees a large measure of agreement on the necessity, if not urgency, of rethinking the objectives of training. But the precise means by which the expected competences should be developed are both more difficult to identify and more controversial.

Uncertainty relates in particular to the roles of, respectively, formal knowledge and experience-based knowledge in the mastery of a professional activity, as well as the setting in which this mastery might be acquired. What can be learned, and can only be learned, in school? What really cannot be acquired in this setting? Does our dual system of training have sufficient flexibility to adapt to new training needs? Does the occupational apprenticeship in its traditional form have a future when compared to the attractions of courses providing general training or full-time vocational education? Do the reforms in progress in the field of occupational training herald a paradigm shift in ways of thinking about the relationships between

Apprentice in a Changing Trade, pages xxiii–xxviii
Copyright © 2011 by Information Age Publishing
All rights of reproduction in any form reserved.

general training and occupational specialization, between knowledge and competence, or between acquired cognitive skills and experience gained? Vocational and technical colleges find themselves very much caught up in these changes and the questions they raise, needing to manage new situations and expectations. How does this affect their adaptation of the content, approaches and goals of training? How in consequence do they manage renovation of the necessary technical facilities?

This book tackles these questions by drawing on a case study, and to be more specific, a study of an occupational training setting in a period in which it was affected by major technological developments, due in particular to the introduction of new computer-assisted manufacturing equipment. Roland Bachmann, head of a college in the Jura mountain region of Switzerland and drawn to our research work, extended an invitation to us to come and observe his management colleagues, teaching staff, and students, and together devote ourselves to understanding what the arrival of new technologies in a training institution means at a concrete level. What problems arise, what solutions emerge, and what paths remain to be explored? The study was begun in 1993, during a period in the history of this technical college marked by an extensive re-equipment project. This involved first the installation of a manufacturing unit of the flexible manufacturing system (FMS) type, followed by a robotic assembly unit. The college's aspiration was then to introduce its apprentices and more particularly future technicians to automated production equipment, conceived within the general perspective of "computer-integrated manufacturing" (CIM).

In order to understand how technical training manages to adapt in a rapidly evolving industrial and socioeconomic environment, we might, for example, have conducted extensive inquiries into the different training institutions in Switzerland that are concerned with occupations involving mechanical construction. Because we were given the opportunity (it is not that often that colleges contact researchers and willingly open their doors to them), we chose a different approach, in monograph style, closer to a case study. We characterize our study, metaphorically, as closer to foraging within a defined area so as to grasp in all their density the questions that arise, rather than carrying out a more general survey from a higher altitude! Each of these ways of gathering data can in its own fashion be useful to an observer studying the changes in a landscape, but the means used in these two kinds of investigation are very different. Given our own preoccupation—the way in which a training institution copes with ongoing technological changes—we chose to focus on a systematic examination of a specific setting during a period rich in events. We were also concerned with verifying on a regular basis whether what we observed here resonates and makes sense in comparable training settings elsewhere.

This investigation required different kinds of data collection. These included analyses of documents relating to the organization and history of the occupational training provided by the Ecole Technique de Sainte-Croix and their relationship to what has happened elsewhere in Switzerland; interviews with members of college management, with teachers, and with students; observations in the workshops of different sessions in the courses in which students are trained in professional practice; video recordings of practical exercises on automation; and a questionnaire study of all the college students.

We took a particular interest in the "disruptions" created by the arrival of new technologies when in one way or another these led to "infringement" of the rules that normally govern the operation of a training situation. Such is the case, for example, when equipment with multiple operating conditions imposes the abnormal requirement of working as a group. By close examination of what happens and what is said in actual training situations, when social interactions arise around complex tasks and problems to be solved, we have sought to develop our understanding of learning processes. We have paid particular attention to those issues involved in all occupational training situations that are at once matters of cognition, relationships, and identity.

This investigation led us to an explicit rejection of simple causal models, which tend to let one suppose that one single teaching approach or one single form of learning will, according to some mechanical logic, be sufficient in and of itself. The pedagogical reality is more complex. It is a setting in which social actors (teachers and students) come together with often different representations, tacit knowledge, objectives, and strategies. In order for the transmission of knowledge and skills to occur here, a sufficient common understanding needs to be established among those involved as to what is to be understood, learned, or produced. On the same basis, all learning is also socialization into an academic or occupational culture. This socialization deserves the most careful scrutiny in a college in which one encounters students with widely varied prior educational careers, and in which the teachers themselves come with different ranges of professional experience.

This research perspective has led us to take different levels of analysis into consideration. These range from the most micro level, as represented by our observations of students grappling with specific technical difficulties, to the most macro level, as represented by the socioeconomic and industrial history of the Jura region of Switzerland and the particular place it occupies in watchmaking and precision mechanics. These areas of activity have been confronted with technological changes that have been destabilizing on both the industrial and the socioeconomic levels, and it is important to locate the Ecole Technique de Sainte-Croix in this context if one is to appreciate the significance of its strong concern to maintain and promote high-quality provision of technical training, adapted to the current expectations of industry.

As we shall see, talking to teachers and their students about the development of automated production is also in a sense to talk about the history of a college, a region, and its inhabitants; it is to encounter views about development but also fears that technological change will accelerate. Our study aimed to grasp the manner in which general technological and socio-occupational issues are reflected in concrete form in the training situations observed.

The first chapter examines the issue of the new competences that are required today in the utilization of information technologies. We begin by considering the changes that new technologies of information and communication have introduced into a wide range of occupational activities. We shall see that, in this context of change, the need is felt within occupational settings to identify what competences are now necessary. Within the training context there is a corresponding quest to understand how responsibilities in these matters should be discharged. However, work concerned with describing the impact of computing tools upon human activities emphasizes the inseparable link between the technical competences involved and both evolution of the socio-occupational picture and reorganization of work within business enterprises. Given this, it becomes very difficult to establish a precise correspondence between the characteristics of a technical device and the competences that its mastery requires. In addition, the multiple and distributed competences necessary often turn out to be collective. How should the college, more accustomed to dealing with individuals than with groups, respond to this?

Talking about the impact of technological innovations and the new competences they call for is one thing, but asking where and in what way these competences can be acquired is quite another. This latter question is addressed in the second chapter. In response to the current crisis in apprenticeships, the development of occupational training provision *in college* is seen as the solution of the future by various political actors. A more pronounced "academicization" of training, combined with several placements in industry, is seen as a good way to develop the general and transferable knowledge demanded in the world of work. What historical points of reference will help us better to grasp the direction of change and the ongoing debates? It is worth recalling that, in the context of Swiss Romande (the French-speaking part of the country), full-time vocational colleges were created around the 1900s, during a period in which the issue then was one of responding to a situation in crisis. The preferred option at the time was to provide, under a single roof, training that was both practical and theoretical. The history of the Ecole Technique de Sainte-Croix belongs fully in this context.

Chapter 3 shifts point of view and level of analysis by examining how this technical college has, over the course of the last 25 years, coped with the need to keep up-to-date in terms of technology so that it could provide its apprentices with a decent introduction to computer-assisted manufacturing. We show how the introduction of new production equipment required strong involvement on the part of the teaching staff. It turns out to be a matter of rethinking learning objectives, of perfecting approaches adapted to training, of redesigning course supports, without forgetting that to these pedagogical activities need to be added significant amounts of installation and maintenance work, and even sometimes the development work that the introduction of new facilities can require.

In the three chapters that follow this, we seek to examine in detail a particular pedagogical situation that is at the heart of this techno-pedagogical inquiry. Here, we refer to the observations we carried out during the course of practical sessions on automation, using the recently acquired FMS manufacturing unit. Chapter 4 first describes the situation observed and then analyzes the interactions between teacher and students over the course of these sessions. Chapter 5 presents an observation and analysis of interactions between students working together in small groups. Chapter 6 steps back a bit from the specifics of the teaching in order to capture the meaning that the partners involved attribute to these practical exercises, drawing on a body of commentaries we collected either during the sessions or in the course of later interviews.

A questionnaire allowed us to put questions to all the students enrolled in the Ecole Technique de Sainte-Croix, and in this way, we sought to establish their opinions about the training they were pursuing, the considerations that had driven their vocational orientation, their representations of learning methods, and their views about the competences required in the occupations they were aiming for. Chapter 7 presents the results of this inquiry and, in particular, examines the manner in which students perceive themselves as future professionals.

Chapter 8 outlines a picture synthesizing the observations undertaken, seeking to identify in these what is found to be challenging about the arrival of new production technologies within a technical college. This chapter poses a question about the effectiveness of a college in terms of its capacity for innovation and its capacity to manage difficulties encountered in the pursuit of training objectives. This capacity is not defined in the abstract but derives from a "college culture," with its own constraints, both positive and negative.

In the concluding chapter, we show how this study contributes to a broader rethinking of the models of learning in training, in this way opening up new directions for research and action. We emphasize in particular how vocational education is made up of multiple forms of training and evolving approaches to learning that cannot be reduced to one simple model. This multifaceted reality of training today offers a veritable open-air pedagogical laboratory for occupational training. Vocational colleges potentially provide settings for observation, thinking, and innovation in education capable of being used increasingly by all sectors of teaching.

CHAPTER 1

RESTRUCTURING OF VOCATIONAL COMPETENCE

THE GROWING PROMINENCE OF COMPUTERIZED TECHNOLOGY

It is now rare to encounter any sphere of employment that has not found itself altered, if not utterly transformed, by the revolution in information and communication technologies. Thus, in the service and commercial sectors, as much as in industrial production, dependence on the computer and upon information networks has become the norm.

Beyond these developments, a range of uses of the computer that would hardly have been imaginable just a few years ago has been strongly developed in these various sectors of working life. Developed initially within the domain of numbers and calculation, the computer subsequently moved into text processing. Then the worlds of sounds and images were in their turn digitalized, as was the communication field. One consequence has been the profound modification of a range of occupations.

Like many other occupations, precision mechanics has found itself profoundly transformed by the computerization of core tasks. The drawing

Apprentice in a Changing Trade, pages 1–6
Copyright © 2011 by Information Age Publishing

1

board has been progressively abandoned in favor of computer-aided design. As a result, the computer has come to bear upon conception as well as production. It is also involved in manufacturing through robot-controlled machine tools that are increasingly integrated within systems of automated production.

TO DEVELOP NEW COMPETENCES?

In Switzerland, in the face of these technological changes, the matter of identifying key skills (also referred to as "key qualifications") has become the focus for a set of proposals and recommendations that are now emerging from a range of sources. For the Swiss Union of Arts and Craft (USAM),

> key qualification are those which do not rapidly become outdated, but remain exploitable for a relatively long time. At issue here are capabilities that go beyond the specific requirements of individual jobs and occupations, such as flexibility, creativity, capacities to learn, to work in teams and to communicate, dispositions that make the worker more flexible and mobile while at the same time enabling him to develop and realise his potential. (1994, pp. 9–10)

In a document on the reform of apprenticeships, the service for occupational training of the Association Suisse des Machines (ASM; 1996), also discusses "general competences" and "capacities for adaptation": "The multitude of means of production, accessory tools and methods, and likewise their rapid evolution requires new qualifications on the part of tomorrow's workers. The search for personnel no longer accords any advantage to specialists possessing extensive knowledge in a circumscribed domain, but to generalists with a broad basic training enabling them to understand processes and adapt rapidly to new areas. The principal mission of the training of apprentices will be … to encourage basic techniques, qualifications like independence, flexibility, a sense of responsibility, the capacity to work in groups and the desire to learn."

The continuing professional development sector is equally involved in this task of identifying new professional competences. The Centre CIM de la Suisse Occidentale (CCSO), the mission of which with respect to competences is to support enterprises engaged in technological innovation, sketches out the new profile for employees in very similar terms. They are called upon to demonstrate:

> multidisciplinary qualification: competence in several domains; capacity to master new tasks; a global vision and motivation for the domain of activities;

> *human qualities:* capacities to work in teams; capacity to manage conflicts; and

responsibilities: identification with the work, concern for improvement; autonomy in the organization of work; a sense of responsibility. (CCSO, 1993)

In the mechanical construction field, industrial authorities also have high general expectations. In an article titled "The Automated Factory Has Need of the Hand of Man," Ebel wrote back in 1989 of the need to be qualified to repair flexible production systems:

> The kind of flexible automation that is at the heart of CIP (computer integrated production) systems cannot function effectively and continuously unless it is entrusted to highly qualified and motivated workers, capable of remedying relatively frequent breakdowns in these complex and sophisticated machines and of resolving problems in the computer programs. (p. 28)

Since 2001, several amendments to the Swiss legislation have granted a growing importance to the development of the apprentices' and tecnicians' "general" and "transversal" (i.e., boundary-crossing) competences (OFFT, 2007).

COMPETENCES EXPECTED AND COMPETENCES EFFECTIVELY REQUIRED

We have given above a sample of the expectations that have been expressed regarding future technicians. But what exactly do we know about the competences specifically linked to mastery of the tools of information technology? Have these been empirically verified or are they merely assumed? Can we be sure that the mastery of these tools really is based on the capacities we imagine? An *a priori* analysis of the task has led some to suppose that computer-assisted manufacture requires knowledge of the different components of a process of automated production, grasping the logic in its entirety, mastering the programs employed, as well as the semiotic systems of representation specific to human–machine interfaces. Perhaps we are inclined to imagine that this activity might require capacities of anticipation, of planning actions, of analysis and resolution of problems in the sense in which these general capacities have been studied within cognitive psychology (Hoc, 1987; Richard, 1990). However, is it really this type of competence that operatives put into practice when they initiate the functioning of a complex system? To be certain that this is indeed the case, observation of the activities of learning and work is indispensable.

To think about the technical competences required for mastery of a device, it is helpful first of all to recognize the different types of relationships between humans and machines. Drawing on the work of Rabardel (1995), we note three approaches to an artifact as a function of how it is understood, first as a technical system (in which case the logic of functioning dominates); second, from the point of view of its functions (the logic of the process of transformation of things); and finally, as a means of action in an instrumental relation (the logic of the activity and of use). As Rabardel observes, these different types of relationships to an artifact are not mutually exclusive, they are complementary. The instrumental relation (logic of use) requires a sufficient knowledge of the system as such, if only to ensure the basic conditions of functioning are satisfied, as well as a minimal comprehension of the process by which objects are transformed, in order to achieve the goals of action.

On which of these levels does the introduction of computing tools have the effect of introducing greater complexity into work activities? To claim that the knowledge required by computer tools is more abstract is not sufficient to justify the conclusion that the activity is thereby rendered more complex. As Stroobants suggests,

> this "abstraction" contains a major ambiguity. The automatisation of an operation most certainly represents an abstraction in the sense that the worker is abstracted from the function performed by the machine. But this disconnection does not imply that his new task will necessarily be more abstract or more "intellectual" than before. (1994, p. 182)

The issue of occupational deskilling brought about by technological changes is controversial. For Stroobants, this debate is itself embedded in the history of industrial production, which has led, in each epoch, to a reappraisal of the precise nature of the occupational competences required. In certain cases, far from a disqualifying effect, the introduction of new technologies seems to serve to enhance the importance of existing experiential knowledge and skills Previously implicit competences emerge as indispensable to the mastery of machines; again we can refer to Stroobants:

> when the formal knowledge incorporated in the instructions and in the machine is apparently radically efficacious, this complement would be nil. From the moment that these techniques encounter their limits, irreducible skills become visible. Characteristics that cannot be automated become specifically human (for example, coping with uncertainty). On the other hand, what can be automated becomes devalued. The machine and its limits have rendered unsuspected qualities visible. (p. 182)

However, as we have established in our own work, fear of an impoverishment of occupational activities remains a very salient preoccupation among those working in the area of precision mechanics; these are expressed in a very direct manner in the responses of the teachers and trainees we have interviewed. They fear that their trades will be reduced to so-called "pushbutton" tasks, circumscribed by automated systems. This concern is most evident among future technicians, who for the most part aspire to do design work, but without yet really knowing how their status, intermediate between that of mechanics and that of engineers, will actually allow them to position themselves in the future work environment. They cannot clearly envisage what kinds of tasks they will be allocated.

RESEARCH ON THE IMPACT OF INFORMATION TOOLS

A first category of research that it is now possible to identify concerns the effect of the activity with tools on the development of new cognitive structures (Säljö, 1999). Thus, in the area of initial training, investigations bear upon the specific learning associated with the new technologies. For example, Aussenac (1987) studied the behavior of students in production techniques utilizing digitally controlled machine tools (CNC machine). From a similar perspective, Lebahar (1987) analyzed the impact of utilization of the CNC machine on the graphic competences of technicians in training; et plus généralement l'impact des outils de conception (CAO) sur l'activité des designers (Lebahar, 2007). One of the conclusions to which this author comes is that: "CNC induces, as a result of the demands of preparation, the editing and the execution of machine tool programs that match their deterministic constraints, a higher level of abstraction of the transformation space of the object. They tend to promote axiomatization and conceptualisation of the object" (Lebahar, 1987, p. 375). These studies of the identification and development of the various cognitive competences related to use of drawing tools and computer-aided design and manufacture (CAD, CAM, etc.) link to work by Greenfield (1993, 1994) on the cognitive benefits that can result from video games, particularly at the level of spatial representation.

Additionally, Rabardel (1995) has examined the manner in which the tools used can structure an individual's activity. He distinguishes several ways in which activity is determined by artifacts, ranging from simple passive structuring in the case of hand tools, which have no functioning of their own, all the way through to the structuring activity of artifacts, which have a knowledge of the operator and have as their objective modifying or guiding the latter's activity, as is the case in certain expert systems. However,

> the artefact does not strictly know how to determine the activity, on the one hand because it is only one of the elements of pre-structuration alongside utilisation schemes, and on the other hand because several other sources of the structuration of activity exist in addition to tools, among them the tasks and prescribed modes of operating; finally, the structuration of the activity is a continuous process through which the subject involves himself in the singularity of situations (in which he participates) and which he manages" (p. 178)

This was particularly evident in an experiment carried out with 14- to 16-year-olds involving the use of a teaching robot, an experiment that aimed at reproducing effects of different forms of control (movable cursor vs. computer keyboard strokes) of a robot's arm and grasping mechanism.

This effect was only partially reproduced, leading the author to summarize the results as follows:

> Use of the robot led subjects to construct representations which could be regarded as belonging to the same family, that of direct control of the hand in the work space. But this is a large family; the possible points of arrival are as numerous as the routes that the subjects could select to achieve them. Multiple representations are functional for a single class of situations and their functionality is also dependent on strategies adopted by the subjects, as we were able to demonstrate in a previous experiment using the same robot. A multiplicity of factors thus indicate that the situations of use of an artefact are in the end specific to each subject. (Rabardel, 1995, p. 181)

It was this that led the author to define the notion of a *relatively required activity*, which issues from the tension between the diverse constraints imposed on the subject (the artifact, the task, the environment, his own competences and capacities, etc.) and the psychological subject himself, a unique and intentional actor.

A body of work analyzed by Blanc, Michel, Villard, and Perret-Clermont (1994), and put to practice in the context of training and professional development, is concerned with the consequences of introducing new technologies (particularly those involving computer-controlled machine tools) upon the cognitive activity and work organization of employees (Barcet, Le Bas, & Mercier, 1983; Wilkinson, 1984; Martin & Scribner, 1991; Martin, 1991, 1992, 1995). This work indicates that the introduction of new devices provokes changes in skills and modes of thinking, but also reveals that these transformations do not depend solely upon tools and their particular characteristics. They depend also on the type of use made of machines, the goals pursued, and the manner in which the tasks enabled by these tools are socially distributed within the organization, with the power struggles that can arise among qualified workers, technicians, and engineers. What is observed in the enterprise is thus not a simple substitution of models of thought and action, but a restructuring and redistribution of these models.

These studies make us aware that the issues of competences arising in the context of technological transformation cannot be approached as if they simply involved creating a relationship between the relevant technical device and appropriate new competences, element by element. To determine the individual and collective knowledge and skills that are involved, it is necessary to take into account modifications in the socioprofessional setting into which new technologies are introduced and in which new relations with machines can be established. How does this dynamic work in the training setting? What new divisions of tasks and responsibilities can be observed, alongside a new relation to the activity of use? These are the issues we examine in the chapters that follow.

CHAPTER 2

WHERE CAN PROFESSIONAL KNOWLEDGE AND SKILLS BE ACQUIRED?

In the current context of technological change, new competences are needed, but where can they be acquired? Can the traditional settings for training, namely colleges, businesses and factories, continue to hold on to their roles, and if so, by following which approaches, and according to which complementary forms? If not, do these new technologies require alternative conceptions of the transmission of professional knowledge?

OCCUPATIONAL LEARNING AS A REFERENCE MODEL

It is useful to first recall the importance of the place occupied by the occupational training sector in Switzerland; in effect close to 70% of young people enter into some form of professional training at the end of their compulsory education, doing so within a dual training system. This system of training is founded on experience and on convictions that are largely shared within Swiss society: that knowledge of a trade is not learned at school desks but in a place of work, or at least in a college workshop insofar

Apprentice in a Changing Trade, pages 7–000

as this latter sufficiently resembles a setting for occupational activities in terms of both the technical equipment available and of the quality of the work undertaken there.

In this conception of occupational learning, the importance of general education (which is to say cultural, scientific, and linguistic) is not neglected; teaching programs have again recently been the object of fundamental reform. Nonetheless, engagement for a prolonged and continuous period in a workplace (or quasi-workplace) is traditionally regarded as an irreplaceable learning experience. The dual system of training is characterized by the desire to preserve the unity between theoretical education and practical experience (in contrast to other possible arrangements, for example, a model of alternation); it is the product of a long history and of a process of negotiation, which, as we shall see later, can be traced back to the end of the 19th century.

Occupational training draws on a division of time devoted, in parallel, to general education and to the acquisition of professional knowledge as well as to the practice of a trade. The specific forms that training can take are certainly diverse, and vary according to whether learning takes place in a vocational college or in a business, as well as with the size of the business, and indeed whether it contains a training division. In each case, though, reference to the dual system remains an organizing principle. We find this in vocational colleges, which, as full-time schools, could present themselves as an alternative model. For now, the organization of training in these establishments reflects the general structure of the dual system. The week is divided into teaching time spent in the classroom and practice time spent in the workshop under the supervision of a professional expert. We shall see later how this kind of training program is structured.

How should the classic learning situation be characterized? Whether this involves a place of work or a vocational college and its workshops, the apprentice is initiated, under the guidance of a master, into the execution of tasks that will allow him or her to progressively assimilate the techniques, gestures, and postures of the profession. One of the basic principles in structuring training is the grading of tasks from the most simple to the most complex. In 3–4 years, the apprentice thus progressively acquires a professional mastery that allows him or her by the end of the course to obtain a Certificate Fédéral de Capacité (CFC). The teacher is allotted the task of guiding and accompanying the apprentice, initially very closely, but then giving him or her progressively more and more responsibility and autonomy. This period of training leads up to a final evaluation in which, in the course of a practical exam, the apprentice must produce a piece independently and within a given time limit. For those who pursue technical training, the final diploma work fills an analogous function of social recognition of acquired competencies. In fact, the production of personal

work that completes and validates professional training is based in the tradition of guilds. The masterpiece was therefore the synthesis of everything
the apprentice had been able to learn and proof that he could become a
master-craftsman. The Compagnonnage[1] thematized and in a certain sense
amplified this training-initiation approach. As De Castéra (1988) observed,

> the masterpiece is a homage to the craft and to those who have passed on
> the tradition for generations. This token is disinterested, its maker receives
> no payment and makes it as a gift to the community. It is the opportunity to
> give of his full technical and moral measure at least once in his life. (p. 103)

This conception of training and its culmination is in one way or another
still very much alive in several occupations and professions.[2]

A MODEL IN CRISIS

It is said that the occupational apprenticeship is in crisis today, by virtue
of various kinds of dysfunction (Dubs, 2007; Fillettaz et al., 2008). This is
not specific to Switzerland. Germany, whose professional training is likewise
founded upon a dual system, is also engaged since many years in questioning the system of apprenticeships (Lattard, 2000). The factors that lay at
the origin of the apprenticeship crisis are numerous, embracing economic
and demographic issues, as well as a changing relationship to training and
trades. Without pretending to offer an exhaustive analysis of the question,
we consider three distinct facets of the problem.

The first is very concrete and concerns the diminishing pool of places
for apprenticeships. This decrease can only partly be explained by demographic changes. The causes are also to be found in the reduced number of
apprenticeships offered by employers. Is this because they judge the costs
of supervising apprentices to have become too high? Is it that the priorities
of large, often multinational companies are such that they do not have the
same concerns about training replacements? This situation has become a
worrying preoccupation for those with the responsibility for professional
training. The Confederation, as much as the Cantons, has taken special
measures to encourage businesses to create apprenticeships. Let us note
that beyond concrete questions of academic and occupational orientation, the scarcity of places has subjective consequences that the statistical
evidence does not reflect. For example, the fact that a young person must

---

1The Compagnonnage was a brotherhood with aims of mutual aid, protection, education, and
   knowledge transmission among its members.
2Within the framework of university training, the masters' dissertation and then the doctoral
   thesis likewise represent work at the completion of studies that plays a decisive role in establishing an affiliation with the university community.

select a vocation that is not his or her preferred option cannot be without consequences for his or her motivation.

Another source of preoccupation concerns the lack of attraction apprenticeships have among young people as compared to more general courses of study. To attempt to remedy this, information campaigns, notably using posters, currently seek to rehabilitate the value of apprenticeships, in particular by working on a renovation of the language, speaking, for example, no longer of the "apprentice" but of the "student of mechanics." The lack of attraction is not, however, easily understood: Is it really a matter of lack of interest in learning a trade rather than a desire to defer commitment to a particular occupational destination together with the difficulties of adult life if at age 15 or 16 this kind of commitment may be seen as premature? The preference at the upper secondary level for general educational courses can be explained in part by a desire to postpone for a few years the entry into the adult world that is implicit in occupational training. Currently, attempts to persuade young people of the value of apprenticeships emphasize that award of the Maturité Professionelle (*a vocational qualification*) opens up the opportunity to pursue professional training all the way through to a vocational university. This emphasis on highly specialized training is certainly seductive, but how is the message received by the very many young people whose own compulsory schooling has ended because they were convinced that they were not fit for extended education? How can this paradox be overcome?

Another reason for the crisis is probably to be found in the limitations of the classical model of apprenticeship in the context of evolving occupations. In effect, the apprenticeship is traditionally associated with an essentially reproductive transmission. The situation is different during times of occupational change. As we have seen in the previous chapter, expectations are different: they have gone beyond the reproduction of knowledge and skills of the older generation and have moved on to the promotion of capacities for adaptation and innovation. This, in consequence, requires the rethinking of learning situations and, in particular, of the role of trainers (Pastré, Mayen, & Vergnaud, 2006; Filliettaz, 2009a, 2009b).

In addition, we can hypothesize that information technologies have contributed in their own way to destabilizing traditional forms of apprenticeship. The classical scheme of progression, which begins with the simplest tasks and moves through successively more and more complex tasks, is difficult to apply with information technology and with programs that from the outset confront the user with all of their richness and complexity. The most effective means of coping with this complexity remain for the present uncertain. Within a pedagogy that should necessarily be caring, we can certainly attempt to construct methodical didactic progress, but the risk then is to offer artificial (academic) routes that bear little relation to the spontaneous learning practices in this area. The work peculiar to apprentices is distinctive, but difficult to plan. The tools of information technology lend themselves to more haphazard, trial and error learning; whether one chooses or not, they themselves introduce a certain didactic disorder into the progression that traditionally structures apprenticeship programs.

Let us again note that computing tools are not without paradoxical effects on pedagogy. To work at a computer is an activity often described as more abstract in the sense that it mediates direct contact with the world of objects. This process of setting concrete action at a distance requires anticipation, planning, and reflection on one's own actions. At the same time, current programs are well- suited to free exploration, to trial and error; the mouse click is often quicker than the learner's thoughts. The computer seems to emphasize a relation of use to the detriment of an understanding of function, to return to the distinction offered by Rabardel (1995) and Verillon and Rabardel (1995). A new relationship between knowledge and skill is in play here. Around computers, a fine-grained management of time for work at the screen and time spent on reflection upon the operations executed or upon those to be carried out becomes a crucial didactic question about the elaboration of new logics of learning. An organization of training in terms of distinct class hours allocated respectively to theory and to practice is not an adequate response at this level.

RETHINKING OCCUPATIONAL LEARNING

A set of measures recommended by those involved in professional training in Switzerland is currently moving in the direction of a deconstruction of training both vertically and horizontally. The initial intention is to redefine apprenticeship, not as a circumscribed and closed period of training but as something that can be pursued up to the tertiary level. It was with this aim in mind that the voctional baccalaureate was conceived, providing the option of access to Hautes Ecoles Spécialisées (HES, also sometimes referred to as Universities of Applied Sciences. A second kind of measure, corresponding to a horizontal deconstruction, bears upon the shrinking number of opportunities for occupational training, with the creation of core curricula that offer, across a group of occupations, an initial level of common training and only later introducing more specific elements of training relevant to one or another occupation. The forms of restructuring that are currently underway all, in one fashion or another, introduce a new approach to the knowledge and competence that are appropriately transmitted to future professionals.

To offer to young people opportunities for training that are at once both flexible and of high quality, school-based training tends to be presented, in the context of the current crisis, as the most appropriate solution. Contact with places of work is not necessarily neglected; mixed solutions are envisaged, for example, combining initial general training on a full-time basis in college followed by training courses carried out partly in the workplace. Generally, the workplace course, designed according to a logic of alternation, is a formula that has growing appeal in the occupational training field.

We cannot fail to be struck on this point by the very different developments in different countries; while Switzerland has come to question the future of its dual system and to recommend a consolidation of that part of the training carried out in college, other countries (the United States, and in particular France) are working to revalue, in different forms, those occupational apprenticeships based in the workplace that have historically been abandoned in favor of academically based training (Brucy & Troger, 2000). In one way or another, the changes that are currently in progress call for a more precise specification of what can be learned only in college and what can be learned only in the work situation (Tuomi-Gröhn & Engeström, 2003; Bailey, Hugues, & Moore, 2004; Samurçay & Pastré, 2004; Yamazumi & Engeström, 2005; Billet, 2002; Durand & Fabre, 2007).

LEARNING A TRADE IN A TECHNICAL COLLEGE

What occupational competencies can be acquired in college has never, in the history of occupational training, been a matter that could be taken for granted. In the French-speaking world, it remains a subject of lively debates, still pursued in one form or another. In their work on the history of technical teaching in France, Pelpel and Trager (1993) describe the conflict that has, from the end of the 19th century, pitted the advocates of learning in school against the workshop and those favoring the workshop against the school:

> On the side of supporters of learning based in production workshops, realism dominates: only genuine experience can teach young people the practice of those trades for which they are destined. It will be driven by work in all its aspects including economic and relational and, of necessity, by confrontation with the most up to date forms of production and the most advanced machinery, for otherwise it would be necessary to finance their production, because this is production machinery. (p. 266)

For the advocates of occupational training who recommend that practice be included in college-based training,

> the so called advantage of real experience turns out in fact to be limited and dangerous; each workshop only has available that machinery necessary to its own production, and it is an illusion to believe that this will always be at the forefront of technical developments. Under the pretext of realism there is a considerable risk of having only a very circumscribed training. (p. 267)

The debate on this issue is certainly not over. It underlies numerous observations we heard at the Ecole Technique de Sainte-Croix during the course of the interviews that we carried out with teachers there. The link between training activities and real professional practice was often mentioned. Some of the remarks made by these teachers would lead one to conclude that teaching and learning in a technical college are less effective than teaching and learning in the classical dual system, precisely because of this absence of "real" work in the former. It is to remedy this that initiatives have been made to introduce within the college program periods of professional practice that are genuinely industrial, along with visits to workshops and courses in companies. Let us also note that, for the students, the professional experience of their practice teacher was perceived very positively from this point of view, providing a source of credibility.

For the teachers themselves, reference to the world of work was very salient in their reactions. Some of them expressed a fear of losing their original competence and professional identity by virtue of prolonged practical training that progressively distanced them from more recent industrial developments or more general developments of knowledge in their area of work. Thus, the manner in which the relation to the world of real work is experienced depends on the direction taken by prior training. The question is particularly sensitive for those teachers who, on the basis of their own basic training and sometimes previous industrial experience, have developed a strong professional identity that in some way takes precedence over that of teacher or trainer. But any generalization in this area turns out to be very difficult, given the wide range of approaches to training to be found among the teachers in a technical college.

However, the tendency today to value the element of technical training that can be provided in college, together with the corresponding trend toward a staff establishment increasingly drawn from higher education, is not without consequences for the approaches to training that are adopted. As shown in the French context by Tanguy's (1991) work, recruitment of teachers with higher diplomas in technology at the expense of holders of a professional qualification alters the content of teaching and the pedagogical approaches adopted; teaching of technical knowledge tends to be substituted for teaching of occupational skills.

Our intention here is to provide some reference points so that we can more adequately grasp, in the Swiss context, the significance of these current developments and debates. We begin with some historical background that raises questions about where full-time trade schools are going and what place they occupy in a system of occupational training more generally characterized by dual functioning. Then we describe, starting with the example of the Ecole Technique de Sainte-Croix, how the practical and theoretical elements of training are combined in a technical college.

WHERE DID THE FULL-TIME SCHOOLS COME FROM?[3]

In the 19th century and in the context of change in the organization and techniques of work, of reaction against the catastrophic human consequences of liberalism, but also of struggle against a decline in the quality of Swiss industrial products, the development of training was first led by individuals from industry, from the Swiss arts and crafts movement,[4] and from local government. According to Tabin (1989, 1990), this development entailed an ambiguous combination, in particular within the Swiss Union of Arts and Crafts (USAM), of a progressive desire to provide workers and young people with social protection and of a more reactionary movement to restore an older order, that of craft guilds and corporations and their privileges. This order was abolished in 1848 by the Constitution of the new Swiss republic and replaced by freedom of commerce and trade. At the federal level, establishment of a system of occupational training was not initiated in Switzerland until the end of the 19th century, leading to the first federal law in 1930.

For the private technical drawing colleges, which have existed since the 18th century, at the apprenticeship level, the situation was chaotic. The industrial revolution had not only forced a large number of workers into unemployment or a situation of extreme poverty, but the introduction of new procedures and equipment had also required qualified labor. Where to find it? The former teachers of the craft industry had become rare and they did not choose to train workers for industry. We then witnessed multidirectional developments: the industry of machines and textiles itself set about training its own labor force. Teaching workshops were opened in large companies. Watchmaking in the Jura established its own colleges (with the support of the communes) (Villiger, 1985).

It is worthy to note that to retain precision mechanics and watchmaking in the Joux valley of the Jura region, the Industrial and Commercial Society (SIC) had, as early as 1878, condemned the poor training situation in this principal economic activity of the region. It commented upon the end of an era in which "one had seen large numbers of foreigners, from every country, come to live in our cold valley in order to learn from our old and venerated experts, over the course of several years, the difficult art of making watches from scratch" (Schindler-Pittet, 1976, p. 11). Long ap-

---

[3] The historical elements presented here, and also the observations that follow in the next two sections, are taken from the following research papers:

> Golay Shilter. (1995). *Le systeme suisse de la formation professionnelle: repères généraux.* Séminaire de psychologie, University of Neuchâtel.
>
> Golay Shilter. (1995). *Regards sur l'organisation et les enjeux de l'enseignement a l'Ecole Technique de Sainte-Croix.* Séminaire de Psychologie, University of Neuchâtel.

[4] Including the Swiss Union of Arts and Crafts (USAM), founded in 1879, and the Industrial and Commercial Society (SIC).

prenticeships became too costly, and young people were required to work in factories without any training. The absence of training led to a shortage of qualified workers and the loss of local skills, such as finishing, to the benefit of other watchmaking cantons (Neuchatel and Geneva). Despite the urgings and efforts of the SIC, the watchmaking college of the Joux valley did not open until 1901. The communes quarreled among themselves and were reluctant to invest their own money. In Sainte-Croix, the SIC also struggled in vain in the 1870s, and the Ecole de Petite Mécanique was not established until 1908. In comparison, Geneva set up its own college in 1823, and in the Canton of Neuchâtel, four colleges had already been created, including Fleurier in 1851, La Chaux-de-Fonds in 1865, Le Locle in 1868, and Neuchatel in 1871.

From the beginning there were two types of colleges in Switzerland: full-time colleges (arts and crafts, watchmaking, woodworking trades, textiles, etc.) mostly in Swiss Romand, and colleges attended part time by apprentices undergoing training within businesses. There were also debates in the crafts and trades context at the end of the 19th century on whether it was desirable to promote a system of full-time education for all or to maintain work-based apprenticeships. The creation of these colleges and these debates shows that a movement had started, but up to now "these efforts remain confined to the limits of a parish, a town, a business or a region" (Villiger, 1985a, p. 46). Meanwhile, the state, both Cantonal and Federal, played almost no role at all.

In 1882–83, because of a shortage of qualified labor and disquiet about the quality of Swiss products, the Confederation launched an "industrial inquiry" in response to complaints from companies on the subject of matters that could hinder their activities. What emerged was the necessity for government action on the issue of occupational training, training of a type one began to appreciate could no longer only be practical. Without any constitutional basis for legislating in this area, the houses of parliament could opt only for a federalist political solution. Since academic teaching is a responsibility of local government, it was left to this level to create and manage professional schools, while the Confederation and the Cantons contributed to their financing. It was thus that between 1890 and 1910, numerous local schools for professional (and academic) improvement were funded (Villiger, 1985a).

The first laws on apprenticeships were cantonal, starting with the Neuchatel law of 1890. The principal objective of these laws was the protection of children and young people in the workplace. Neuchatel also established an apprenticeship final examination, which was initially optional but became compulsory in 1909. On the matter of examinations, until then it had been the USAM and other professional bodies that played an organizing role. The gradual takeover of occupational training at the federal level took a decisive step forward in 1908 with the addition to the Constitution of the Confederation's right to legislate on industrial, commercial, arts, and trade matters, and notably on the right to work. Then the presence of a large proportion of foreign skilled workers in some occupations, workers who disappeared during World War I, drew attention to the need to establish a reserve of a trained, indigenous labor force. The labor unions also began to take an interest in the question of exams becoming compulsory more or less everywhere; all these influences were leading to the drafting of federal law. But its gestation was a long one, reflecting both the differences among those involved and the economic considerations. As Tabin (1989, p. 17) notes, "regularisation of the legal situation on apprenticeships came to have effects on the conditions of competition and came to place companies in an equal position regarding the definition of an apprenticeship and the practice of a trade." It was thus not until 1930 that the first federal law was passed on occupational training. This defined the basic conditions for an apprenticeship (a minimum duration of one year; professional teaching and compulsory examinations; obligations of the employer toward the apprentice; etc.). If the crisis delayed the implementation of the law, in contrast, unemployment stimulated the organization of all kinds of courses and workshops.

THE ECOLE TECHNIQUE DE SAINTE-CROIX: HISTORICAL BACKGROUND

Creation of a technical college at Sainte-Croix has to be set in the historical context described above. The story of the creation of this college, insofar as it is presented in the brochure published on the occasion of its 75th anniversary (Mellana, 1883), faithfully illustrates the more general history of technical teaching and industry in the Jura region of Switzerland:

> In the story of Sainte-Croix, the word "crisis" often arises. It was during the recession that prevailed from 1866 that, for the first time, the question of occupational training arose. On the 17th of September, 1870, the Industrial and Commercial Society of Sainte-Croix, prompted by the inadequacy of certain workers in watch-making and musical instruments, charged Monsieur Gilliéron, college professor, with the responsibility of giving lessons in mechanics and technical drawing.

But it was not until 1908, after long negotiations, that the SIC opened its "true" Ecole de Petite Mécanique.

As elsewhere in the Jura, the Sainte-Croix region had seen its industry born in the 15th century with the exploitation of iron ore, which then gave way to lacemaking, and subsequently watchmaking and, at the beginning of this century, music boxes. On each occasion, the appearance of "new technologies," in association with other factors that we will not go into here,

precipitated a decline of industries that had previously been locally dominant, along with transformations that were more or less successful. These
"crises" were not only economic. The organization of work changed radically (working at home, traditionally significant in the watchmaking sector,
was supplanted by the development of factories), and liberalism in the matter of rights of practice and commerce and the accompanying deregulation
combined to undermine systems for the transmission of knowledge and
skills. These last themselves changed and developed in response to unforeseen currents (the influence of the United States, for example). Animated
by intentions that were simultaneously socially concerned and highly con-
servative, because they wished to revert to an earlier order of corporations,
it was the crafts and trades movement that responded first (Tabin, 1989,
1990). The Sainte-Croix SIC, which, as we have already seen, played a central role in the initiative that was to become the ETSC, belonged to this
movement.[5]

Of the significant dates in the history of the Ecole Technique de Sainte-
Croix, the brochure mentions the introduction of new techniques (plastic
molding in 1966, the introduction of computer-controlled machine tools
in 1973) alongside the introduction of new training schemes (the technical
baccalaureate in 1969, the training of technicians in operations management and construction in 1970, and industrial computing in 1979).[6]

Unfortunately, this brochure only gives dates without any accompanying
detail or commentary, despite devoting many lines to a description of the
industrial history of the region and the context at the time the college was
established. This is a shame because identification and analysis of the occasions on which new techniques, knowledge, and training were introduced
into the curriculum could considerably enrich our understanding both of
the internal dynamics of a college and of the links relating it to technological evolution.

Other bits of information about the development of the Ecole Technique de Sainte-Croix were provided to us in the course of our interviews
and in other, more informal ways. Thus, we learned that in 1969, members
of the management team created SwissPerfo, a business specializing in the
manufacturing of industrial products and CIM teaching aids, which they
provided to the school as well as worldwide. The college also bought out the
equipment of a business that failed in 1993. Additionally, the school, which
had for a long time been dependent on the commune of Sainte-Croix, is
now maintained by the Canton of Vaud.

---

[5] Let us also recall, with respect to the major role played by this body, that the professional
school of the SIC in Lausanne had already trained thousands of students and apprentices.

[6] To this list should be added the creation of training in electronics in 1985 (transferred to
Yverdon in 1999), as well as the setting-up of innovative general training in information
technology.

The history of the Ecole Technique de Sainte-Croix is closely analogous to that of neighboring establishments in the Jura region. A study dealing more particularly with the Joux valley technical school (Schindler-Pittet, 1976) clearly shows how the life of this establishment reflected the ups and downs of watchmaking, a regional industry closely linked to economic circumstances while being strongly emblematic of local identity. Economic crisis and unemployment can affect college numbers in different ways: in one direction because a number of apprentices remain longer in the school, in another when applicant numbers drop because the prospect of later unemployment discourages young people from preparing for occupations in crisis. For those in charge, it was a continual struggle at the financial level to renew equipment, but also to convince others of the necessity of diversifying training (in this case, toward mechanics and electronics). Let us again note that the links with local businesses were very strong because the institution was financed by some of them and its advisors included representatives of these enterprises while commissions were produced for them. In brief, these trade schools fulfill multiple roles at the regional level, roles that are at once economic, technical, identity-related, and political. In addition, they compensate for disparities between the apprenticeships offered and the demand for training, while sustaining otherwise "disappearing" crafts, such as violin maker and wood sculptor (Wettestein, Bossy, Dommann, & Villiger, 1989, p. 130).

INSTRUCTION IN THEORY AND PRACTICAL TRAINING UNDER A SINGLE ROOF: THE CASE OF THE ECOLE TECHNIQUE DE SAINTE-CROIX

We have examined the context in which the trade schools saw their time come so that we could look in more detail at the history of the Ecole Technique de Sainte-Croix. We now need to consider in more detail how training is organized so that it can provide under one roof the acquisition of both the theoretical and the practical knowledge specific to each course of training. Requirements for professional knowledge are fixed by the rules for apprenticeships established by the Office Federal de l'Industrie et des Arts et Metiers (OFIAMT),[7] along with the hours to be devoted to each discipline. The objectives and the hourly allocations for the areas of general culture and sport are the subject of a separate scheme of study. These requirements provide a general framework, which, the teachers told us, must sometimes be adapted as a function of the specifics of regional industries,

---

[7] Following a reorganization carried out in the federal administration, the responsibilities of this former office are now integrated with those of the *Office Federal de la Formation Professionelle et de la Technologie.*

the resources available, and indeed the strengths and weaknesses of their students with respect to the knowledge required for the final examinations.

The Training of Apprentices in a Technical College

One part of the training program consists of time spent on practice in the workshop, representing about 60% of the training schedule, a proportion that slightly increases over the 4 years of the apprenticeship. This training is provided by a teacher responsible for the activities taking place in the workshop. The remaining time is devoted to theoretical instruction. This latter consists of three parts: *professional knowledge*, *general culture*, and *scientific disciplines*.

The various branches of *professional knowledge* provide the apprentices with the knowledge they require to pursue their professions. These courses deal, for example, with general electronics, the properties of materials, and additional technical drawing. Several of the teachers we questioned found the programs of professional knowledge very demanding, in particular those for electricians; in the view of one of them, "The work required is enormous, indeed superhuman."

General culture includes German, English, French, accounting, economics, and civics education. At the Ecole Technique de Sainte-Croix, the French teacher saw his work with the apprentices as "a last chance to compensate for the deficiencies of their earlier schooling." He goes over the basics of grammar with students who have reading difficulties and dislike this subject. As for English, the principal aim is to be capable of "getting by" in the eventuality of a stay in an English-speaking country. The instructor responsible for the course in commerce told us that he teaches primarily on the basis of concrete examples, such as the creation of a business, producing a budget, etc. Course requirements and teaching methods are left to the discretion of instructors who must adapt these goals to the level of their students and often work with groups of different levels.

Scientific disciplines (physics and mathematics). These have the smallest allocation of time. From five sessions in the first year, it declines to two sessions in the second, and then disappears from the program for the electricians, while for the mechanics it is replaced by a session on vocational arithmetic.

The Training of Technicians

Introduced into the Ecole Technique de Sainte-Croix in 1970, the training of technicians was recognized at the federal level with the law on professional training in 1978. At the professional level, the technicians are trained to assume the functions of supervision. But the technological developments and the change of the educational system (notably with the creation of

Universities of Applied Sciences) call for reconsideration and perhaps even a new definition of the functions and the training of technicians (Garnier, 1994).

The Ecole Technique de Sainte-Croix numbers around 40 trainee technicians and offers three courses: "project management and production," "mechanical construction," and "industrial computing." The first two deal with the design and construction of apparatus and machines, with an emphasis in the first course on the management of production. The computer technicians learn to respond by computer to technical problems and to deal with automated production systems, networks, and office installations. Their training is provided by 2 years of full-time study at the technical school. In the three courses, the final year is divided between one "semester" of 30 weeks, and a second of 7 weeks devoted entirely to diploma work. As regards the weekly timetable, the 45 separate sessions of the training program are divided in the following manner:

Practical training (20–22 sessions). This consists of "technical office" activities and practical work. The mechanized construction course contains the largest element of practice while that of industrial computing contains the smallest. In the practical sessions we were able to observe the engagement of students in the tasks, carrying out their work in a relatively autonomous fashion. Generally, the variety of training backgrounds they come from and the individual projects make this training of the technicians sufficiently individualized.

Theoretical training (23–25 sessions). This includes teaching the professional knowledge (11–13 sessions) that accompanies the practical work; teaching of scientific knowledge (seven sessions), and teaching of general knowledge (five sessions). The scientific disciplines are the same for the three courses: physics, mechanics, and mathematics. The mathematics teacher observed that although the level at the beginning is not very high, rapid progress is made during the course of the year. The branches of general knowledge are French, German, English, political economy, and business. Teaching of languages was introduced very early on at the Ecole Technique de Sainte-Croix, which had recognized the need before other institutions However, languages are not heavily represented in the final examinations, and the English teacher told us that students often only seem to discover later why mastery of languages is important in the professional domain.

A LABORATORY FOR PROFESSIONAL TRAINING

Through their ambition to integrate on the one hand practical training (in the college workshops, where trade skills are acquired) and on the other the development in their students of more general knowledge, the technical colleges *de facto* embody the problems of the dual system. However, the close association of practical work classes with classes devoted to theory encourages a search for a pedagogical relationship between these different opportunities for training, based on a model that we may call flexible alternation or "micro-alternation."

During our frequent visits to the Ecole Technique de Sainte-Croix site, we were able to see that full-time schooling covers a wider variety of teaching arrangements than is apparent simply from examining the course timetable. In fact, the time devoted to classes, exercises, practical work, workshop sessions, the diploma project, and individual work turns out to overlap considerably, and this is probably even more the case within a small establishment in which the same teaching staff often delivers both theoretical courses and, via their responsibility for workshops, practical training. It is not unusual to observe time in the workshop being devoted to the provision of complementary theoretical explanations or, conversely, practical work being introduced, according to need, into theory sessions.

Through the close and flexible articulation of training sessions that they achieve, these institutions deserve the closest attention; in our view, in terms of the learning processes at work within them, they represent a valuable laboratory for the study of professional training. Apart from the larger institutional restructuring in progress, we think it is necessary today to refine the observations made of the characteristics of situations in which professional knowledge and skills are combined, of the time spent in instruction and learning by trial and error, and of the time spent in individual development and that spent working in groups. The general categories employed to designate different training structures (dual system, apprenticeship, alternation, full-time trade school) by themselves cover neither the diversity of training practices employed nor the breadth and complexity of experience to which trainers and apprentices are exposed in the transmission and appropriation of new professional competences.

By taking on the task of achieving a functional integration of practical with theoretical training, a technical college occupies a pivotal position between the world of training and that of work. This interface position is not, however, as stable and well established as one might think. Without doubt there is a regular need to rework it in response to various developments and changes taking place in the technical domain (notably reflecting the increasing proliferation of information technology), in conceptions of the act of learning and processes of training, and also in the relations between generations, between "experts" and "novices," as well as in the aspirations of young people and the manner in which all this is reflected in society at large.

CHAPTER 3

INTRODUCTION OF MANUFACTURING SYSTEMS INTO A COLLEGE

The Views of the Teachers Involved

How does a vocational training college respond to the challenge of introducing new technologies? What are the concrete repercussions for the functioning of the institution, for the training programs, for the teaching activities, and for the students?

Over the course of this chapter, we shall be hearing in particular the views of those responsible for training, as well as those teachers who have found themselves involved in the different stages of major technical development projects in the field of computer-assisted design and manufacture. At the beginning of the 1990s, when the first contacts were established between our research team and the management of the Ecole Technique de Sainte-Croix, this school had just completed a major development with the installation of a teaching facility incorporating a flexible manufacturing system (FMS), the first step in building toward an automated production

Apprentice in a Changing Trade, pages 23–56

workshop. This point in time was therefore particularly opportune for providing insight into the demands of new technical equipment when introduced into the training program.

We describe what the teachers communicated to us in the course of various interviews, always trying to preserve the richness of their observations. These observations were sometimes summarized on the basis of interview notes; in other cases, we had transcriptions of recordings of the interviews. In this latter case, to avoid involving the reader in laborious and unnecessary detail, the transcriptions are not exact reproductions of the style of the oral communication.

THREE OVERLAPPING THEMES

To organize the presentation of what we heard and learned, we focus on three dimensions corresponding to three broad themes: the delivery and installation of new technical equipment; the formulation of learning objectives; and the approaches to training put into operation.

The first of them concerns the *commissioning of equipment* as experienced by those who found themselves entrusted with the task of technological upgrading within the institution, from initial conception to installation, and including the implementation of new equipment and its pedagogical uses. The interviews conducted with teachers revealed the extent to which different pieces of equipment were laden with history within the institution. Each stage of technical development was experienced as an adventure, an epic saga in which success seemed utterly dependent on the energy and tenacity of the teachers charged with its execution. Their involvement in the initial phases of the process profoundly affected the pedagogical engagement that followed. From this point of view, the stage of acquisition and commissioning of a new facility was not a preliminary stage that was unconnected to the training put into place once the equipment was installed and capable of serving training goals.[1]

The second theme bears upon *learning objectives*, and the level of mastery of the new production technologies that the teachers wish their students to achieve. We will see that the teachers gave particular emphasis to the impact of computer-assisted manufacture in transforming the nature of the technical activity; in the words of one teacher, this activity becomes, among other things, "more cerebral," because all the operations and their interconnections must be anticipated and then represented using coding

---

[1] On this point it is possible to establish a relationship between the creation and the use of means of teaching within the more general domain of teaching. The fact that teachers may use in class either resources available "off-the peg" or those they have themselves created plays an important role in the didactic process, but a role that as yet has been little studied (Perret & Runtz-Christian, 1993).

systems. It is on the basis of this general observation that the issue of the competences to be developed is discussed and considered.

The third theme concerns the *training approaches* that teachers informed us they had to develop in consequence. How do the technological changes affect their way of thinking about the practice of training? Do these tend to "disrupt" current conceptions and practices in the area of professional didactics, or is it possible to "mold" them to well-established pedagogical approaches?[2] How does new teaching content find a place in the established training structure, in the weekly timetable, or in the organization of examinations?

TECHNICAL EQUIPMENT DISCUSSED IN THE INTERVIEWS

To train their students in the idea of computer-assisted manufacture, as well as adults undertaking further training in this area, the Ecole Technique de Sainte-Croix both developed and brought in an array of increasingly complex equipment. In this area of activity, innovations unfolded in large steps. The first step, one taken somewhat earlier, involved the introduction of computer numerically controlled machine tools. The Ecole Technique de Saints-Croix, a pioneering college in this area, has been designing and constructing this kind of equipment since the 1970s so that students could be initiated in their uses. This will be the first aspect that we consider, taking into consideration the chronology of the technical renewal that has marked the life of this institution.

Other interviews covered equipment acquired by the college more recently, at the beginning of the 1990s, equipment destined to be incorporated into an overall plan for computer-integrated manufacturing (CIM).[3] The following equipment was involved: a didactic FMS unit; a unit for robotic assembly; and a program for management of computer-assisted production. Each of these elements gave rise to somewhat different approaches to facilities. It is for this reason that we examine successively what the teachers had to say in each case.

It is helpful, however, to understand the underlying thread that links these successive technological innovations. An institution such as the Ecole Technique tends to follow general developmental trends within the world of industry. The evolution of automated manufacture has, in effect, followed a series of stages and a succession of developments, each of which was aimed at a greater integration of the different elements of production

---

[2] In the field of continuing education, Ferrand, Le Goff, Malglaive, and Orofiamma (1987) note that training in new technologies does not necessarily require new pedagogical practices. Is the same true for initial training?

[3] Behind this major re-equipment project lays the program of action, research, development, and training that the Confederation has supported since 1989 with the aim of underpinning the introduction of apparatus for computer-integrated manufacturing into Switzerland.

in order to improve the efficiency and flexibility of the system as a whole (in the sense of constituting a *flexible workshop*, indeed a *flexible business*).

Note, however, that the stages in the creation of facilities presented here do not encompass all the technological developments that have been undertaken within the college. The introduction of automated manufacturing facilities certainly represents the major component of the innovations in the Ecole Technique de Sainte-Croix, but other areas of activity were equally affected by the introduction of new technologies.[4]

FIRST ASPECT: DIGITALLY CONTROLLED MACHINES

Stroobants (1993) characterizes this equipment and its development in the following manner:

> Digitally controlled machines (CNC) have been established in industry since the 1960s. As their name implies, these involved hybrid equipment, consisting of a machine tool—true to a type and its functions (turning, drilling, cutting, etc.)—and a control mechanism—a robot transmitting operating instructions to the machine. Thus the director of the control mechanism in question constitutes a manufacturing programme, in which is stored the information corresponding to the operations for driving and steering the machine.... The digitalisation of instructions, and then the development of micro-processors thus led to the introduction, in the 1970s, of digital control with calculation which made it possible to introduce or modify a programme directly via a key-board. (p. 164)

How Did the Ecole Technique de Sainte-Croix Become Equipped with Digitally Controlled Machines?

Construction of the first digitally controlled machine tool at the Ecole Technique de Sainte- Croix took place in 1975. Two teachers in particular played a prominent role in this project. One was responsible for the mechanical side, the other for the computing element. They executed this project outside their normal teaching duties; the students in the college were consequently not involved. Who presided over the launch of this project, and how did it unfold? The details on these matters, acquired in the course of interviews, can be summarized as follows:

---

[4] This is particularly true of electronics, where programs now make it possible to draw electrical circuits on the computer and then simulate their operation so that they can be tested before actually being constructed. The computing sector is equally marked by the development of systems of exploitation, languages, and technologies that underpin in particular the creation of information networks. The teaching of more general subjects has also been affected by the introduction of new computing aids: notably, teaching programs have been provided to students for language learning.

Digital control has been employed in large companies from the 1960s, but the computers required were huge machines, too costly for a college. How, then could the students be introduced to its use? It happened that in 1970 the Ecole Technique had built for the forestry service an apparatus to measure the diameter of trees that involved recording on punched tape.

Hand punching did not last long because the punching in of each code was laborious and every error meant the process had to be completed again from the very beginning. A card reader-writer was introduced and continued in use for 4–5 years. Then the college acquired magnetic tape, and finally it was possible to store programs on hard discs. This development on the computing side required the involvement of computer scientists and led to the development of "true" digital control, operating with ISO codes. For the electronics aspects, before the creation of an electronics section within Ecole Technique, "those of us with some knowledge pitched in, soldering circuits in the evenings."

To initiate students into digital control at the time, teaching equipment had to be chosen because of the very high cost of industrial machinery. In addition, the acquisition of such machines had the drawback that the students were allowed to access these had to be limited out of fear of harmful accidents during their use.

With respect to the mechanical aspects, the first machine was only capable at the beginning of engraving straight lines in relatively soft material. Then progressively it became possible to engrave or cut obliques and circles. Until 1984, the digitally controlled machines were made up from elements constructed entirely in-house. From 1985 onward we saw the introduction of Sinumerik machines, built by Siemens.

The Ecole Technique de Sainte-Croix finally possessed five centers for teaching machining, along with one engraver and one cutter, to train its students in the use of digitally controlled machine tools. These machines evoked a range of reactions among the teachers.

Concerning the five teaching centers for digitally controlled machining: *the exercises accompanying the course in "Theory and practice of computer numerical control" were based on these machines. With them it was possible to use softer materials that could tolerate errors in a way that was not possible with production machinery.* The instructors said that they preferred using these five teaching machines to a large industrial production center that allowed less error and was not designed for students to get involved in and learn. *There was no need for something too good, an overly expensive machine on which the instructor would end up doing everything out of fear that the students would break it. The aim of education is to risk mistakes under conditions such that when they are made there are no serious consequences.*

Of the engraver guided by a Sinumerik controller: *It could remove shavings, and cut with a 10mm tool. One could, for example, machine the frontal plaques of a control panel in thin material.*

Of the cutter on which the Sinumerik controlled was installed by the technicians of the college: *It was the only one capable of cutting pieces of normal sizes, but it did not have an automatic tool loader, as "modern" machines currently have.*

We might note first of all that none of these machines was bought as a finished article by the college. All of them were designed, assembled, modified, or completed within the college, with the collaboration of Swissperfo.[5] But it is not certain that, in the future, technical developments of this scope will continue to be realized within the college itself. The acquisition of new machinery today seems to involve delivery of machines that are ready to run. *If the financial support requested had been accepted by the State, The Ecole Technique would have been able to acquire new digitally controlled machinery that was ready to run. A request had in fact been made to support purchase by the college of two manufacturing centers and two CNC (computer numerically controlled) lathes. This equipment was justified by the fact that it is now possible to pass the practical exam for completion of an apprenticeship certificate based in part on CNC. The college does not currently offer this option; the gap remains to be filled.*

Our second observation concerns the perception of the machines themselves. Several remarks on this score drew a distinction between the educational machines and the production machines, along with the distinct functions that they respectively filled in training. The instructor responsible for the "CNC theory and practice" course pointed to the educational machines and said: *Here it's an exercise; we work with resin. As for a mechanic, he works in overalls and with lubricants; that's what you do in the workshops at the end of the second year and in the third and fourth years.* Viewed from the workshops, the educational machines certainly represent something modern, but as one of the workshop heads puts it, *Unfortunately they are just educational. That's okay for demonstrations but they are not robust enough for metalworking; if one tries, everything vibrates. In the workshop there's a solid machine with modern digital control, but there is no tool feed and it does not work on four axes. It's dated.*

What Training Objectives are Pursued?

The teachers believe it is essential that their students develop competence in the area of digital control. *If they leave the college without having done CNC, it would give the school a bad reputation. It would be aberrant; nowadays, CNC is everywhere.*

---

[5] This enterprise, initially called Perfo, was set up in 1970 on the initiative of a former director and several teachers of the Ecole Technique. It first specialized in the production of punch tape, but the business then grew and became oriented to the production of digitally controlled machinery. Over the years, it retained close links with industrial development and training activities. The Swissperfo engineers had in particular supported the development and maintenance of the equipment at the college. Several of the college's teachers had also contributed, sometimes with their students, to the development of prototypes. It was within the context of this collaboration that it was possible to put together both the hardware and the software elements of the manufacturing unit.

What objectives are envisaged in this area? *At the end of training, the students should be capable of programming any part and manufacture it in the workshop, starting from a drawing and with materials provided. They must know how to program the digital control codes to regulate the machines and the tools; they should be capable of anticipating and imagining the manufacture without having to make five attempts to get their program to work.*

The exam requirements can be summarized in three points: *produce* a machining program on the basis of a drawing of a part; *draw* a part on the basis of a program; *correct* a program. These learning objectives are commented upon in the following terms: *It is necessary to analyze manufacture, which is to say predict the operations in the correct order with the right tools, as a function of the characteristics of the part. Some plunge into the activity without thinking about it. It is important above all to be methodical. We don't need these little geniuses who throw themselves in and break the machines; those people who have too much self-confidence are dangerous people. Me, if I was a boss, I would not employ someone like that.* Is it difficult for them to be methodical? *Yes, but this can be learned. In conventional manufacture, the order of operations is self-evident. But with digital control a method is necessary because it is more abstract. You have to give coordinates, indications to the machine, things you do not have to do with other machines. With conventional machines, you more quickly see what will not work.*

Another teacher characterizes what is particular to computer numerical control as follows: *With the conventional machine, one makes a part in a cascade; one can get there in stages. With computer numerical control, it is necessary to envisage the whole process, from A to Z; it's more cerebral. It is necessary to sit at the desk and analyze the operational phases. Some prefer to rush to a machine and get on with it; they hate picking up pencil and paper. These students are miserable with digital control.*

The trainees have to draw a part on the basis of a program and vice versa. They have to be capable of correcting a program. *It is typical of the situation that arises in professional practice; one must be able to see where there is a problem (where this is perhaps a keystroke error). The College's machines indicate the nature of the error. To correct these, one has to know the digital control codes and use theoretical knowledge and figure out what does not seem consistent. For example, to verify the order of movements, or the diameter of the drill used in relation to the radius of the cut to be made. It is a matter of being systematic. It is here that there are problems; often they skip a stage.*

Knowing how to correct a program; that's always useful. Certainly today there is increasingly assisted programming. But 80% of parts are still made on equipment like that available here, equipment that machines on two axes. The new four axes machines are necessary to machine complex shapes (molds, for example) using complex movements.... We still work with direct programming (programming on the digital control keyboard). We think with the hand. We do the calculations ourselves, introducing each instruction, while with the advanced machines more and more you give them general indications, and the programs take control of the calculations and other decisions. This basic mastery of CNC coding is still judged to be useful: *In 10 years, there will still be machines like those the students use. Besides, their machines already have several computer-aided functions, such as the "pocketing" function to machine pockets.*

Are the apprentices sufficiently prepared for work in industry? *Yes, even if they come across other machines, they must know how to read the manuals and cope.* Nonetheless, an expansion is envisaged of the training provided in this area. *If computer numerical control represents 30% of the practical hours, they will also do lathe work and it will be necessary to work on machines with tool changers, for larger operations. Some of these things are possible in the "CNC theory and practice" course. But the teaching machines are not suitable for steel and in the workshop they only have a computer-controlled cutter.*

What expectations do employers have of the students they take on? According to the head of the mechanics section, the ideal for them would be for the students to be instantly capable, for them to have perfect knowledge of the machines used by the employer. *They ask for too much here!*

Do the students have this capacity for rapid adaptation? *Yes, they learn fast in a business, but they leave fast when they discover they are button pushers. In effect, an enterprise gives a graduating apprentice a position as machine operator. He enters the data prepared by the technician in charge of planning the machining, and monitors the machine, which is a job, but one that turns out to be less interesting than expected. So, if students are interested at the outset, attracted by the prestige of digital control and automation, they are quickly sick of it. At least in a small company, they have the chance of becoming a programmer-operator. What's interesting in digital control is work as a development technician operating across the range, making installations, etc.*

The CNC Machine to be "Tamed"

The mechanics apprentices encounter CNC on the one hand in the workshop practical sessions, which continue until the fourth year, and on the other in the course titled "CNC Theory and Practice," which forms part of the program designated as "theoretical." This course consists of 200 sessions (five weekly classes during the second year of training). According to the timetable, each Monday there is one hour of theory and four of practice; in fact, the teacher regularly moves back and forth between theoretical presentation and application: *It's more effective for comprehension, for holding the attention and sustaining the concentration of the apprentices.* For the exercises, different types of machining are successively introduced, and students begin with engraving *because no tool correction is needed; it's the simplest.*

How do students experience the transition from conventional machining to digital control? *Preliminary experience with conventional machining is necessary, but the method of approach is different for computer numerical control. At the beginning they are surprised; there are no handles to turn. But that pleases them, they quickly take to it. Some of the students do then get stuck; we are well equipped and all this is so modern. For the mechanics apprentices, the screen is a priori complicated. I understand them because I've experienced this. When I moved on to digital control the first time I worried about everything. But really it is very simple!*

Those who are bothered by it spend very little time on computer numerical control, because it is not required in the practical exam. Those who are keen, I leave with the machines and use various stratagems with them and they founder, and founder some more, and this is how they learn.... At the beginning they call me to press the start button. They are afraid. But I show them a trick: reduce the speed so that you can see what is happening. On conventional machines you do such and such a thing and it moves in response while with computer numerical control everything is prepared in advance so they are afraid of the consequences of their errors. But this fear declines; our generation had more fear than theirs, because this lot, they have computers at home! And here one can tame the machine by reducing the speed; it's simple to do.

The teachers in charge of the practical sessions have created a way of using the CNC machines that takes the form of an introductory guide for beginners, a complete and detailed set of instructions that indicate step by step what needs to be done and explains why. Their method of working provides the principles of application for the individual who knows how to program in theory but who must now learn how to use the machines. The production of such a guide has proved to be necessary because *it is difficult to find everything in the vast pile of documentation produced by the manufacturer.*

It is possible to see, at the level of general organization of the workshop practical sessions, the strong organizing role provided by the methodical progression through the different exercises and pieces of work to be completed. The students are assigned to machines. A list of exercises fixes progression through the tasks. There are rotations and adaptations following personal progress. The instructor has a chart allowing him to check that each student has completed all the operations and worked on all the machines. But each individual remains responsible for being able to work on the different lathes without limiting himself to a single model. These progressive exercises are sometimes interrupted to produce work to fill orders.

At certain times, there is work for clients. It would be tempting only to put the best of the students on to this, but if I'm going to have to give them more help anyway I make sure that the students all have a go because it motivates them.... Often these jobs require CNC because the parts are more complex (such as, for example, a floating brake disc for a motorbike). If there are no orders, we invent work. I make a measuring instrument for the college. Each student makes a part of it. For the assembly work, I create subgroups because it's difficult. If there is a specialty, something that will not arise again and that is interesting, the students are assembled around the machine and are given explanations, a dose of theory. At any moment in the workshop you can see students gathered around a machine for a group explanation.

For the exercises that are subject to assessment, something that occurs four times a semester, the students receive a sheet with a drawing and a time limit. The teacher has the same sheet with the list of assessment criteria. The teachers involved decided some time ago to rationalize this process in the direction of the demands that students will face in the final exam at the conclusion of their studies (CFC). *There are measurable, observable, and quantifiable criteria and the students see this sheet and the marks are discussed with them. They try it on a bit over particular marks, but in general they take it well; they are all well aware of the goal, to pass the CFC. Is that their principal goal? Yes, they don't see much past this, though you try to explain some of it to them....*

Group work is perceived differently by the teachers depending on whether it occurs in the "CNC theory and practice" course (working in pairs here is commonplace, as the first of the following comment makes clear or in the practical sessions in the workshops (here, work is traditionally carried out alone). In the CNC course, *for the course exercises, the students are divided up so that all the machines are used. In general, they are two to a machine. That's the ideal; one of them reads out the code and the other types it in. And it's good that they are two, to check for errors.* In the workshop, *the problem of working in teams is that you have one of them working and all the others watching. Even in pairs, there is always one who has the hands-on experience. In the workshop, they work alone if possible, and then they can't avoid being involved.*

Summary

Within the domain of digitally controlled machines, the Ecole Technique de Sainte-Croix has been a pioneering institution in developing, from the 1970s onward, ad hoc equipment for training purposes. This technical development, requiring prolonged effort, has clearly been experienced as an epic endeavor; it has drawn upon the expertise of many individuals, particularly in the areas of electronics and computing, something new for the Ecole Technique: *those of us with some knowledge pitched in, soldering circuits in the evenings.*

The CNC machines initially developed at the Ecole Technique de Sainte-Croix were designed for teaching. In the interviews there were often questions about the distinctive features of teaching equipment conceived first of all for learning and not for production (in contrast to industrial machinery). In this respect, the digitally controlled machines seem to occupy an intermediate position at the intersection of different projects and approaches to training. On the one hand, they belong to the province of professional practice in precision mechanics, and on this basis are located in the mechanics workshops, where the apprentices train to master the trade. On the other hand, CNC is the focus of teaching that combines theoretical material with practical work. While the workshop traditionally values production machines that allow student-apprentices to become competent with "genuine" tools in a quasi–real work context, for others, the purpose of practical work is to illustrate and give concrete substance to a lesson; they start from a more " academic" perspective on training and for this they need equipment shaped to this particular educational purpose.

Depending on the point of view adopted, it is then either the limitations of the educational machines that are discussed—they *are not robust enough to machine metal*—or their value to training—*they allow errors that a production machine would not support.*

As regards the competences aimed for, it is interesting to note what the teachers say about the importance accorded to general analytical capacities, to anticipation, and to the ability to picture the machining (*some of them throw themselves into the activity without thinking!*). The need to be methodical is similarly emphasized (*it's a matter of being systematic; it's here that problems arise because often they skip a step*). The capacity to adapt to different industrial equipment is also invoked (*if they come across other machines, they must know how to read the manuals and cope*). Beyond the statements of general objectives, it is acknowledged that, within these, different levels of competence can be distinguished, according to whether it is a matter of competence in designing or correcting a digital control program or whether it is competence in using a computer numerically controlled machine. The roles of anticipation, planning, and visualization are different in these two cases.

SECOND ASPECT: A FLEXIBLE MANUFACTURING SYSTEM UNIT FOR MACHINING

A flexible manufacturing system (FMS) unit is a set of machines that are digitally controlled, interconnected, and linked to one another by an automated transport system.[6] The whole is supported by a computer system with a high capacity for scheduling and adaptation, which serves the following functions: *data storage* (digital control programs, data for particular tools); *communication* (transmitting programs, tool correction, dialogue with the terminals); *scheduling* (defining production orders, managing deadlines); *piloting* in real time (making decisions to optimize the functioning of the FSM unit); *graphic visualization* of the installation; and *monitoring* (alarms, errors, etc.).

The unit installed at the Ecole Technique consists of two machining positions, attachment positions, industrial-scale palettes, a storage bin, a tool controller, and an automatic transport system or automated guided vehicle (AGV). It provides an educational device that allows students to familiarize themselves with the operation of a flexible unit from the conception of a part all the way through to its manufacture. It is described as educational

---

[6] For a general description of this system, we draw upon the elements of an article on the Ecole Technique de Sainte-Croix that appeared in CIM/Vaud Bulletin, no. 33, September 1994.

because its set of tools is intended to work on light "exercise" material (synthetic resins) and not on metal. This choice has a number of advantages, including those of *safety*, arising from the nature of the materials that are worked and the option of machining at lower speeds, and *visibility*, based on the absence of protective screens or the covers that are normally required on an industrial machine. It is thus possible to observe close up what the machine is doing, something that should facilitate understanding of the operations involved.

How Does an Educational Establishment Manage to Equip Itself with an FSM Machining Unit?

We draw attention here to two aspects of the question showing that this achievement reflects the fruits of a partnership of different training authorities, business enterprises and institutions, as well as that its implementation within the college was founded on the involvement and expertise of teachers charged with the problem.

To acquire such equipment, the Ecole Technique de Sainte-Croix effectively relied on collaboration with companies in the region and in particular with Swissperfo, associated with the college and specializing in the design and production of machines intended as much for industry as for instruction.

Given the very high cost of an educational flexible manufacturing system—between 500,000 and 900,000 Swiss Francs, depending on the extent of integration aimed for—the college had requested and received substantial funds, awarded by the Commission for the Encouragement of Scientific Research (CERS) and by the federal "training offensive" program. The project as a whole envisaged the development of a computer-integrated manufacturing production workshop and the setting-up of training for the college's apprentices and technicians, as well as for adults pursuing continuing professional development.

The project was distributed among a network of partners; links were formed with the Reuge Company in Sainte-Croix, itself engaged in the automation of its production of base-unit mechanisms for musical boxes, and also with the Ecole Polytechnique Federale de Lausanne (EPFL) and the engineering school at Yverdon. Over the years, some of the collaborative arrangements declined, in particular because of breaks in the Confederation financing of the project, while new collaborations were established, notably that with the computer-integrated manufacturing center in Geneva.

We can again note that equipping the Ecole Technique de Sainte-Croix with educational equipment relevant to CIM was not an isolated operation in the sense that other training establishments drew on the experience developed in this area at Sainte-Croix. The sale of machines developed with Swissperfo supported the creation of relationships with several occupational training institutions in other countries (Portugal, Brazil, Malta, etc.). The sale of a complex product almost inevitably has to be followed by movement into the training of installers and operators, if further development of the equipment delivered to meet the client's needs is to be guaranteed. It has been possible to establish these forms of exchange both through long-distance communication (primarily by fax) and through direct interpersonal contact (training courses for overseas technicians at the Ecole Technique). The college has thus been able to build up experience in the transfer of technological competence. Although not explicitly defined as "distance learning," part of the experience it has acquired does in fact relate to this field of activity.

In the opinion of the current director of the Ecole Technique de Sainte-Croix, the degree of latitude allowed to the college to pursue work on the development of automated machines and on commercialization is not sufficient. In comparison to earlier investments, the director believes that the college currently functions only in a reactive mode and no longer proactively. That is to say, it confines itself to responding to the approaches of current partners and clients without looking for new contracts. This issue arises very concretely with respect to the Flexcell program developed at Sainte-Croix to control the FMS unit. Its creation required an enormous investment in terms of hours of work. Should this product now be abandoned or should the work continue to develop the program, make it more widely known, and seek its commercial exploitation? For the management of the Ecole Technique, the ideal here would be to establish a close collaboration with a local company.

Within the college, the teachers are well aware of how much they benefited at the beginning of the 1990s from opportunities and conditions that were particularly favorable to the development of wide-ranging equipment projects. Such conditions are not seen as easily recreated. As the teacher in charge of the FMS unit put it: *In the future there will certainly no longer be such dramatic activity with the college involved in the development of such an advanced system. Compared to what goes on in a company, here we are currently at the same level. It is possible to keep up with the flow so far as anything well defined is concerned, but not to develop new systems that cost millions of francs.*

Budgetary constraints are the first to be mentioned. We have to broaden our perspective here and take into account the involvement of other factors, both objective and subjective: perception of the future, both of the college itself and of its options for setting up collaborations with business; fears about the future autonomy of colleges within a system of professional training, which is currently the subject of a political initiative toward centralization; and beliefs about public finances and indeed regional economic development.

The installation of an educational machining unit required not just financial support and the creation of particular partnerships but of equal importance professional involvement supported by the management and the senior teaching staff. This task and this responsibility were articulated in the following terms by one instructor: *The demands are considerable. The teacher responsible must take care of maintenance, development, tidying up, etc. Is it possible to estimate the amount of time all this requires? In any case, the necessary means are never available. Nonetheless, one gets involved in this costly operation because it is an opportunity for a young teacher to establish his position and make a name for himself in uncertain times for the profession.*

Another aspect of professional involvement that is represented by taking on responsibility for a complex operation is the range of expertise that must be mobilized: *Flexibility on the part of the lead teacher is indispensable in a small establishment. I deal with traditional machining, with automation, with FAO, with the electronics, and with wiring. If I was at a polytechnic college, I would be able to specialize and only work on a single system. That isn't possible at the Ecole Technique. Pursuing one's own continuing professional development is essential; I'm taking several courses to ensure I remain up to date. When your position is at risk you have to invest.*

What Levels of Competence are Aimed For?

An educational machining unit within the college represents a training resource that can be used in different ways, depending on the learning objectives pursued and according to the type of professional competence targeted. What knowledge and skills and what levels of competence does the college aim for? The question is particularly relevant to the training of technicians.

Must the technicians who are undergoing training understand the overall functioning of a machining unit? Must they learn to use it, to repair it, to adapt it, or even to develop it? What competences are expected in the area of automated manufacture? For the instructor in charge of this training, there are several aspects to consider. *The technicians can be led to use a system like this one but that will not necessarily be exactly the same type. Thus, they must have used and understood one system; this will help them a lot to use and understand another one. Some of them are going to develop such systems—I am thinking of computer technicians—they are going to develop automatic control systems or a machine, or a workshop; I don't know exactly. What is sure is that they will have development tasks. For them, understanding how one can organize data and make connections between pieces of data, it's a gold mine; being able to take a data base such as Search Query Language and interrogate it; having several PCs working simultaneously and communicating with each other. Understanding all this organization, it is truly precious.*

Next there will be some, and perhaps they are the majority, who will be technicians and who will find themselves taking delivery of an automated system in their company, a system that will have been designed by someone else. They will have the responsibility of making it work. And this is a very important aspect: they must be able to ensure the smooth functioning of the system and look after its maintenance. They will be testers and that is an entire occupation in itself. It is necessary for them to learn all the tricks, everything that can happen, and learn how to make a systematic test. It matters that a system be communicative, that it records everything it does so that errors can be retrieved; it needs to have a black box (a "log book"). This last point, I give it a lot of emphasis, I provide examples, they go through a log book..., they must check through it and realize that "here, there's an operator error," or "here, there is something unexplained," or indeed that everything is currently okay....

They can then be users, developers, or even testers. From these three perspectives, the training given on the unit is useful to them. But it can also be decisive; in a business, is it worth the effort of moving in the direction of greater integration? For example, if four digitally controlled machines are in operation, is it worth the trouble of connecting them together? They will have an idea of the cost represented in doing this, of what it could involve at the mechanical level or in terms of computing; they will have the elements to make a decision.

In the course of specifying the competences that the technicians need to acquire, the question of the transfer of acquired knowledge—that is to say, the capacity to use this knowledge when faced with other machines in different contexts—is a major theme that came up at several points in the exchanges.

Do the students encounter the same types of machines in industry? *This is not so important. If one learns the basic principles of these devices, one can easily adapt to other equipment. It's true that nothing is standardized, but these are only variants.* Will they use the APS program for computer-assisted manufacture? *It is basic knowledge that is readily transportable beyond the college; the students are very likely to encounter this program elsewhere. It's a staple, in the same way that a secretary needs to understand word processing, a technician needs to understand computer-assisted manufacture. They are going to come across APS, or if not that then they will encounter a very similar computer-aided manufacturing system.* And what about the Flexcell software (developed at Sainte-Croix)? *The students are not going to come across this program as such elsewhere. No workshop management system can be transplanted as it is, because actually each case is unique. It's like the organization of a company; you never find two that are exactly the same. What is involved in the piloting of a workshop, there will be certain concepts that are going to be encountered, but it will never be equivalent.*

The general principles, the basic information, the management of tools, these are going to be encountered in all programs, but the appearance of the displays, the button pushing, all this will be different. It's natural, you can never as a teacher have a system that the whole world uses. It's like when you learn to drive a car; the first takes you

20 hours and the second half an hour. It is somewhat similar with computer-assisted manufacture; they put 30 hours into understanding this system, and if they have to change systems they put in maybe 10 hours.

The issue of the competences to be acquired also raises a prior question about the basic knowledge and skills that represent the indispensable prerequisites for really being able to benefit from and get something out of training. What is the nature of these preliminary competences that are necessary to understanding and mastering a flexible manufacturing system unit?

They need some minimal acquaintance with computing, if they have used a PC operating Windows, things like that because we make use of it; it's a culture that they must have acquired, no matter where.... Within the college? *Yes, for the computing technicians; mind you, the others also work on PCs with Windows but they have no special course; they learn it in their practice. As regards machining, you also hope that they have some minimal knowledge here of cutting and turning.*[7] *I am not going to teach them how to calculate cutting speeds! This has some relevance to CNC, but this should also be learned beforehand. At the end of the day, I don't concern myself much with knowing if the cutting speeds are appropriate from an industrial point of view; we work with material that tolerates quite a lot of error, because this is not the object of my teaching. If it were necessary to take account of this in addition to the problems they have with computer-assisted manufacture, if tools broke every time a student entered the wrong parameter, one would never manage to teach everything.* Nonetheless, the role of previous experience with conventional machining is not minimized. *It is important for the technicians to have handled the material in order to be able to understand anything about feasibility, parts, materials, their properties.*

By virtue of their previous experiences, not all the technicians have the same background and in particular the same experience of computer-controlled machines. *What happens then is that we alternate with one week in two on the CNC course, one on the flexible manufacturing system course. We have done this for the past year. Thus, they were learning CNC at the same time that we started on FMS; and then, when one really needs CNC, they've already acquired it. It's a problem with the technicians; they have different training, with gaps in different places, and one doesn't know what they have done before, and at the end of the day one needs to have filled in the gaps and raised everyone to the same level.*

Will this move in the direction of creating an option, a specialization in computer-integrated manufacturing (CIM), and is this a direction in which industry is currently moving? *I don't believe so, not much in Switzerland, in our region. It would be the case with Peugeot, they are going to have a big demand for people trained on FMS and CIM; we should get closer to them, we could take their material, we would check that the knowledge provided could be transferable there,*

---

[7] The technical students' previous training was very diverse; some of them have a qualification in mechanics and have thus acquired a solid knowledge of traditional machining, and others are electricians or even computer technicians.

that it would be worth the effort. But here, there is not much demand. There are very few companies that are moving into this, except for computer-assisted manufacture, and CNC of course. People are equipped for computer-assisted manufacture. First, they buy a CNC, and then they introduce computer-assisted manufacture. From this point of view the 90 hours of CFAO out of the 120 are a good investment because our technicians have every chance of encountering exactly this. The 30 hours spent in the FMS unit is the cherry on the cake that enables them, should they ever find ... or certainly in the future, it is possible this will be useful for putting two or three machines together, devising a smaller system than this one, but based on the same concepts. But I believe that there is no specific demand on a large scale currently. At best, there could be a little more. There are people who find work because they have a good basic foundation of programming knowledge, and this is in demand.

Designing the A to Z of an Approach to Training

The acquisition of up-to-date equipment does not automatically lead to educational use that is immediately optimal. As one instructor emphasized, a key factor is to be found in the motivation of the senior teachers who find themselves assigned the responsibility of making a unit work and devising a training scheme. *When the teachers are not motivated then the new equipment is not used, or possibly there will be 2 or 3 hours a year to demonstrate some very limited use of it. There is no compulsory course to be given on these machines. If they are not used, no one is bothered. The equipment remains idle. It serves as window dressing for the college and occasional demonstrations for visitors.*

How do you design training around a machining unit that is made up of a complex, segmented system with several parts? *The problem of training in this area is first of all to assemble the structure of a course, because this does not exist ready made. The program and the teaching material have to be constructed. In all other subjects, you have course structures, even in automation.... You have things that exist. The trainer will himself have taken courses in this area. There are also exams and textbooks. But for a new system like this, there is nothing. So the teaching has to be organized and thought through: what should be taught and in what order should one do it?*

What form does this task of structuring the teaching take in the areas of knowledge concerned? *In FMS, there are two major parts; there is computer-assisted manufacture, which is to say the drawing of the part and the design of the machining using a program called APS. This is a relatively well-defined base. The manufacturer provides me with examples of parts and it is easier to set written tests because I give them a part to produce with given constraints of machining, materials, tools, etc., and they do this on the computer. The result is measurable; this fits in well enough with college teaching; it's easy enough to include. Then there is the other part, Flexcell, and this is the piece that is more difficult to cover. Because it is a product truly unique to our college, there is not the slightest chance of coming across it in this form in a company; instead, we must try to derive concepts from Flexcell, things that will be useful to them, and we do this when we can teach in subgroups.*

It is noteworthy that the content of the course includes a section devoted to different systems for the transport of parts within a unit, and comparison of these, with the option of studying *in situ* the live operation of an automatic guided vehicle (AGV) system, namely a self-guided vehicle that undertakes the transport of parts between different workstations or storage bins. *One should understand the limitations of an AGV, the time it needs because it can only do a little at a time; it doesn't have arms everywhere in the workshop, while a transfer chain works in all places at the same time. Here we work with the AGV, we examine the technical solutions employed and the problems encountered. It's a matter of exposing them to what goes on in the world of industry, of giving them an idea of what exists out there.*

When a new course is introduced, a very concrete question that arises is to find for it, or rather to create for it, the space necessary in the overall program of study. Put another way, how do we manage to insert new material into an institution's program? When the training timetable is already very full, adjustments have to be made and new allocations have to be found. The solution adopted in the present case was as follows: *We have a course here called CNC-FMS (3 hours a week out of the first year training program for technicians), which involves 120 hours in all. Of these, 60 are for CNC, providing some foundation, and 60 for FMS, of which 30 concentrate on APS. There are only 30 hours that are truly devoted to the unit.* Do these 120 hours, within the training program as a whole, represent a large enough component? *Yes, it's around 8% of the entire program, which is natural enough; there are theoretical subjects, general technical subjects (electronics, automation, etc.), and everything that takes up half the time of the technicians and that concerns their specific trade: construction for those in manufacturing, operations, and computing for the others. There is something here that they will have in common. It's a "plus," a "new technology" signature that will help them to understand complex systems. The weight given to it is quite appropriate. If we had twice as much time to spend on Flexcell we would be able to fill it anyway. We have had Brazilian trainees who worked 3 months full time on top of this, because they wanted to become users of the system, they wanted to understand all its tricks. But we do not train technicians at the college for this purpose; we are not training specialists in Flexcell. It is not that the subject is too weak; rather, one has to know when to stop. One has to say to oneself: for now one wants them to have a clear idea of this system, to understand the basic concepts, and there may be just a few aspects that can be considered in a little more depth.*

How does the course unfold? *When I present the course to them, for me it is a patchwork of different parts that are linked together by the system itself. I begin by giving them a demonstration of the system in sequence. That is to say, we spend 2 hours manufacturing parts; they are going to see the elements develop, to be perfected, and this is going to arouse their interest a bit; they are going to say to themselves, "Hey, this works!" The first time that they see it working, they are quite amazed. They draw a part together on the screen, and they say "Is that what we are going to do?" and a short time later the parts are made; one can make anything one wants, etc. I give them a little bit of motivation with this surprise. Then later they ask "How does this work?" and they go on to acquire the elements one after the other. Next, there is an initial phase that is the study of the information contained in the flexible manufacturing system, which is achieved first in a very simple fashion using a module called "image," which shows the information. Thus here they have to recover the information, the tool corrections, what has happened to the palettes, etc., but on the basis of a program designed for the purpose so that they are already beginning to operate the system. And on the next occasion we move further down with direct access via SQL (the database language). Thus here they go to a PC and they type in instructions so that we can retrieve from the database a list of the palettes, a list of the tools, the tables, etc., and in this way they learn SQL. It is a language that requires writing requests in a standard format and one can interrogate the database. And this is how Flexcell works; all the Flexcell modules work this way. But a Flexcell user does not need to do it with SQL. For our part, we want them to understand it because they are perhaps going to need it on occasions to reprogram, to make alterations to an order, or to grasp what is going on.... The exercises with SQL consist in going to consult the database, but to do this they have to be able to understand its structure. (...). In this area, 20% of the time is devoted to use and 80% to understanding how it works.*

In understanding how the unit functions, the emphasis is placed on the decision-making process. *How can a computer make decisions, let alone sensible or even rapid and effective ones, given it is dumb as it can be because it only does what it is instructed to do? Coming to grips with its decision-making principles is an interesting part of the course. How to respond when all of a sudden one receives information that a part has just been stopped at the attachment point; what is one to do about it? Should it be left on a machine? And if so, why on that one? Should it be stored while waiting for the machine to become available? There are plenty of potential cases like this.... How does the computer, with the thousands of pieces of information that make up its database, make decisions?*

Within the practical work context, it can, however, prove difficult to reconcile these objectives of understanding with the objectives of control, and this can be a potential source of tension: *The choice we make to emphasize understanding rather than use of the equipment can rebound on us during the practical work at the end of training. There we ask the students to make a product, to be users, in order to refresh their ideas. But because they have spent very little time being users, they stumble over all kinds of problems. They are in a way like good garage mechanics who don't know how to drive well! The students take this badly; two years after some limited practice and then returning to the system, for them to use a system on which they have had so little training is difficult. They get things wrong all the time. During the practical work, I am constantly being asked to give them some help. But this is also the goal; it is important that they are confronted with a real situation, with a precise objective to be attained. To reach this point they are going to come up against difficulties because they no longer know the way very well; they are in the forest and don't know the path; they get stuck and we guide them. I proceed in this way rather than providing a fully signposted route, because with the latter they are not going to learn anything.*

However, this teacher wonders if the way in which this practical work is designed, given all the difficulties that students encounter, does not entail too many negative consequences relative to the interest it creates in automated manufacture using FMS: *At the beginning they are very attracted to FMS, they like APS and see that parts are made rapidly, but at the end when they come back to all this, it's like a jungle. Even if the fact of having to do everything themselves is something positive, it can still leave them with a bad impression.*

The fact that this practical work is not undertaken until the end of the second year of training, while the theory course is given in the first year, is probably a factor that needs to be taken into account. This teacher wonders whether the practical work should not be introduced much earlier. The current structure had been thought to have the benefit that *this would be fresh in their heads when they left college.* If the practical work had been integrated into the first year program, *they would have forgotten a lot by the end of the second, yet they should not have forgotten this when they leave the college.*

This issue is not without connection to the more general question of student motivation, regarded by the teachers as weak among the apprentices as well as among the technicians, while the problem does not arise at all within the context of continuing professional development. *When I teach evening courses, it is completely different—no marks, no need for assessment. The participants are like sponges, wanting to absorb everything, while with the average student, let alone the poor student, you have to force them to get into things; the usual means to put pressure on them is to grade their work so that they are obliged to take it in, otherwise.... And we see it very clearly here; if I set three pieces of written work and I then have only one or two sessions remaining to demonstrate things, absenteeism increases enormously and the kids no longer listen. One half is very motivated but the other...*

We should note that these same students, described as poorly motivated, can nonetheless prove themselves to be tenaciously, even passionately, engaged in long-drawn-out tasks, in particular during the production of their personal work for the diploma. Consequently, the opinion that the trainers have of their students must be viewed and interpreted within very specific contexts.

Summary

The acquisition by the college of an FMS unit was, it is true, made possible by conditions present at the end of the 1980s that were particularly favorable to collaboration and financing, and all this within the climate created by the Confederation to encourage CIM projects. But, as we have just seen, the acquisition of these state-of-the-art machines was also made as part of a continuing effort by the Ecole Technique to upgrade its equipment, an effort that can be traced back to the 1970s with the introduction of computer numerically controlled machine tools.

Adapting an FMS machining unit to the aims of the training program required a highly sustained effort, particularly on the part of the teacher responsible, and this was as true for the technical level (putting the system into operation and maintaining it) as for the educational (designing the content of the course and structuring the practical work).

The objectives of learning are not easily defined, in particular by virtue of the wide variety of professional requirements that this training must satisfy (operator, developer, or indeed tester of systems). Generally, the current training puts more emphasis on understanding the composite parts and the functioning of an FMS unit than on skilled operation of the equipment. Now, the students do in fact find themselves, during their practical work, in the position of "operators" without really having trained to manage this kind of task; this experience is not without stressor feelings of doubt about their own competence (*when they come back to all this, its like a jungle... it can still leave them with a bad impression*). The fact that training on the FMS unit was designed as an introduction for all the technicians, whatever their professional specialization, also had as an unforeseen and even paradoxical consequence that it gave students the impression that the subject matter was peripheral. The students, in effect, tended to see it as secondary because it did not bear upon the core competences on which the identity of each strand of training was founded (production management, mechanical construction, industrial computing).

The introduction of new course material that is directed at students with differing professional orientations also raises problems of organization, in particular for the arrangement of the programs and the timetable. What place is to be accorded to this new subject? How can it be incorporated into the existing curriculum? A technical college, probably more than any other training establishment, finds itself confronted with the need to make these choices: redistributing and updating its teaching programs.

The question of transfer of acquired knowledge was raised several times in the comments the teachers made. They expressed their preoccupation with emphasizing in training the knowledge and skills that their students will be called upon to mobilize when they are subsequently employed. This issue of transfer is complex and requires taking account of the specific purposes of knowledge. One program is likely to be encountered again in an industrial context while this might not be the case for another. In each case, specific considerations arise regarding what will and what will not be transferable.

One final point we would like to make here concerns the variety of previous training that students have had. Certain adjustments have to be made in the way that teaching of automation proceeds, in particular when students do not have sufficient prior knowledge of digitally controlled machines. The teacher should be able to count on a degree of broad familiarity with computing on the part of his students, though not necessarily specific knowledge. For us, the manner in which the diversity of initial levels is managed in the training of technicians remains in large part unknown. The social interactions that take place within small work groups during the course of training, interactions that, as we observed, are frequent and often lively among students with very diverse previous experience, surely play an important role in the acquisition of the basic technical background that teachers desire. But further observation is still necessary to confirm that students do indeed fill in any gaps they have.

THIRD ASPECT: AN ASSEMBLY UNIT USING ROBOTICS

The assembly unit installed at the Ecole Technique consists of an assembly line with palette transport (transfer chain) and a robot. It is expected that in the future this unit will be integrated with sets of other machines (screwdrivers, riveters, etc.). This unit, supplied by a specialist company, is of industry standard in the sense that it was not designed with educational goals in mind. In this respect, its introduction to the Ecole Technique has characteristics and a history quite different to those of the machining unit described in the previous section.

From the Order to Installation

The evidence on which we draw here to describe the arrival of the assembly unit at the Ecole Technique was collected at two points in time. The first included interviews we conducted in the autumn of 1993 (time 1) with the deans and senior teaching staff involved in the project, and then during the course of a coordination meeting between the Ecole Technique management and the manufacturer, just before delivery of the assembly unit. Following this delivery at the beginning of 1994, several months went by with the unit on standby, awaiting, in particular, additional funds and essential complementary materials. It was in March 1996 (time 2) that we reestablished contact with the teacher, who had, in the interim, found himself responsible for commissioning the equipment and organizing an *ad hoc* course.

The order placed by the Ecole Technique with the specialist company consisted of a palette transport system mounted on rails with points, in the form of a large square. There was, additionally, a robot "donated" by the company in exchange for an arrangement with the Ecole Technique to host visits by clients of the donating company, as well as making the unit available for training days organized by the company for its clients. The subsequent developments and supplementary payments were to be examined at a convenient point in the future, and no precise plan was formulated at the time.

To train himself in the operation of this unit and the use of the robot, the member of staff responsible for the project at the Ecole Technique counted on getting complete documentation. No course, he told us, would be requested from the manufacturer; such courses, requiring several days, were judged too costly and of questionable effectiveness. Time for feeling one's way around and progressive familiarization with the equipment seemed the best strategy. *Training oneself over a few weeks of groping around is very different to a couple of days of packaged explanations. The first approach, in my experience, is preferable.*

Within the Ecole Technique , who specifically was to be given this job? For the dean to whom we put this question, identifying someone who was both competent and available was not a trivial matter. Should they take on someone external (an unattractive solution given the financial circumstances of the college at the time) or adjust the specifications to fit an existing teacher?

The senior teacher chosen for this task was certainly interested in the job but was worried about the amount of work involved (he could devote a few hours to it, but could not spend weeks, let alone months, making adjustments to the equipment and getting it to work). In addition, he found it difficult to arrange effective training with students around a huge machine that has its limitations and inflexibilities: *On this type of equipment, one cannot multiply the work positions to give everyone a chance to do something. While some students are on the machine, one has to occupy the others elsewhere. Moreover, it is not easy to devise independent work with material that is not without danger. The CIM equipment is important to the college and above all for its reputation as an "up to date" institution, but it is not easy to devise an effective training structure around it.... One has to organize the class group into smaller groups around the unit.... The risk of breakdown is considerable, and this can provoke loss of attention, even messing about.*

The documentation provided for their clients by manufacturers can often provide the basis for the development of supporting course material; sometimes this documentation even contains exercises that are readily exploitable as teaching material. For example, in a course on automatics, I managed to get hold of teaching material that I was able to use with my students; it allowed me to put together a course in 6 days. If the supplier of this unit had had something equivalent this would have represented a considerable savings in time.

The teacher involved in the project had wanted to negotiate, during the meeting planned with the manufacturer of the unit, the delivery of a system that worked and that could at the minimum assemble an ordinary part, even a simple part. He compared this type of equipment to a forest and expected the designers to point out a route by which he could cross the forest and reach a goal (the assembly of a part). On this basis, he would feel ready to explore other possible routes and variants by himself. But without the assurance that there was at least one possible route, he would not get involved in the operation; "*the investment would be too great,*" he told us.

During the course of the meeting, in which we took part, between the Ecole Technique management and the staff from the unit's manufacturer, it emerged that the rationale of the equipment and requirements of training do not necessarily coincide immediately. We do not think the same way about a machine for learning and a production machine. The manufacturers of automated machinery design and produce machines for their industrial clients that are able to manage the assembly of well-defined products, something that obliges them to set up the equipment in a very precise way for a specific use in advance of delivery. From a training perspective, the expectation is not the same; the teacher wants a machine capable of effecting the assembly of a range of parts, even quite ordinary ones, much in the manner of constructing something from Lego parts, according to the needs of training and demonstration. From an educational perspective, it is not the product to be assembled that counts, but the opportunity provided for insight into the processes involved in an assembly unit.[8]

It was above all with respect to the programming capabilities of the equipment that the disparity between educational and industrial aims made itself felt most strongly. On the day before delivery of the unit, no precise configuration of the programming material had been offered by the manufacturers, who were themselves still waiting for specifications from the Ecole Technique, specifications that were difficult to provide for the very reason that this project had an open and flexible character. Uncertainties had likewise persisted regarding the additional facilities still needed to make the unit work, leaving it inoperative for a long time.

The issue of ensuring safety in the vicinity of the robot (*the rapid movements of its arms could knock a bull senseless!*) had also revealed that equipment designed for industry cannot be transposed into a learning establishment

---

[8] This, for example, is what Parmentier and Vivet (1992) sought to do when they developed an educational robotics system based on didactic micro-robots constructed out of Fischertechnic parts (a sophisticated version of Lego bricks). They describe the equipment produced as follows: "The pedagogical robots are generally guided by domestic micro-computers, using a programming language that is generally simple and pedagogic (this explains the frequent use of LOGO) and by an appropriate interface system. The classic concepts of guidance and control are used, those of degree of freedom, of coordination, of learning a trajectory by points, and of initialization of movement. However, we should add here certain ideas of our own such as that of transparency to allow presentation to the learner, of the role of the different elements" (p. 76). This experiment in training is also reported in Vivet (1992).

without thinking through the particular hazards it can represent for inexperienced apprentices.

Here we jump forward around 10 years in the story of the installation of the assembly unit at the Ecole Technique to hear from the instructor who was finally given this job. *The director had asked me at the beginning of the year if I would agree to taking on this unit. By then it was crumbling into dust. I had looked at what was involved; we lacked a program, interfaces, all kinds of things, and in consequence the unit did not work. I am not even talking of the unit as a whole, just the robot. Now it is beginning to run; I spent a considerable amount of time over 11 months to make it run, 11 months looking for solutions.*

The equipment consists of three different automatons, and each also has its own language. As you see, we do nothing simple here! As I had no blueprints available, no precise documentation beyond a very general manual, it was necessary to make systematic tests to determine what input led to what outcome.

As regards the robot, it had been ordered a dozen years ago, which is to say it is currently completely out of date. Nonetheless, this is what I have to cope with; it is a very particular language that runs on an old operating system. Consequently, it is rather forbidding for the computer technicians because it is not going to give them anything they are going to find in industry; they will have to adapt to the sometimes older material that they come across.

Currently we have basic facilities allowing applications that are certainly educational but that can be directly translated to an industrial context. For the present we work with plastic blocks. One plan is to make a Lego piece, an assembly carried out by the robot and then transferred using the palette system. And then I have a project for putting the mechanism of a music box in its container, that is to say assembling the movement in the box. For this it will be necessary to make further adaptations, in particular making pincer grips. I am right at the beginning with this. It's here that we will be able to work in groups, involving the construction technicians in making the pincer grips; these will be produced in the workshop. But we should not make too much of this; the point for me is the teaching; it is not a matter of creating a magnificent structure that one is going to have perform to impress the gallery; that would serve no purpose.

Developing an Ad Hoc Approach to Training

The problems of training on the machining unit and the assembly unit are quite different. Effectively, the computer logic for controlling a robot is not the same as that for controlling machine tools. Consequently, the teachers see little potential for transfer of experience gained by students in the machining unit. They recognize that they will have to develop *ad hoc* training objectives and approaches. The goals are to familiarize them with the programming of the robot and with synchronization of the robot with the unit; finally, there will be a third issue, which concerns the switching of points for different palettes as a function of their content.

For this first teaching experiment, 20 course hours have been put into the annual program. The teacher who was in charge of it had prepared a range of supporting materials for the course relating to the numerous technical elements involved in the functioning of the unit, as well as a set of exercises. Sessions on practical applications, attended by some students, are for the present included in these 20 hours. In the future, the teacher thinks that it will be possible to integrate these into the semestrial "practical hours." Likewise, diploma work could be introduced.

Summary

The assembly unit was the subject of an order placed with a company specializing in robotics. We might have expected that ordering equipment in this way would have lightened the task for college staff and required less effort than "in-house" projects, developing facilities from the beginning within the college. In the event, it turned out to be nothing of the sort; having equipment delivered does not necessarily simplify life, quite the contrary! In this case there is a possible explanation. The desire of the Ecole Technique to possess an "open" assembly unit, namely one open to a range of uses and adaptations relevant to training goals, led the manufacturer to deliver "unfinished" equipment, leaving the college to provide the additional features needed to put it into operation as desired. These requirements turned out to be complex and clearly demanded considerable effort.

Putting in place a teaching program around this unit (at a time when it was still in the process of being constructed) points to a certain tension between the concern to be able to give a well- structured course that can, with some confidence, present students with the knowledge needed to understand and manage the equipment, and the desire to involve students in development work, in making the equipment operational and in testing it with all the unforeseen difficulties and hours of patient casting about in search of solutions that this entails. This time spent by teachers and students in collaborative research is, in our view, an important form of training in which the students have the opportunity to observe firsthand their teacher exercising his competence, which is to say observing an expert resolve unforeseen problems, formulate hypotheses, invent solutions, etc. This time, however, seems to be experienced quite differently by the teachers and the students; the latter endure this as a provisional or transitional phase awaiting the moment when the unit will be fully operational and running smoothly. As a result, the practical courses on a unit still in development retain for the present a poorly established status, while the accompanying teaching remains in a very early stage of development and holds little interest for the students. To this is to be added the fact that the robot was ordered a dozen years ago: "...*it is a very particular language that runs on an old operating system. Consequently, it is rather forbidding for the computer technicians.*" This comment could moreover lead us to ask ourselves about the aging of "new technologies," and about what this term might mean for young technicians.

Let us again note that for the teachers, a machining or assembly unit represents at the pedagogical level a break with the organization of workshops, each of which traditionally provided a separate work place for each individual. The organization and division of tasks, as well as the forms of collaboration between students, it turns out, must be rethought to achieve the best match of a new technical environment with the aims of training.

FOURTH ASPECT: A SOFTWARE TO MANAGE THE PROCESS OF PRODUCTION (GPAO)[9]

A system for management of computer-assisted production draws on a data base that provides the company with a detailed description of its products and the means for their manufacture. As Hatchuel and Molet (1992) explain it,

> the purpose of a GPAO system is to schedule the number and dates of production of each of the elements of manufacture, consistent with commercial predictions, but also with the existing relations of components between products. It takes account of the production time required for each part, the supply details relevant to each supplier, and finally the stocks available at each stage of the planning. In addition, as soon as one or other of the elements is modified, it will on request recalculate a new plan of action, calling attention to any delays or discrepancies that could result. Then it derives a manufacturing plan, the costs of the work that will be involved for each machine, within the time horizon considered, and also identifying over-capacities or bottlenecks that must be resolved. GPAO systems thus produce the automation of a complex chain of operations that were formerly extremely long and demanding to examine. (pp. 143–144)

The report prepared by the senior staff member responsible for this area of training (Dugon, 1993) indicates the criteria that governed the choice of the software with which technicians taking the "operations management" option currently work. Strictly educational criteria, connected to the constraints of the training, are included. The specifications for the GPAO software that the college wanted list a dozen or more criteria:

- Strictly technical characteristics
- General qualities (flexibility, power, recent design)
- Institutional requirements (produced in Switzerland)

---

[9] Gestion de la Production Assistée par Ordinateur.

- Requirements for use adapted to the college and to work with a group of students (multi-users, multicompany, can be integrated with the college's CFAO facilities)
- Educational requirements (simple to use, offers ease of use for teaching)

The college did not in fact seek a teaching software; instead, it considered several "professional" software programs that were available on the market. One of these turned out to provide a good fit, primarily by virtue of its simplicity, with the work that had been carried out manually by the technicians up to this point. In addition, included with this software were introductory materials (transparencies, a book, demonstrations on disk) and this also played a part in the decision to adopt it.

Ease of use and the rapidity with which it can be put into operation are important criteria in the choice of a computer program. As the author of the report expressed it: *Our objective is to train the users of GPAO and not the users of one particular program. We had a bad experience with a high-performance CAO/FAO program, which, because of its complexity, we were never able to use for teaching.*

The training objectives were formulated in the following terms: *The technician taking the "operations management" option must know the basics of production management; know how to put into place a structure for a contemporary form of production; evaluate a GPAO system, install it, put it into operation, and use it, as well as train staff.*

For this last aspect we have confined ourselves to examining the report upon which the choice of a computer-assisted management system (GPAO) had been based. In particular, what emerges is how interlinked the technical and pedagogical aspects considered were in making the purchase decision. The informal exchanges we had with the teaching staff in charge of this educational assignment revealed no significant difficulties encountered in the introduction of this software.

VARIED TECHNICAL FACILITIES THAT ALL PROVED TO BE DEMANDING

We have first of all retraced the history of the introduction of digitally controlled machines at the Ecole Technique, and then looked into the more recent arrival of facilities that enable an even more integrated automation of the manufacturing process (a machining unit, an assembly unit, GPAO software). We have reported the views of those responsible for training and of the senior teaching staff most directly involved in the development and putting into operation of these new facilities. Let us now review the principal issues and observations that have emerged, organizing them into three recurrent themes.

Strong Staff Engagement

The issues surrounding the arrival of new machinery and the business of putting it into operation in a training establishment are numerous; these issues are as much technical, financial, institutional, and staff-related as they are educational. Here we would point to the importance of the engagement of those people who had, at any given moment, charge of the realization of a re-equipment project. The circumstances of such realization certainly varied from one project to another, but in each case strong staff engagement proved to be vital. The development and maintenance of a complex system, such as a flexible manufacturing system unit, calls for sustained effort, which turns out to be indispensable to the viability of the project; without this, the newest technologies might remain unused and risk becoming outdated even more rapidly.

This first observation raises a set of questions related to the status of technical development work in a college context. Who in a technical training establishment is willing to provide this particular kind of effort? Who has the necessary skills? Is this the kind of investment that one only makes once in one's career, at one stage or another in one's working life as a teacher (Huberman, 1989)? What gains from involvement in such a task might be derived by a teacher in terms of personal satisfaction, the respect of colleagues, professional interest, continuing professional development, or promotion? To answer these questions we need to examine the widely varied career paths of teachers in a technical college. The management of human resources is probably no less important in the training arena than it is in the business context.

Is staff engagement, often experienced as extra work, inevitable whenever an institution takes on new technical facilities, or is it the consequence of failing to adequately anticipate the factors that need to be taken into account together with routine underestimation of the complexity of the work to be done?[10] The delivery of "ready to run" equipment seems to offer a more economical solution in terms of human costs, but as we have seen it does not radically alter the nature of the problem. There will remain a major installation task to be accomplished, including adjustment and modification of equipment.

In the teachers' job descriptions, the technical development work tends to be added to teaching duties. Most often it has to take precedence over these duties because of the necessity of operational facilities for training.

---

[10] It would be interesting to examine how the methods of "participative anticipation," developed and put into practice in industrial enterprises that are faced with the management of major transformations, might be adapted and transposed to training projects. On this subject, see in particular the contribution of Blatti (1992) in the context of the Centre CIM de Suisse Occidentale (CCSO).

Nonetheless, the development work itself represents a fertile opportunity for learning when the students are also involved in it. For these latter, the fact of being able to interact with, and perhaps even collaborate with, someone who demonstrates not only a capacity to teach but also professional expertise in the development and completion of a project, has considerable pedagogical advantages. At the Ecole Technique there is a tradition of involving some of the students, on a voluntary basis, in the realization of college projects, but this remains an occasional practice, pursued when circumstances permit. We believe that there would be considerable benefit in designing a closer interrelation between teaching activities and this technical development work, the educational exploitation of which often remains marginal.

Technical Knowledge and Occupational Knowledge

Questioned about the competences that they regard as central, the teachers list a range of knowledge and skills that they know by experience is relevant and valued. Here it is of interest to note that, in the course of the interviews, the aims of training formulated first of all in rather general terms were often spontaneously illustrated, made concrete or contextualized in order to give them meaning, and teachers would clarify what they were speaking about by reference to real occupational conditions. Thus, for example, with respect to a CNC machine, the teacher concerned began by setting out a general objective "they must be capable of correcting a program," and then straight away qualified this with the following detail "…it is typical of what occurs in professional practice; one has to see if there is a problem, perhaps it's a keystroke error." By his use of language, the teacher thus spontaneously provides a definition that is not unrelated to the approach to the operationalization of learning aims characteristic of objective-based education. Let us again note that, if a competence is perhaps above all a "situated competence" (Le Boterf, 1994), then the best way to describe it may be to characterize some aspects of its application, in particular by means of examples drawn from the world of work.

However, the future professional work of student-technicians is difficult to foresee. The industrial realities that they are going to encounter vary widely. Faced with this uncertainty, teachers are led to emphasize understanding of the general principles that underpin the workings of a technical device, principles that will be common to different types of industrial equipment. The preoccupation with developing a general understanding indirectly raises the issue of transferring knowledge acquired in one context to a different context.

Everyone would certainly agree with the general proposition that a college should furnish transferable knowledge, but when the issue is examined more closely and in relation to the different kinds of knowledge transmitted and the different equipment and computer languages used, transferability proves to have a number of specific aspects that need to be identified. For example, in their future professional practice, what kinds of software are students likely to come across and what other kinds are they unlikely to ever encounter? What characteristics of the equipment and tasks on which they will work at the Ecole Technique will they have the occasion to reencounter in the future? In each case, the question of transfer arises in quite specific form. This refinement of perspective on the matter of transfer, such as arises concretely with respect to different teaching contents, deserves to be pursued and systematized. Various theoretical analyses can make a contribution here (e.g., Toupin, 1995; Meirieu & Develay, 1996). The challenge is to link a general approach to broad competences with issues that arise locally in the course of training, and to make this link in terms of the different knowledge and skills tackled.

The issue of knowledge transfer is of direct interest to the students. As we saw earlier, they are very ready to express hurried judgments on the relevance of what they can gain from "college" technologies that are in their eyes too distant from industrial realities or their own future working lives. We believe that the students would be very interested in being involved in an exercise in systematic reflection on the nature of just what is transferred from a training situation to a work situation.

Developing a Training Approach: An Individual or a Collective Task?

When new equipment is introduced, how is training set up? The staff member in charge of a machining unit (or an assembly unit) sees himself as responsible for organizing his teaching (classes and practical work). It seems to go without saying that this is an individual task that is taken on according to apparently well-established patterns that we can characterize as follows: the construction of a course requires in the first place some analytical work; the different elements of the technical system to be taught constitute so many chapters or subsections of the course; each course unit then gives rise to the creation of exercises. Practical work is then devised to encourage a more integrated use of the knowledge acquired in the course. To get into this process, the teacher considers beforehand whether documentation provided by a manufacturer or from other sources (technical charts, plans, exercises, existing courses, etc.) can be adapted and exploited for his own teaching.

This procedure seems sufficiently familiar and well understood by teachers to require almost no comment. And yet we ask whether, when confronted with new training issues, and in particular when faced with the challenge of initiating students in the operation of a complex unit that requires teamwork to cope with the numerous tasks involved, the traditional approaches to course construction really remain appropriate. In effect, these inevitably result in a large amount of time being devoted to the cumulative introduction of knowledge rather than an integrated implementation of acquired knowledge. The design of practical work, as well as the habitual practice of relating this to the course, certainly needs to be reexamined. Each teacher seeks out and experiments with adaptations on his own account, but there is probably a task here that could be undertaken at the collective level. The re-equipment and technological development projects, at least in their initial phases, involve the college management and the teachers coming together in committees and working parties. Why is this not also the case for setting up the pedagogical aspects of these projects? Pedagogical innovation is certainly not in essence a more individual matter than is technological development. In our view, there is no shortage of pedagogical questions that deserve to be worked upon at an organizational level.

One question that will require collective work is that of the pedagogical status of educational machines designed for learning and industrial machinery designed in the first instance for production. Let us recall in a few words what is involved here: the machines on which the precision mechanics apprentices train in the workshops are traditionally industry standard; here they learn to manage "real" tools (lathes, cutters, grinders, etc.), even if some of them are not of very recent manufacture. The concept of an "educational" machine was introduced with the development of automation so as to be able to initiate apprentices in automated manufacture. The range of educational machinery introduced at the Ecole Technique corresponds to the fact of a certain displacement of the learning aims. The first goal is no longer to practice the operation of a machine tool up to the level of perfection, but to understand the operation and use of an automated manufacturing system (starting with a computer numerically controlled machine and moving all the way through to an entire system for computer-integrated manufacturing). To do this, the educational machine tool does not need to have the sturdiness and speed that is typical of a production machine; the alternative of machining lighter material such as resin, rather than working with metal, offers numerous advantages (economy, visibility of the process, safety, the opportunity to proceed by trial and error).

Various observations made by the teachers seem to cast doubt on the value of the educational machines, suggesting that their position and their virtues are not yet fully established. How is the activity performed on an educational system really perceived? In what contexts and by whom is it taken seriously, and in what other contexts does it seem to lack "professional" credibility, because it is associated with the domain of school exercises? The weight of tradition seems to be important here; working in a mechanical workshop is associated with an image of students who work "in oil-stained overalls," and this image can in certain cases constitute an obstacle to the idea that relevant training can be provided on educational machines.

In the matter of educational tools, the Ecole Technique nonetheless possesses a rich store of experience, both internal to the college but also enlarged by the development and commercialization of several teaching machines that have required the establishment of numerous contacts with different sites of professional training both in Switzerland and abroad. But the educational assumptions and the training practices put into effect in each case do not seem to have been documented or capitalized upon. The presence of educational equipment within the Ecole Technique tends to reflect a matter of fact that is not questioned: this equipment forms part of a learning environment that is taken for granted, a heritage that one tends to make the most of.

Thinking about the contributions and the limitations of educational machines in professional training is in our view important because it inevitably encounters another very closely linked question, namely that of knowledge transfer that we raised earlier in the context of the competences envisaged. Using machines that were designed for learning only makes sense to the extent that it is possible to transfer knowledge and skills acquired on these to real professional situations. Such effects have been reported by Vivet (1992), whose work in the area of robotics confirms the appropriateness of introducing purely educational machines to train workers in new production technologies.

Machines at the Intersection of Different Intentions

What the principal actors involved in training provision have told us about the new technologies introduced into their establishments has revealed a certain number of tensions relating to the complex position these machines occupy in the domain of professional training. In the comments these tensions provoked, this equipment became almost systematically compared to other equipment. Their mode of existence seems to rely on comparisons that are principally organized on two dimensions.

The first of these classifies equipment facilities into those that are conceived as purely educationally at one extreme and those that are strictly industrial at the other. Thus, as we have just seen, within the Ecole Technique's own workshops, educational machines were routinely compared to so-called production machines that were also present within the college.

On the second dimension of comparison, all the machines possessed by the college were contrasted with the machines with which business enterprises were equipped (or with which they were believed to be equipped). We should note that this latter dimension of comparison is something of a composite; it can variously embrace such features as the quality, precision, robustness, speed or even age of the machine tools and other equipment compared. The dominant preoccupation here is whether the college is technically up-to-date compared to the world of work.

In other terms, the college machines belong to two worlds, to that of training (these facilities are here for learning) and to that of the industrial world (the world of genuine machines). Additionally, they are located with respect to another dimension that runs from dilapidated and outdated facilities to cutting-edge facilities.

Each individual sees the college machines through the lens of subjective evaluation, and this seems to be the most commonly adopted perspective. Creating opportunities to clarify these views and evaluations, to compare and check them, would in our view be a more beneficial approach. The organization of visits to, and even short courses in, business enterprises that the Ecole Technique is now seeking to develop will certainly help to provide the apprentices and technicians with the best benchmarks for appreciating both the reality of the industrial environment in their region and the merits of the technical equipment their college possesses.

Thinking through the development of technical facilities in a training establishment, and in the process giving consideration to both their educational and industrial relevance and to the subjective perceptions that those involved have of these facilities, probably represents a key task for a technical college that is today concerned about the quality and effectiveness of the learning environment it creates within its walls.

CHAPTER 4

WHAT HAPPENS IN THE COURSE OF PRACTICAL WORK?

With this chapter, the presentation of our research takes a bigger step. Up to this point, in studying various documents and conducting interviews, we have remained in some fashion on the threshold of the workshops, upstream from the educational situations that take place there. We hoped in this way to gain some appreciation of the context, the organization, the technologies involved, and the purposes of the training pursued. But once the threshold is crossed, what do we observe? What goes on during these practical sessions, which make up around half of the training time spent within a technical college?

From our first visits to the mechanical and electronics workshops at the Ecole Technique de Sainte-Croix, we were particularly interested in the practical sessions and the manner in which the work undertaken was supervised and guided by the staff running the workshops. From the point of view of learning processes and the sociocognitive processes involved, these training situations immediately seemed to us very rich, much more so than the traditional educational discourse had intimated. These occasions of

Apprentice in a Changing Trade, pages 57–78

professional training are generally represented as periods of progressive mastery of more and more complex tasks, and as the "mere" practical application of knowledge acquired previously during a course. But this only partly reflects the reality.

In order to understand more adequately what is played out in the course of the activity itself, a systematic observation of what is done, said, and learned seemed necessary to us. We chose to put practical work on automation in particular "under the microscope." This work brings future technicians in the final stages of their training into contact with a task involving computer-assisted design and manufacture. The practical work sessions had some interesting features. They were an opportunity for students to review, make use of, and integrate the entire body of knowledge acquired over the course of 2 years of training. The activity also has the advantage of forming a whole; the machining that students must design and program as their first task is then executed, and this allows them to observe the practical consequences of the machining options they have chosen. In this respect, these practical sessions are similar to a real work situation in which a technician needs to mobilize and integrate the different pieces of knowledge that he has already acquired. Here we shall see the manner in which work groups cope with the different stages of production, and in particular how they seek to overcome the difficulties encountered.

THE SITUATION OBSERVED

Our observations were carried out in the course of practical sessions on automation conducted by the student technicians in small groups. For them the task first required design of the schedule for manufacturing a part using software for computer-assisted design, then transferring this plan to the computer guiding the machining unit, and finally initiating the automated fabrication of their part.

This task had to be completed in a relatively short period, 3–4 hours. The first part of this was carried out on the computer by the students. The software interface presents a series of pull-down menus on the screen, each containing submenus. The software also provides a series of windows and dialogue boxes. Each time one of these is completed (by clicking on the chosen options or by entering values), and if the solution is correct, the next window opens. In addition, the computer provides information at the bottom of the screen about the procedure to be carried out at each step (e.g., "select geometries"). It also transmits error messages. Finally, it provides opportunities to visualize and check the steps already completed in the manufacturing sequence.

The software used is a computing tool developed for industry and used for training purposes. It is an instrument that allows the generation of a manufacturing schedule without the need to code each operation and each piece of information one by one, as typically has to be done in the direct scheduling of machining on a computer numerically controlled machine. In effect, once it knows what shape to machine, in what direction and to what depth, and as long as it has already been given a number of other parameters, the program itself carries out the calculations and the coding that directs the work of the tool on the digitally controlled machine.

Our observations related to 10 student technicians, all of them young people (despite the desire of the college to open itself up to a wider age range). They were 20–25 years old and organized into four work groups. These groups had already worked together in other practical work sessions. The students did not all have the same level of experience of either conventional machining or of digitally controlled machines.

The entire activity of these groups, from design all the way through to the actual machining of the part, was filmed with two cameras, one focused on the computer screen, the other on the work group. Synchronized (split screen) editing of the two recordings was then produced for the purposes of analysis.

TEACHING WITH VARIED DEMANDS

We begin by presenting an initial analysis of our observations, concentrating on the interactions that took place over the course of this activity between the teacher who organized these practical sessions and the work groups of students that were formed. We examine the manner in which a teacher shapes, guides, and monitors the activities of his students in the workshop. Other analyses, focusing on forms of collaboration among students and on the significance they attach to this training situation, are presented in later chapters.

Issues surrounding the nature of a teacher's role arise in very concrete form within an institution devoted to professional training. Many times at the Ecole Technique de Sainte-Croix we came across the following pedagogical debate: within the context of activities in the workshop, how can the students be guided and helped while at the same time allowing them the degree of autonomy and responsibility essential to high-quality training? Put in other terms, how can the teacher be involved while nonetheless not being too involved? This debate indirectly expresses a worry about monitoring the step-by-step work of the students so closely that there will not be sufficient opportunity for them to make the necessary experiments with the application of their own knowledge and competences. This is a source of tension for several of the teachers wanting to see capacities for initiative and independent work developing in their students. They feel that, in effect, they have often directed, guided, and supervised their students' work in too close a manner, providing a level of support that could almost be described as "mothering."[1]

At the Ecole Technique, the observations made to us about the autonomy of the learner seemed to relate to two models of learning. One puts the emphasis on the role of experience itself in the act of learning (here the teachers referred to Dewey's idea of *learning by doing*, John Dewey having developed the concept of self-education based on experience at the beginning of the 20th century). The other stresses autonomy as the culmination of successful learning, autonomy as something to be proven in the final examination, in the course of strictly individual work without any external help or resources available. The first perspective treats autonomy as a process integral to and a condition necessary to learning. The second treats it as a product, which is to say as the outcome of a period of learning. How, in each case, is the apprentice's autonomy favored in practice? The pedagogical roles are numerous: teacher, trainer, organizer, coordinator, supervisor, accompanist, mediator, supporter, guide, and tutor.[2]

What professional faces are reflected in the practices observed in the context of practical work on automation? Within the dynamics of the work groups, what is the role of the teacher in the unfolding of the activity undertaken? Is this role primarily confined to defining the task and redirecting it when necessary? Is it to check that everything is done properly? Is it to lead, coordinate, assist, help out, or stimulate the students? Is it to give them explanations and additional instructions? Or are the teachers' tasks

---

[1] Developing autonomy turns out to be a difficult and paradoxical task, as Moyne (1982) has shown in the context of experiments on autonomous work carried out in France at the second stage of secondary education, and indeed as we have observed for ourselves in a French high school (Perret, 1978). The ideas of autonomy and self-directed learning, as well as that of self-training, continue to be the object of a series of studies concerned with achieving a better grasp of the activities of adult apprentices in the dynamics of learning itself (Carre, Moisan, & Poisson, 1997; Barbot & Camatarri, 1999; Carré, 2006).

[2] Interactions that are characterized by the establishment of an asymmetrical relationship in which one of the partners demonstrates the intention to teach, train, explain, help, or even guide a learner (pupil, student, or apprentice) have been the object of different kinds of analyses. One already well-established line of research, taking a descriptive perspective, focuses on the pedagogical communication in the classroom and on analysis of teaching behavior. This approach has led to the development of a large number of observational coding schemes. Grasping the precise role of the interactions observed requires an appropriate theory of learning processes. Bruner's work on the role of the mediator in the orientation of training has helped in providing a framework for understanding the role of interactions with persons as resources in the construction of knowledge (see, e.g., Aumont & Mesnier, 1992; Barth, 1994; Jarvela, 1995; Mayen, 2000; Durand & Filliettaz, 2009). Following Vygotsky and, more generally, a number of Russian researchers (e.g., Leontiev and Galperin, but also many others), a lot of work has addressed analysis of the relations between novices and experts (McLane & Wertsch, 1986; Wynnikamen, 1990; Mercer & Fisher, 1992; Forman & McPhail, 1993; Rogoff, 1995). Here the *a priori* theory adopted is that knowledge is transmitted from expert to novice, the latter appropriating this knowledge by successive steps, deploying the behaviors supported by his or her expert partner.

and functions different from all these things? Are some particular events more suitable than others as occasions to encourage *modeling* (providing a model) or *scaffolding* (support) based on an asymmetric relationship?

Pedagogical roles are also liable to change within the course of a single activity. Each stage of the work can effectively involve a different role on the part of the teacher. For this reason, our analysis of the practical sessions on automation will distinguish three phases:

1. Presentation of the task and instructions.
2. The design phase, during the course of which the students' activity is focused on the software that will make it possible to set parameters and program the successive machining operations on the computer.
3. The phase in which the machining unit is put into operation, a phase that calls for an understanding of the logic according to which the equipment operates and a mastery of the connections among the different elements of the system.

We look into these three phases successively and examine the nature of the didactic interactions that are involved in each case.

WHEN THE TEACHER INTRODUCES THE TASK AND THE INSTRUCTIONS

Orally Communicated Instructions

We are at the very beginning of the afternoon; the students have returned to the practical work classroom. The teacher distributes the work to different groups, following a rotation of pre-established tasks, and then asks the two groups who will be working on the machining unit on this particular afternoon to join him and collect all the information they will need. We reproduce here what the teacher says about the instructions to the two groups concerned. The teacher's remarks are designated by T, the comments and questions of the students by P.

T: *So the aim of this practical work is on the one hand to make a part like this one* (T indicates the part)...*okay? On the other hand, it is to do some revision on APS[3] and on Flexcell[4] and also to show you the link from AUTOCAD[5] through to machining, via APS. So, the AUTOCAD–APS link: you don't need to touch AUTOCAD, you have a file in DXF format; that is an exchange format that can be used by APS. Neither AUTOCAD nor APS normally works with DXF files. But it's an exchange*

---

[3] APS: Name of the software used for designing the machining on a computer.
[4] Flexcell: Name of the software that manages the database for operating the machining unit.
[5] AUTOCAD: Software for technical drawing and computer-assisted design (CAD), used by technicians in the building industry.

format. It's like language; if you don't have the same mother tongue, you are going to understand by speaking English. It's the same thing between AUTOCAD and APS. AUTOCAD knows how to write in DXF format. APS knows how to read DXF format.

First job, that will be to open a file called TP34.DX, which is on a diskette in APS, and then manage to machine this part, and perhaps to define certain missing elements. It will be necessary to follow certain restrictions, in terms of speed, in terms of the maximum number of attempts, even while trying to limit the machining time of the program. Let's say 10 minutes; that's the order of magnitude of a program that is getting toward being correct. 10 minutes...

P: *How long have the other groups taken...?*
T: *I think they have had 9 minutes, 15, 9 minutes, something like that*
P: (reactions, laughing) *7 minutes, who needs more...?*
T: *Okay, the part on APS will take you around 2 hours I imagine, perhaps a bit more, perhaps a bit less. Once you have the digital control program, a second part, which I hope that the two groups will be able to do—if not, it will be the first that does it, this will be to start up the unit with Flexcell. Now, there are different modules to be started from different positions. I will help you a little; you will have to plan to say what will be done to the parts of this type here, and then you are going to machine them for real. Agreed?* (Inaudible reaction by the students.) *Does this make sense? Next we need to decide on a division between the two groups; I suggest that this group uses the MPF130 program and the other uses the MPF131; those are the two free numbers and the manufacturing orders associated with these, it's OF10, and OF11 for the 131. Unless they are wrong, it's written 130 and 131, that's a given, and then OF10 and OF11. Agreed? Then I think you can go and get on with it. I suggest if you are agreed that the first group works here, because in the second one of the students has not taken the APS course.{*

We begin by analyzing these instructions and considering the nature of the initial information given by the teacher. The issue here is appreciating the nature of the reference points provided to the students to help them do the exercise better.[6]

---

[6] Research into processes of problem solving emphasizes the importance of the initial representation that any individual mobilizes when he or she engages in a task (Richard, 1990). Here, one could equally appeal to the classical distinction, introduced by Galperine, between the executive aspect of an action and the orienting aspect. The basis of orientation to the action plays a determining role in the entire performance because it includes all the constitutive elements of an initial representation of an action to be performed, in particular representations of the goal to be pursued, the approaches to be adopted, and the constraints to be considered. The idea of an orientation base first allowed Russian psychologists to analyze the progressive training of relatively simple actions linked to the school learning of young children (Talyzina, 1968). More recent research has returned to this theoretical framework to analyze training in the technically complex actions that, for example, need to be mastered by the operators of nuclear power plants (Podolski, 1993).

An initial content analysis made it possible to identify the following elements in these instructions:

- Information about the goal to be pursued: *make a part like this one (...) do some revision on APS and Flexcell (...) show you the link from AUTOCAD through to machining, via APS.*
- Explanations: *Neither AUTOCAD nor APS normally work with DXF files. But it's an exchange format.* The explanation then draws on an analogy: *It's like language, if neither you nor I...*
- The procedure to be adopted: *First job, that will be to open a file... and then manage to machine this part, and perhaps to define certain missing elements.*
- The constraints to be taken into account: *It will be necessary to follow certain restrictions, in terms of speed, in terms of the maximum number of attempts, even while trying to limit the machining time of the program.*
- Information on the way in which matters will proceed in general: *the part on APS will take you around 2 hours I imagine; once you have the digital control program, a second part (...) this will be to start up the unit with Flexcell with different modules to be started from different positions.*
- Organization of the work: *Next it is necessary to decide on a division between the two groups; I suggest that the first group use* [rare occurrence of the subjunctive in English!] *the MPF130 program and the other use the MPF131 (...) I think you can go and get on with it. I suggest if you are agreed that the first group works here.*
- On the instructor's role: *I will help you a little.*

By virtue of the variety and precision of the directions they contain, these instructions demonstrate the concern the teacher has about getting the activity going in an effective fashion by providing the students with a base for orientation that is as complete as possible. Additionally, at several points, the teacher checks that they are following his presentation of the instructions. This is reflected in the questions that punctuate the presentation: *Is this okay? Does this make sense? Agreed?*

The interventions made by the students during the course of these instructions are interesting in this respect. They are informative about the activity undertaken by students in the process of adjusting to the task and forming a representation of it. For example, following the indication the teacher gives of the machining time it would be appropriate to achieve, the students ask about the time taken by the groups who had previously done this practical work. The machining time needs to be checked in order to obtain the "correct" time (according to the terms used by the teacher), and this seems to be interpreted by the students from a competitive perspective, even if with a dash of humor. The challenge is, therefore, not just to produce a piece of machining within an acceptable time but to achieve the best time!

Interventions by students in the course of the presentation of a task are often more frequent, as we have witnessed on other occasions with other work groups. Students seem to want to confirm their understanding of the task and the knowledge they will need to apply point by point. They also come to anticipate the teacher's instructions by asking about the machining time, this even before he had mentioned it: *Do you have a base time for the program? How much is it necessary to do?*

When presentation of the task is more of a dialogue and the teacher is interrupted at every step, this can give the impression that the instructions have been formulated less rigorously. In fact, it is nothing of the sort. This kind of dialogue gives us a glimpse of the extent to which instructions constitute more than an act of formulating an initial message that is intended simply to be listened to by the students. The delivery of instructions in effect immediately engages the students in a process in which they interpret the task (the goals to be pursued, the data to be taken into account, the constraints to be considered) and anticipate the means to be used to navigate toward its successful resolution. In some manner, they are already engaged in the process before the instructions are completed.

Written Instructions

Orally communicated instructions are not the only basis for orientation. We also need to take into account the other reference points on which students are able to draw to understand what is involved and what is expected of them. What are these?

The most concrete and available element in the business of getting on with the work consists of a series of written instructions given to each group by the teacher and summarizing in a few lines the goals of these practical sessions and the work stages to be completed. On a second sheet are repeated the particular commands that will be needed to move between files in the computer programs; this information is provided as a memory aid.

We will see that these instruction sheets are not referred to by the teacher during the oral presentation of the activity. They probably form part of customary practice, their presence and use being sufficient in and of themselves to require no explicit mention; the students had these sheets in front of them anyway.

The students' reading of these two pages always turned out to be incomplete. For example, a sentence concerning the relationship to be established was phrased in the following terms: "the report of this practical session will mention all the necessary steps that are not indicated in the practical work text or in the attached sheets." This element of the instructions will only be considered once the activity is under way, and then sometimes only at the end of an activity, when a student reminds the group that their teacher expects the delivery of a report.

Other Elements of Orientation

Let us again observe that oral and written instructions are not the only supports on which the students can draw to learn the task that confronts them and to give them an idea of its requirements. In the course of the first practical work session that took place on the FMS unit, the students who did not belong to the first group engaged in this task were able to look over what their fellow students were doing. In this respect they had the opportunity to form an initial, albeit rather general, idea of the required activity.

In addition, the students do not find themselves faced with an unknown technical device encountered for the very first time. These students will have received instruction about the machining unit during the previous year and will also have completed several exercises with respect to its component parts. In addition, putting the equipment as a whole into operation will have been the subject of a demonstration by the teacher. What these students will have done and seen done on the unit, even if it was several months before, certainly helps to give some meaning to the instructions they heard.

The evaluative criteria to which the teacher will refer in assessing the work undertaken and in awarding a mark will already have been communicated in some degree. Certain criteria, such as succeeding in machining the part, seem to go without saying. In contrast, other criteria, such as the capacity to work independently, are not always recognized. In the course of the activity, as we will see, some groups question the teacher repeatedly, while others do so rarely, without knowing how he will take this into account in deciding the final mark to be awarded for the work carried out. Moreover, students will later contest the relevance of this latter criterion, leading the teacher to change his mode of evaluation on this point.

It was on the basis of this collection of varied elements that we came to identify how the students construct for themselves a representation of what they have to do.

THE TEACHER'S INTERVENTIONS
IN THE COURSE OF THE ACTIVITY

Over the first phase of the activity, the group is gathered around a computer to program the machining. We now examine when and in what way the teacher is called in to help, and with what frequency. Furthermore, does he intervene on his own initiative or at the request of the students?

The work groups observed here do not all seek the teacher's help in the same manner; one group may request help a dozen times while another may request assistance only once. Clearly, the groups resort to the aid of the teacher to widely varying degrees. In addition, the sequences in the course of which the teacher intervenes are also widely varied in length, ranging from a brief interaction on a specific point to an exchange of 100 speaking turns. To what are these differences due? Several explanations can be given.

We might naively expect that recourse to the teacher's help is linked to the students' levels of knowledge, and we might also think that the absence of requests for help from the teacher is an indication of mastery of the task. But this is not what happens in reality. There is no clear relationship between the number of interventions by the teacher and success at the task. In particular, the most autonomous group does not on this basis seem to have any greater capacity to master the task, in fact quite the contrary. These observations confirm the findings from other research (Kiyake & Norman, 1979; Nelson-Le Gall, 1985) showing that students having difficulties generally make fewer requests for help than others.

Do the different reactions across groups depend on their perceptions of the teacher's expectations? Is it perceived as possible, tolerated, or even legitimate to approach the teacher while they are working? Is it the effect of a general uncertainty about the correct manner in which to proceed? To ask questions is also to take a risk, given that this reveals one's lack of confidence, one's difficulties, the gaps in one's knowledge, or one's lack of competence. Conversely, to put questions to the teacher can also be a way of according oneself value, of showing one's interest, one's insight, and one's intelligence by posing "good questions." Taking this risk is going to depend in particular on the manner in which the questions are received by the teacher and on the responses they provoke: Is this the beginning of an interesting and instructive exchange with the teacher or merely an irritation for him? Additionally, there is the way in which such "autonomy" is evaluated by the teacher, evidenced by the mark he gives in his final evaluation of their work.

Constitutive of a didactic contract, the regulation of exchanges between teacher and students is not established anew from one day to the next. It is forged over the course of time, over a period of weeks of working together, in the form of a set of rules, usually implicit, that underpin the functioning of exchanges and the perception of expectations (Schubauer-Leoni, 1986). What is the nature of the contract established in these practical work sessions regarding the availability of the teacher? Apparently, no particular standard is strictly enforced. Certainly, there is a general expectation on the part of the teacher that the students will work autonomously. But a set of particular circumstances (the time that has elapsed since instruction on the FMS unit given in the previous year, the complexity of putting the unit into operation, the relatively short time available) can encourage the teacher to provide his assistance. In addition, he informs them of this explicitly in the instructions, when he tells the students that with respect to the second phase of the work, "*I will help you a little.*" In this particular context we can understand that students may come to interpret the opportunity to seek the teacher's help in different ways; some will be determined to manage by themselves while others will not hesitate to ask for support every time any significant difficulty is encountered or, more simply, when they feel the need for some reassurance about their approach to the work.

What Initiates an Intervention by the Teacher?

Three-quarters of the teacher's interventions are made following a specific request from the students. In the following example, the students find themselves faced with a new situation that creates uncertainty about the drawing on which to rely: *we've never done this!* One of them then goes to seek out the teacher, who is currently occupied with another group.

1P1: This isn't working, we're never going to do this!
2P2: *(Gets up to go and find the instructor, who joins the group.)*
3P1: For the depth, the perspective, we have all the sides in agreement but… we cannot retrace everything; normally, you should be able to use the profile plan.
4T: Ah, the agreement between the two views.
5P1: Yes, the two views.
6T: Ah! You have to leave out a little; they've come back in the form of a drawing; it's actually a 2D drawing.
7P1: You can't make alterations?
8T: No, because it cannot make a correspondence all by itself between the lines.
9P1: We have to redo everything, retrace everything.
10T: Yes, just the depths.{\DIA}

As the following extract shows, it emerges that this request is made in stages. In the second speaking turn, an initial attempt to consult the teacher is launched by one of the students (P1), but by turn 16, it is his partner (P2) who has made up his mind. The teacher (T) finally intervenes at turn 18. The problem encountered concerned the necessity or otherwise of designating on the drawing of the part the lines to be taken into account for machining.

1P1: But, it's … this thingamajig, no but there has to be a system here
2P2: Where is C [the teacher]?
3P1: There has to be a system without drawing the lines, because then there is no point in drawing the part if it's you who still has to say "you must do this, you must do that"

4P2: You may joke but that's the way it is

5P1: Okay, stop then, we are not here to lose time, eh

6P1: Yes, okay

7P2: (...)

8P1: You bastard!

9P1: Yes, but we can't work like this if there are computing devices that are to help someone, they are not for...

10P2:I am sitting here looking at this, it makes (...)

11P1:Huh?

12P2:Why has it gone red now?

13P1:But because it has (...) I think it has really simplified the program!

14P2:What?

15P1:It seems really simple

16P2:No, it's not hopeless, wait, I'll go and see C [the teacher] it's not possible, it's not possible

17P1:Take a break

18T: The problem here, what is it?

19P2:It's that I've made the lines appear in red because I've machined from above

20T: Yep

21P2:Then I'd like to take this out then I have (...) with the program but even so it stays on the screen [this does not make sense to me— something missing? Or is it me?]

22M: That is shown in red because you have indicated that that was to be machined

(...)

How is the decision made within a group to call upon the assistance of the teacher? We never saw agreement among the students on this matter: They do not take the time to discuss among themselves whether they should at any given moment seek the teacher's help. The decision depends on individual initiative. It is often an impulsive response born of irritation with a persistent difficulty. Thus, appealing to the teacher is often a means of calming a working atmosphere that has become oppressive. Also, the teacher who comes to a work group on his own initiative implicitly gives the group the opportunity of settling all unresolved questions and potential sources of tension.

In the sequences in which no request is made, the exchange occurs because the teacher himself comes to the group to see how work is progressing. Let us note that when the teacher is led to give his attention to a group without having been called by them, it can occur either in a fortuitous manner because his attention has been attracted by some unexpected incident (abnormal noises, excessive moving about of students, sustained laughter, etc.) or deliberately because he wants to follow the work of one group more closely, knowing that they lack expertise. Under these circumstances, when no initial request is made, one can nonetheless distinguish two scenarios according to whether the teacher approaches and immediately questions the group, as the following extract shows. The group has managed to complete the programming for the machining, and the teacher comes to examine the work completed.

1T: So?

2P: Good, we've finished it.

3T: So, is it okay? It's not bad, that. It's already better there. Size 13.087, why not? Good, do you know the order of the tools you will use?

4P: It's obvious: 1, 2, 3.

5T: Yes, but I mean to say, what type?

6P: Diameter 8, cut of 8, cut of 3...

7T: Good, has that been saved?

8P: We've saved that in there, but now we are here...

9T: I just want to see if...if above this... We are agreed, 11 minutes, the speeds... What have you specified for the material?

10P: ETSC

11T: Resin? The advance of 288 is not really much.

12P: You, you said not to change anything.

13T: That's right, but normally you need 432. Why have you started with that? Ah! For the large cut, it's right. Okay, then now we will go into Flexcell. What is it called?

In the second scenario, the teacher begins by watching in silence what the students are doing. The effect of his presence is then to spark off questions, as if the students benefit from having the teacher available for a moment to be questioned on some point or another. An example:

1P1: *(In response to the teacher's presence)* Hello

2P2: Come on! What are you waiting for? We need to engrave.

3P1: We need to engrave. Okay, quick, quick "machine," "tool"

4P2: Which grinding is it?

5P1: "Cut." Cut a groove.

6P2: There isn't an engraving

7P1: You do it with the drill bit

8T: You do it with a cutter of 3

9P2: But there is nothing at the end

10T: No, no

11P1:Cutter, diameter 3, come on!

12P1:You should have said that before.

13T: There is something missing there

The variety of forms in which support is provided for the students' work leads us back to the issue raised earlier of their autonomy. This autonomy turns out to consist of a dimension that is cognitive but also socioemotional, because it is concerned with emotional resolution of persistent difficulties or divergences of opinion within the group.

How Is an Intervention by the Teacher Concluded? Who Takes the Initiative In This?

After having examined the ways in which an interaction sequence is initiated, we now turn our attention to the manner in which a teacher-student interaction is brought to an end. We should point out straight away that identifying the end of a sequence with any precision is never straightforward; it is rare to find statements that mark the end of an exchange as clearly as the following one does:

T: Try to cover this; I'll leave you to do it and then you call me
P: Okay, okay, no problem.

More often, the exchange seems to dry up by itself. This seems to occur in three scenarios:

1. The students have been given the answers they wanted and are thus sorted out; the teacher can then withdraw. In fact, the sequences analyzed rarely consist of a single question that brings forth the expected answer from the teacher that will allow the activity to continue. The sequences consist of successive questions that tend to follow on from one another, so that one cannot readily determine which answer brings the exchange to a close.

1P: Sir, the safety level, what does it do exactly?
2T: It moves down to there; it is going to come over the part like that.
3P: How much do you have to have above the part?
4T: So as not to worry, me I put in 10; in any event you should have 5. 20 or 10 is okay. Ah, you've put 16 minutes, there we are! It is not for that reason that it takes more time.
5P: It's not that? One and a half minutes to change the tools, isn't that a bit much?
6T: Yes, but that's three tool changes; you are using three tools.
7P: It takes as much as that?

It also happens that the teacher, thinking the intervention with the group has been completed, makes to leave but is immediately called back by a request for related information. This is what happens, for example, in the following extract, after the 9P2 speaking turn:

1P1: What is engraving 3d, 4d, 5d; me, I don't know?
2T: Why do you need that?
3P1: To engrave that
4M: You want to make a line with your cutter!?
5P2: Well, me, I want to make a rough cut / finish
6T: Yep
7P2: I'm doing everything okay. Depth, you take minus 0.5, engraving: number of passes, you have to put what, 3? 5?
8P1: You're kidding me!
9P2; Okay, I am just going to put 4
The teacher makes a move to leave but one of the students calls out to him:
10P: Hey, you talked about this change of operation, is it necessary to show how you do it?
11T: In the machine menu
12E: That's good.{\DIA}

2. In some cases, the teacher seems at some point to not want to give any more help or information, probably to avoid having to do the work for the students.

3. Finally, some interactions come to an end because the students are manifestly returning to the task. They now have an idea how to move forward with what they are doing and become reengaged in the activity, as expressed in particular by the postures they adopt, reoriented around the computer. The teacher can then withdraw; his presence is no longer needed.{\NL}

What Information Does the Teacher Provide in the Course of an Interaction?

Up to now, we have been concerned with the manner in which the interaction with the teacher is initiated and the fashion in which it is concluded. Here, our concern is to examine what is said and what types of assistance the teacher provides in the course of an interaction sequence. The information provided is, in general, either conceptual (taking the form of explanation) or procedural (relating to operations).

Explanatory mode. The teacher is led in the course of his interventions to define certain ideas. This is then expressed by recalling theoretical elements covered earlier in the course. These explanations are in fact not very numerous. For example, the teacher is led to clarify the meaning of two distinct commands, "group" and "assemble."

    1P: It's right then. So it's right; I did "group" before
    2T: Okay, even so, a little point about "group." "Group" and "assemble," they are not the same thing. "Group," you can group one thing here, another thing there.
    3P: "Assemble," you put things together
    4T: "Assemble," that is to say that it becomes a single element.{\DIA}

A second example concerns the meaning of "safety level."

    1P: Sir, the safety level, what does it do exactly?
    2T: It moves down to there; it is going to come over the part like that.

Procedural mode: The activity of the students is focused on the success of the machining, so that "how do you do it?" then prompts the question "why do it like that?" A predominant place is accorded to procedural instructions, as much in the exchanges that occur among the students as in the interventions of the teacher. In this practical work context, students seem more concerned about being successful than about understanding. The following extract shows how the teacher can be called on to give a set of procedural instructions when he is asked: "What do you do in order to...?"

    1P: Now then, what do you do in order to remove these lines here so that you no longer see anything?
    2T: Okay, you have the option of displaying only one of the operations, so there you have in the machine menu "edit operation."
    3P: "Edit operation"
    4T: That's it, and then there between the operation of tool 1, tool 2, or tool 3, either hidden or displayed, you choose "hide," for example, entering "select operation 1."
    5P: You go to 1, you click on 1.
    6T: Anyway, it goes by tool, huh? Agreed?
    7P: Hidden or displayed. Okay, but it's the same thing.
    8T: If you now do "escape" you are only going to see...you are only going to see the operations with the number 8 cutting tool, which remains the most legible, huh, even so?

An Exchange Aimed at Diagnosis

The teacher is not always in a situation in which he is able to immediately offer useful advice. He sometimes lacks information about what the students have done or how their work has progressed. Some time spent in observation or investigation is then necessary for making a diagnosis. It is very much this purpose that seems to be served, for example, in the following exchange:

1P: It takes as much as that?

2T: Me, I rather had the impression that it is these shapes here that take the time, no?

3P: It's true there because the machine, it machines, it does a bit there, for example, and then it does this end here and then this end here, this little end here

4T: How many passes have you got here?

5P: Two times, I believe.

6T: Why?

7P: How many of what?

8T: Passes

9P: Meaning?

10T: Meaning for this depth here how many of them? One time or two times?

11P: Two times.

12T: And the same for that one?

13P: Yes.

14T: Twice for that?

15P: Okay, huh, we must check

16T: Yes, but I think it's there that it doesn't work

Note that these diagnostic interactions occur only rarely. More often the teacher identifies the nature of the problem very rapidly. The questions addressed to the teacher admittedly give him some clues, but in general it is by observing the work the students are doing before even intervening, or in the course of the exchange, that he decides on what kind of intervention is appropriate.

We must now examine the role of the teacher's interventions in the dynamics of a group's work. The first question relates to the utility of these interventions. Are they vital to completion of the work? In the absence of an intervention would the work of the group remain stuck or does intervention only speed it up by a few minutes? It is very difficult to give a confident answer to this question, but we offer the hypothesis that most often the impact of a teacher's interventions consists of some gain in time; the students would be able to work unaided but with a cost in time and, representing a more significant problem, delays that undoubtedly would exceed the time slot allocated to this activity. The findings from research by Merrill (1995) also point to this conclusion. Merrill's research compared two groups of students presented with a series of exercises, one group assisted by a tutor, the other group working independently. The effect of tutoring essentially resided in the more rapid completion of the exercises, but no greater mastery was achieved.

WHEN THE TEACHER INTERVENES AS A COORDINATOR

The second phase of the practical work sessions is characterized by interactions that are very different from those that have been examined up to this point. The activities of groups are no longer confined to the work station on which they had been programming the machining. It is now a matter of putting the entire machining unit into operation, and this requires transfer of the file, getting several programs running on different computers, and preparation of the principal components of the unit: the attachment point, the automated palette transport system, the CNC machine tool, and the storage unit.

Consequently, to organize this entire process, the teacher plays a coordinating role in the manner of someone in charge of a team, allocating tasks and supervising the entire operation. Compared to the first phase, the presence of the teacher is more crucial here, and his support more sustained. It is no longer possible to identify circumscribed sequences of help as we did in the course of the first phase. In contrast, we can inverse the perspective and pay attention to islets of autonomy or areas of initiative that students sometimes seek to preserve or inhabit within an activity that is now essentially controlled and managed by the teacher.

This shift in functioning does not really surprise the students. Manifestly, they do not have enough assured knowledge of the entire FMS unit to manage the numerous connections that are required to put it into operation by themselves. The role of organizer or coordinator filled by the teacher is apparent from the beginning of this second phase of activity:

1T: *With the "image" program, there won't be any problem; it must be started up when everything is ready. Likewise "Systrans," it has a place, it's right in the middle of the table over there by the group of eight PCs, it's the one that is connected to "Rado," there isn't any choice. "Planif," we are just going to launch that one at the beginning to specify the quantity of parts to be made, we are going to say 3 OF10 parts, 3 OF11 parts. "Realtime" can be run on any PC. "SAISIE" we will not need. "Manuel 1" we will need there where we attach. It can be put elsewhere but that would not be very clever. We are going to use Machine 2 because … I have more confidence in it; we must switch it on, take the readings.*

2P: *Why not the 1?*

3T: *Because sometimes when it changes tools and when it does that fast enough, it uncouples, and that will make us lose half an hour.*

4P: *How?*

5M: *It's a problem with the servers, which are too limited; that is to say, I think the current detection is too strong. So it often decouples, in particular when it is all on automatic. Because it takes a lot of time to reinitialize, you have to take the part out manually, you have to re-register the machine as ready, but we don't have that risk over here. So, we are going to start Machine 2 on the PC in the back row on the right, and on that we will analyze your two digital control programs.*

Right from the start, putting the machining unit into operation is presented as the business of the teacher. Taking charge of the activity in this way expresses not only his coordinating role but also his experience and professional competence. The exchange about the choice of Machine 2, more reliable than Machine 1, is significant in this respect. What is involved here is no longer the kind of knowledge transmitted in the course, but knowledge founded on experience: "Sometimes when it changes tools and when it does that fast enough, it uncouples, and that will make us lose half an hour." Moreover, he justifies his choice in the first person: "I have more confidence in it." In this way he locates himself as being the workshop boss, not just a specialist in automation but a more authoritative expert on the assets and weaknesses of a particular machining unit. Note that for the teacher, the fact of having contributed to the development of this unit, which is to some extent in the eyes of the students "his" unit, certainly plays a significant part in creating the possibility of adopting, when necessary, the role of "professional-expert," in addition to or even in preference to the role of "master-instructor."[7]

In the course of this second phase of the practical work session, once the activity is under way, we find three types of engagement by the teacher; these vary from a position of momentary "didactic withdrawal," so as to allow the students their own direct experience, to a complete engagement in the task when the technical difficulties encountered require all his expertise.

Occasions Allowing for the Student's Own Experience

One example will suffice to illustrate this approach. Following an exchange with the students and a check on their manufacturing program, the teacher noticed an error on the screen; the part had not been placed at coordinates (0:0). Now, positioning in this way is essential if the tools are to be correctly located to machine the part within the space occupied by the machine. But this error is not communicated to the students. The teacher's

---

[7] This leads us to ask, as a counterpoint, what happens when a new teacher "inherits" equipment and becomes responsible for its use in teaching without having participated in its development? How does he then inhabit the roles of expert and teacher?

frown, nonetheless, leads the students to suspect something. Manifestly, the didactic strategy adopted here rests on the conviction that there is a benefit in students being directly confronted with errors and obstacles, and the teacher should not solve every problem in advance for them; he should not make the road too easy.

This strategy was seldom applied so explicitly by the teacher as in the example given above. This may be related to the fact that not all errors have the capacity to provide the same impact or the same cognitive interest. It is also true that certain kinds of errors must, without question, be corrected before machining, if damage is to be avoided. One of the fears present among the students, and also for the teacher, relates to the risk that the machine tools will in fact come to "machine" themselves in a badly programmed auto-destructive movement.

Occasions for Guidance

On several occasions, the teacher was led to give students directives on what they should do. Note that guiding their action in this way was often done in an indirect fashion in the course of close questioning. We can see here a desire to help the students while at the same time encouraging them to reflect upon the manner in which the activity is unfolding. Here is an example of an intervention using this interrogation mode:

> T: After the check list, what have you not done yet? Where do you stop? The last operation you did on your PC, what was it?{\DIA}

Occasions for Resolution of Shared Problems

At other moments, the teacher finds himself in a situation with the students in which all of them are searching for the solution. Their interactions are then entirely oriented to a search for the cause of the difficulty and, if the teacher and the students all take part in this, it is in a spirit of collaboration. We observed this type of interaction, for example, during an episode in which the machine had started to machine the part in a totally unexpected fashion. Neither the teacher nor the students instantly understood what was going on or how this anomaly had arisen. It was at the end of a shared search that they came to identify the source of the error, and this on the basis of a decisive clue: the data in the file opened by the computer. The file containing the students' work with their machining program had been saved under an invalid name, and because of this, an old file originating from another work group had been loaded by the machine.

To summarize, in the course of a single practical work session, the teacher can enact several roles. One is a didactic role, that of *trainer*, adopted when his concern is to prompt the students to think or indeed when he leaves them to their own experiences. Another is the role of organizer-instructor, which as team leader involves giving everyone the information they need to manage the task properly. A third role, finally, is that of *engineer*, who is able to adequately master the technicalities of the equipment in the event of breakdowns, unforeseen difficulties, or other complex problems requiring resolution.

How do these roles overlap and follow on from one another over the course of the action itself? Different variables seem to come into play. The level of complexity of the tasks to be handled in large part guides the teacher's conduct. The nature of the difficulties encountered, whether or not they are foreseeable, also plays an important part. Additionally, yet other dimensions can be involved. The degree of commitment or engagement of students in the ongoing activity, the time available, or indeed the risk of doing damage can all persuade the teacher to adopt one role in preference to another.

THE SPECIFICS OF A PEDAGOGY FOR PROFESSIONAL TRAINING

The observations described in this chapter have shown us that it is not possible to reduce the role of a teacher operating within a workshop to some simple intervention model. There is a contiguous occurrence of different roles for want of which pedagogical incoherence would prevail. The various roles fill complementary functions. That of master engineer in particular caught our attention; it helped to establish the role and the credibility of the master teacher in the eyes of the students.

But when in reality do the students have the opportunity to observe their master engineer in action, exercising his professional competence? We have seen that this happens in the course of particular phases, such as that in which a machining unit is started up and particularly when there are unforeseen difficulties or breakdowns. The teacher is then led for a moment to take the reins. As soon as the critical moment is past, he can withdraw from direct involvement in the action to leave them to take their task in hand and resume their job of being students.

The training potential of these unscheduled opportunities does not always seem to be appreciated by those involved. These occasions seem to be experienced by some of them as moments of hesitation in the course of which students sometimes seem to be putting the technical abilities of their teacher to the test; how will he cope? Generally, these situations seem to make everyone ill at ease, and they are in a hurry to escape. Breakdowns in some fashion come momentarily to destabilize the pedagogical relationship, while paradoxically at another level they consolidate this relationship.

The interactions between teacher and students within a workshop seem to be marked by a paradoxical dynamic; the more expert the teacher, and the more he is master of his subject, the greater the probability that none of his competence in action will be seen; his interventions are then confined to the range of didactic support. In contrast, when the teacher finds himself in difficulties or searching for a solution, he shows himself to his students as someone enacting his expertise. The situation is formative in that the students become witnesses to the activities of a professional whose skills are on display to be seen and recognized by others. This situation seems to be experienced as a pedagogical discomfort, which undermines its value.

The situations that most likely offer students the best opportunity to observe their "master engineer" in action are those of work involving teachers and students together in a technological development project. The Ecole Technique de Sainte-Croix does not lack for experiences of this kind. In the course of its history, different pieces of equipment have been produced with the collaboration of the college's own students. Quite recently, for example, we were able to observe the way in which students were involved, over the course of several hours of practical work, in setting up the commands for a newly acquired robot. Training opportunities of these kinds seem to be negotiated with students interested in matters beyond the established teaching program, and often even outside any scheduled sessions. However, these periods of collaborative work do not seem to be thought of entirely as time spent in training, but rather as transitional periods waiting for a new piece of equipment to be produced, adjusted, and fully mastered so that finally it will be possible to organize teaching structured around completed and reliable facilities.

What representation do the teacher and his students have of the characteristics of an effective training situation? What do they believe about what is possible to learn in different interaction contexts, contexts varying from highly autonomous forms of work to closely guided activities or activities shared with a master expert? What opportunities do the students have to think about these issues or to decide for themselves on the effectiveness of this or that training situation?

In the workshops of a technical college, different pedagogical models intersect and coexist, models derived from academic traditions and those taken from systems of occupational apprenticeship. The relationship between such models is complex. It constitutes an entire history of its own, as Pelpel and Troger (1993) have shown with respect to college workshops and the debates to which they have given rise in the French context. With Fillettaz (2009; Fillettaz et al., 2008) we think that the issue currently is not so much one of knowing which pedagogical models relating to training can be borrowed from the world of academic education or the world of work, but one of identifying more accurately the specifics of the approaches to learning that this sector has put into practice. Our observation of effective pedagogical practices has revealed to us the richness of what goes on in a college workshop. It has the potential to provide an invaluable basis for thinking about the pedagogy of professional training today.

CHAPTER 5

INTERACTING AND SUCCEEDING

When students are initiated in small groups into computer-assisted manu-facture, what approach do they take to collaboration? How do they interact with one another? What benefits do they gain? Here again we look at the practical work sessions on automation, the setting that was the focus for our observations in Chapter 4. This time we concentrate on the kind of sociocognitive interactions that can be observed in a real training situation of this kind. We do not repeat here a description of the tasks undertaken by these future technicians nor our approach involving filmed observations. The reader who wishes to be refreshed on these matters can review the introduction to the previous chapter.

The analyses presented in this chapter were undertaken by Danièle Golay Schilter. They are drawn from the research document by Daniele Golay Schilter, with Anne-Nelly Perret-Clermont, Jean- Francois Perret, Franco De Guglielmo, and Jean-Philippe Chavey (1997), titled "Aux prises avec l'informatique industrielle: collaboration et demarches de travail chez des eleves techniciens," Séminaire de Psychologie, University of Neuchâtel.

QUESTIONS TO GUIDE OBSERVATIONS

To approach the interactions among apprentices and attempt to come to grips with their dynamics, it is possible today to draw upon a large body of work with widely varied theoretical and methodological orientations (for a review, see in particular Dillenbourg, Baker, Blay, & O'Malley, 1996). Much of this work has been based on young children working in groups on different kinds of tasks. When we turn to adults in professional training, will we find the same general processes that have up to now been described in accounting for sociocognitive interactions? In particular, will we be able to observe in the training situations we are studying the confrontations of viewpoints and sociocognitive conflicts that have been shown in a series of experimental studies to initiate cognitive restructuring (Emler & Valiant, 1982; Doise & Mugny, 1981; Perret-Clermont & Nicolet, 1988; Light & Blaye, 1989; Bearison, 1991; Perret-Clermont, 1996; Perret-Clermont, Carugati, & Oates, 2004; Schwarz et al., 2008)? What benefits can young adults derive from a confrontation of points of view in the course of a task? Are cognitive re-elaborations going to bear upon their understanding of the task and its goal, or upon the knowledge that the task mobilizes? Or are conflictual interactions instead more likely to produce changes in conflict resolution strategies among apprentices (Gilly, Fraisse, & Roux, 1988; Blaye, 1989; Tartas, Baucal, & Perret-Clermont, 2010)?

What will be the approaches to collaboration by which each partner contributes complementary elements? Do the students observed, when involved in joint action, actually talk to each other? Discussion and explanation have often been considered to be helpful in the resolution of tasks for two principal reasons: they allow a sharing of goals, of a definition of the problem and of the sense that is made of the task; and discussion allows analysis of the problem, exchange of ideas, and indeed evaluation of options before deciding together on an approach to take (Pontecorvo, 1990; Howe, Tolmie, Green, & MacKenzie, 1995; Plety, 1996; Howe & Tolmie, 1999; Mercer & Wegerif, 1999; Mercer & Sams, 2006; Schwarz et al, 2008). But some studies have also shown that the negotiation and "conflict resolution" type of discussion has little influence on the performance of the groups studied (Perret-Clermont, 1980; Jackson, Fletscher, & Messer, 1992; Hoyles, Healy, & Pozzi, 1992; Darnon, Butera, & Mugny, 2008). We try to determine whether these processes are involved in the practical work sessions we observed.

Will we also find *an implicit or explicit distribution of roles and tasks* among those involved? The review of experimental research on group processes produced by Moscovici and Paicheler (1973), together with work conducted from an ergonomic perspective (Leplat, 1993), has shown that tasks of different kinds, if they are to be completed efficiently, require specific kinds of organization of the work group. How does this operate with respect to a complex industrial computing task? Will there in fact be a distribution of roles, and if there is, will this occur in a conscious way or more implicitly? Will this evolve in the course of growing familiarity with the activity concerned? Will such a distribution be reflected primarily in who speaks, in decision making and the exercise of power, and in the development of these in the course of the interaction, as Saint-Dizier, Trognon, and Grossen (1995) have shown? Is there negotiation of respective positions and the relative status of the participants, either prior to or during the course of the activity? Will we observe any taking of control, and will this positively contribute to the objective of the collaboration? Previous research has revealed the considerable attention devoted by participants to management of their position and their self-image, indeed their identity, in situations that we might have imagined were primarily devoted to the resolution of purely intellectual problems (Flahaut, 1978; Vion, 1992; Schubauer-Leoni, 1986; Grossen, Liengme Bessire, & Perret-Clermont, 1997; Muller & Perret-Clermont, 1999).

The characteristics of the task and of the computing tools used are both equally liable to influence the forms of collaboration that arise (Littleton & Light, 1999). Within a work group, the way in which control of the keyboard and mouse is or is not shared is the first sensitive issue, as Blaye, Light, and Rubstov (1992) have observed. Other research has focused on analysis of the role and effect of instruments that transmit to learners various signals and information, such as error messages (Blaye et al., 1992; Light & Blaye, 1989; Hoyles, Healy, & Sutherland, 1990).

To summarize, we are interested in the forms of collaboration that are established in work groups, the manner in which learners confronted with a complex piece of work organize their activity and distribute the various tasks, and roles and responsibilities for taking the initiative. We observe how over the course of the action the work groups manage their exchanges and any differences in viewpoints that emerge. We also identify the problem-solving approaches adopted by the work groups. We are, as well, attentive to the attitude of students confronted with an unforeseen situation, to the reactions aroused, and to the resources then mobilized.

HOW DO WORK GROUPS REACT
WHEN FACED WITH DIFFICULTY?

Among the many hours of video recording collected of practical work sessions on automation, we found our attention drawn to a series of difficulties that were encountered with particular frequency by the students. One of these, which the four groups filmed had encountered at one point or another, involved determination of the values corresponding to the different machining depths needed to be taken into account by the program (we describe these depths in Box 1). Here we shall pay particular attention to

---

BOX 1. Technical Data Defining the Difficulty of Determining the Working Depths of the Tool

In the beginning, the students must establish various parameters to be provided to the computer: the material composition of the part to be machined, the tool to be chosen, the tool's direction of work, and also the method for selecting the holes to be made. They then have to enter into the program the values in millimeters for each working depth of the tool (Figures 1 and 2).

These values correspond to the distance between the surface of the part, defined as depth zero, and each of the following depths:

- *The safety depth:* level at which the machine is going to position the tool above the part.
- *Rapid approach:* the level to which the tool descends rapidly toward the part; this allows a time savings in effecting the machining.
- *The reference surface:* this is the surface of the part, the point at which the tool comes into contact with the surface.
- The *depth* of machining to be made, which will either be that reached in the hole by the full diameter of the tool, or that reached by the tip of the tool.

The correct solution requires that the values given for each depth follow a decreasing order. For example: safety depth: $Z = 10$ mm. Rapid approach: $Z = 2$ mm Reference surface: $Z = 0$ mm. Machining depth: $z = -12$ mm, given by the tool diameter. In the case that concerns us, the students use a drill, and for this tool the program automatically recalculates the depth at the tip. Thus, given a machining depth of -12 mm "at the diameter," this becomes a depth of -17 mm.

The reference surface for the machine, the "absolute zero," according to the expression used by the students, corresponds to the position of the vice or clamp. If we machine a pocket starting from the initial surface of the part, the reference surface is itself going to be 0. If the pocket that is machined, or the hole that is bored, is located at the bottom of an existing void, the reference surface can, under certain conditions, be lowered as a function of the depth of this void to save time.

During milling, when students enter values that do not conform to a decreasing order (e.g., a rapid approach that is above the safety depth) or if they forget to indicate the depth by means of a negative sign, the program remains at the first window, emits an audible beep, and gives a message noting the order that the values in question need to follow.

---

the reactions provoked by this difficulty and the manner in which it is managed and then overcome by the students.

Presentation of our observations will be made in two parts. To give the reader a very concrete idea at the outset of the kinds of data with which we

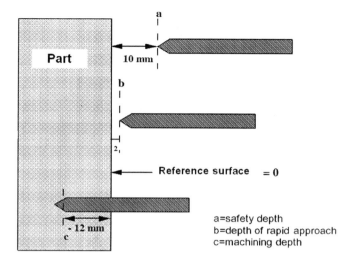

FIGURE 5.1. Successive levels of the tool's approach.

have worked, we begin with the analysis of interactions observed between two students confronted at a particular point in their work with the difficulty raised by determining the exact values for machining. Then we present and discuss a set of observations made of each of the four groups.

To describe the students' forms of collaboration, as well as their approaches to the work and to problem solving, we have not proceeded on the basis of a coding of behaviors in terms of pre-established categories, but via analysis of their interactions. By interaction we mean both a series of actions and exchanges between partners and the properties of these actions, which is to say the reciprocal influence that the partners thus exercise via their respective actions (Trognon, 1991). From this point of view, the interaction constitutes a single process in which the actors concurrently (re)define the

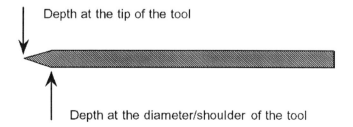

FIGURE 5.2. The two options for indicating the depth of the hole.

meaning of the situation, develop their relationship, display their feelings, undertake cognitive activity, and act on their environment (Grossen et al., 1997). Such an approach requires recourse to a fine-grained description of the exchanges and actions; we have included here changes in the state of the computer program, such as movement from one window (or dialogue box) to another, screen messages written in natural language and audible signals (beeps), as well as displays of different graphical presentations, in particular those representing the machining to be undertaken.

ANALYSIS OF INTERACTIONS BETWEEN TWO STUDENTS

The group consists of two students, Alain and Louis, who are following the "mechanical construction" syllabus. Alain is a mechanic-electrician by training and Louis is a mechanic. Having first tried out at an engineering college, the latter came directly into the second year of the course at the Ecole Technique and had, therefore, not attended the course on computer-assisted manufacture, carried out with the FMS machining unit.

Here is the transcription[2] and analysis of a sequence of about 15 minutes in which these students found themselves faced with the choice of what values to enter for the tool's working depths, a choice that raised several difficulties. These students had already been working together for an hour and a half. They now needed to cut two holes at the bottom of a pocket that had already been machined. We successively distinguish and analyze four phases making up this sequence.

Phase 1: Deciding on the Machining Operation

The sequence begins with a discussion between the two students on the manner in which the work should be pursued. Alain proposes drilling, but Louis is opposed to this because with the tool they are going to use (a 6mm cutter), they can still program a machining operation involving the cutting of two holes. After a brief discussion, Alain adopts his colleague's point of view.

1APS:	**Displays a drawing of the part**
2A:	There is the drilling to do now

[2] Transcription conventions:
characters in bold = dialogue between students and the computer
                   (actions performed on the computer; modifications to information
                   displayed by the program, messages, etc.)
// = uncompleted utterance cut off by the other's interruption
___ = overlap
characters in italics = non-verbal or paralinguistic communications; posture, gesture, tone of
                voice
CAPITALS = the names of menus, commands or contents of dialogue boxes.

3L: Yep. No, "we" should still use the same cutter to do the two holes there (*he takes a part already machined and indicates something in it*), because that is a six //

4A: Hey, wait, there is already an interior (*he points to something on the screen*). Oh yes, no...

5L: No//

6A: ...the interior, it's done

7L: ...because if we have holes of six, it'll work well, but if //

8A: <u>We are making a pocket</u> (*with a hesitant tone*)...

9L: ...<u>if we have the six cutter</u>

10A: (*with greater certainty*) <u>We are making a pocket</u>. (*During the exchange between 4A and 7L, the two students are looking at each other*)

11L: Exactly, we should make another between the others (*still holding the part in his hands, he mimes the gesture of making a hole while emitting a whistle and looking at A*).

The exchange is initiated by Alain. With statement 2A, this student introduces the treatment of a new subject (pursuit of the requirements of the practical work session) by stating, "There is the drilling to do now." Louis accepts this new conversational topic but reacts to 2A with an "argued disagreement" (Gilly et al., 1988). Statement 3L effectively contains an objection ("No"), a different solution ("We should still use the same cutter to do the two holes there"), and an explanation ("Because that is a six"). Faced with this disagreement, Alain cuts into Louis's speaking turn and without offering an argument advances an alternative solution ("there is already an interior"), a solution that he himself then abandons right away. Confronted with the determination with which Louis continues to support his position, Alain interrupts again. First of all, rather hesitantly (8A) and then with more confidence (10A) he says, "We are making a pocket." In relation to the implicit question ("What should we be doing in this practical work session?") that begins the exchange and that is immediately shared by Louis, 8A and 10A thus play a dual role: by mentioning the pocket, Alain on the one hand ceases to dispute the idea of cutting, *de facto* going along with Louis, but on the other hand he brings about a shift in the confrontation; his statements no longer concern "what to do" (from now on tacitly accepted), but "how can it be done?" They are no longer involved in determining the goal but in searching for procedures to attain it. Louis (11L) accepts the procedure indicated by Alain and, with a touch of humor, brings the exchange to a close.

From the point of view of the approach to work, this first sequence shows us two students engaged in a process of organizing their activity. In 2A and 3L, they express above all their desire to continue the exercise through the definition of a specific and intermediate stage in the (long) progress toward the solution that the practical work sessions require. The disagreement that breaks out serves to provide this stage with negotiated contents (goals and certain procedures). This approach is verbal; no modification is made to the program, and the actions (pointing to the screen and indicating the already machined part) occur only to support the argument. Alain, hesitant, does not advance any argument and the thinking behind his observations (4A and 6A) is not available to us. This makes our understanding of the exchange more difficult.

Alain and Louis provide here a type of collaboration characterized by a balance in the frequencies of their respective contributions. A group sentiment is expressed in the systematic recourse to "we." If it is Alain who initiates the exchange and who introduces the themes, it is Louis who defends his proposition with assurance, using hypothetico-deductive reasoning. He emerges as the one who evaluates the proposals and who can decide on closure of the exchange. Moreover, he is in command of the computer.

Louis makes a whole series of choices (display of the part, options for control of the tool, selection of the shapes for the interior, the "pocket" mode of machining) before coming to the window of the program dealing with the tool's working depths.

12L: Okay, now ZOOM, because I can't see anything here, me…
Clicks on SCREEN.

13APS: **Displays the SCREEN menu.**

14L: **In the SCREEN menu, he selects the option ZOOM WINDOW.**
….ZOOM WINDOW
He selects an area of the image of the part using the pointer.

15APS: **Displays an enlarged image of the area to be machined.**

16L: (*to another student*) What have you got to laugh at, Luca?

17L: There it is. MACHINE
Selects MACHINE.

18APS: **Displays the MACHINE menu.**

19L: **Clicks on the option ORIENTATION OF THE TOOL.**

20APS: **Displays the window ORIENTATION OF THE TOOL.**

21L: **Leaves the default option NOTHING TO CHANGE.**
INTERIOR
Clicks on INTERIOR and then on OK.

22APS: **Returns to the image of the area of the part to be machined.**

23L: There it is.
Clicks on the circumference of the hole to be machined, located at the base of the part.

24APS: **Displays the symbol for the tool and its position within the circumference selected.**

25L:And then we do this (*in a somewhat hesitant tone*) (*he indicates the other hole with the pointer*)

Clicks on the circumference of the other hole as well.

(*during all this A watches the screen*)

26APS: **Displays the symbol for the tool and its position within the second**

circumference selected.

27A: No, after

28L: No, come on, we will save time, hey!

29L: POCKET

Selects MACHINE.

30APS: **Displays the MACHINE menu.**

31L: **Clicks on POCKET.**

32APS: **Displays the POCKET window.**

33L: **Retains the default option POCKET CONTOUR, clicks on POCKET IN**

SPIRAL (CIRCLES), retains GEOMETRIES: SELECTED and SIDES: VERTICAL and clicks on OK.

34APS: **Displays the window SPIRAL POCKET in which there are depths of working to be specified for the tool. Values are already displayed: Safety depth = 20, rapid approach = 2, reference surface = 0, machining depth = 0.**

(*A turns his head toward a noise outside, and then turns back to the screen and touches his ear.*)

In statement 12L, Louis takes on the initiative to carry out what the two students have previously decided (cutting of two holes via the creation of a pocket). In addition, this statement marks a transition to action in the form of the entry of inputs into the program. In his dialogue with the computer by means of the mouse, Louis first produces an enlargement of the area of the part that will be the focus of the machining and does this "…because I can't see anything here, me…" (12L). Statement 25L ("And then we do this"), produced in a somewhat hesitant tone, provokes a little conflict between the two. Louis wants to select the two pockets for machining at this point, while Alain prefers that they initially concentrate only on the first one. Louis's explanation ("No, come on, we will save time") seems to convince him immediately. The dialogue between Louis and the program can then be pursued without difficulty up to 34APS.

The communication that Louis initiates with APS unfolds very rapidly. The program *outputs* provide no surprises for a student who displays a certain mastery of the operations. It is he who decides on the approach and largely makes the choices independently. All the same, in the course of his communication with APS, Louis verbalizes the actions he takes (12L: "Okay,

now ZOOM, because I can't see anything here, me..."; 29L: "POCKET").
Alain, distracted by everything going on around him, seems to remain in
the background and to leave all the decisions to Louis. Statement 27A constitutes the only exception during a phase in which it is Louis who initiates, decides, proposes, and evaluates. Louis proceeds with assurance, while
Alain is rather passive.

Phase 2: Choice of Values: From Disagreement to Apparent Consensus

The students must now decide the levels of descent of the cutter toward
the part and the depths of the pockets to be machined. The work continues
with three situations (34APS–53A, 54L–67A, and 68L–82L) in which the
students confront one another in a contradictory manner; one reacts to a
proposition made by the other by arguing his disagreement or by suggesting an alternative.

> 34APS: **Displays the window SPIRAL POCKET in which there are
> depths of working to be specified for the tool. Values are
> already displayed:
> Safety depth = 20, rapid approach = 2
> reference surface = 0,
> machining depth = 0.**

During this time, A turns his head toward a noise outside and then returns his gaze to the screen, a hand to his ear.

> 35L: DEPTH (*he points to the depth of the cut*), ah, now how do we do it?
> (*he points a finger to the dialogue box in question*), Ah, then we have
> to change the re-fer-ence! (*he looks at A who touches himself behind
> the head*)
>
> 36A: That's why the others took so much time, you remember//
>
> 37L: Because they started higher up
>
> 38A: ...because they made it higher (*during this exchange, the two stu-
> dents are looking at each other*)
>
> 39L: We should at least start (*he measures the part, he checks the already
> machined part, the mouse and the keyboard*).
>
> 40L: It's two millimeters (pause), minus two (pause), minus two.
>
> 41A: (*looking elsewhere, distracted, but at the end of 40, he points to the
> part[?] in L's hand and says*): It's not possible! If your reference
> point is there...//
>
> 42L: Ah...//
>
> 43A: ...and if you have to come down to there...//

44L: ...depth of cut! Now we have given the reference point there (*he gestures toward the screen that displays the window with DEPTH OF CUT*).

45A: Yes, but then if the reference point is there, that would mean rather less, less...(*he points to the part*)

46L: No, but the reference point there, that is the depth of the cut, that is to say if you have your reference here// (*he points to the screen*)

47A: Yep

48L: You go down two (*he points to the part and mimics the descent of the tool with his finger*)

49A: Yep, but you can't leave zero (*He points to the screen. During the exchange (36–37) they are looking at each other and at the same time pointing to the screen and the part*)

50L: But we change after (*he shows something*)

51A: Ah, there it is, agreed

52L: minus two

53A: Okay minus two. **Types –2 for DEPTH OF CUT.**

The APS software displays a window that contains the values used in the previous machining, and Louis, without pausing at the first two depths, identifies a problem (35L: "DEPTH, ah, now how do we do it?") and then provides an initial response to it "Ah, then we have to change the re-fer-ence" (35L). In the exchanges 36A to 39L, and 38A, the two students seem to be in agreement that time is lost by starting too high, something that a change in the reference surface allows them to avoid. In effect, Alain implicitly accepts Louis's proposition in justifying it by an example drawn from observation of groups that had preceded them in these practical exercises. Louis then suggests a value (40L: "It's two millimeters, minus two, ... minus two") derived from a measure taken of the part, and thus it is not exactly clear what it relates to. Alain responds to 40L, rejecting the suggestion (41A: "It's not possible!...) and, for the first time, justifies his disagreement. He sticks to his position, despite Louis's pauses and counterarguments.

Understanding the point of view of each of the students and the way in which they arrive at agreement in 51A–53A remains difficult. The rapidity of the solution seems to show that the disagreement was based on an initial misunderstanding; we might say that, in effect, for Alain the measure indicated by his colleague concerned the reference surface and not the cutting depth. This equivocation is nonetheless engendered, in part, by Louis himself. Effectively, at the beginning of the exchange he pronounces the need to change the reference ("... we have to change the re-fer-ence!" he says in a chant); but in the argument he employs it then seems that his measurement specifies a depth of cut ("...that is the depth of the cut, that is to say if you have your reference here, you go down two").

Although a confrontation developed between the two students concerning the values to be set for the reference surface and the depth of cut, there was in contrast implicit agreement on the other two values that appeared within the window displayed by 34APS (Safety depth = 20, and rapid approach = 2). Effectively, these two values were directly incorporated into the new operation without any discussion.

It is always Louis who begins the discussion and moves the work forward (35L, 39L, 40L, 52L). But Alain's presence is much stronger than this suggests; for example, he operates the keyboard. Even if it is Louis who defines the situation and suggests a general solution (namely, to change the reference), putting this solution into effect depends on its becoming a shared decision; Louis does not move directly to action by himself, in contrast to what we observed in the first sequence in the preceding phase. The search for agreement proceeds via a "contradictory confrontation" (Gilly et al., 1988), a confrontation that follows on from formal reasoning in which hypothesis and deduction predominate.

The exchange from 54L to 67A is in part an interlude or digression. It is begun by Louis, who, referring to the consequences of decisions made earlier, suggests modifying the reference surface of a previously programmed machining.

> *54L:* And then you know something else, we are also going to modify this, because here, to do...., because here when it is going to do the contour for that, it starts again from the top (*illustrative gesture of the finger imitating the cutter above the part*), it does the contour, once it has done that for us, we give it the reference point (*glances exchanged between the partners and toward the part*) (*A takes control of the mouse again*)
>
> 55A: No, you can't do anything about that, because the machine does that itself (*he points to the screen*), it does that itself, what you said.
>
> 56L: No, because ... once you have done, because at the beginning it does the contour here, you see, and worse when you say the point of reference, it's in relation to that, the machine begins again from the top, it comes down to two millimeters, to three millimeters (*he shows the movements of the tool on the part*) (*During the exchange the two are looking at each other*) // ...
>
> 57A: Ah! (*touches himself on the chin*) //
>
> 58L: And worse it does the finishing all around the circle...
>
> 59A: I knew that, I knew that...
>
> 60L: And worse once it has to do the hexagon, there //
>
> 61A: Yep, <u>it starts again at zero</u>

62L:	It starts again right from the top//
63A:	We are losing time
64L:	Yep, it... (*he makes circles in the air with his finger*)//
65A:	It's machining for nothing
66L:	Exactly
67A:	That's why the others took more than 17 minutes.

In terms of the content discussed, we may briefly note that once again the students refer to the machining situation, in particular the descending path of the cutter and that they agree on not starting too high so as not to lose time. Again the choices made by other groups provide them with counterexamples here. This concern about the evaluation criterion their teacher had set out (make the machining time short), already expressed earlier, is revealed again in turns 63A to 67A. It is this shared preoccupation with speed of execution and gaining time compared to "the others" that most often drives the solutions proposed and that underpins the joint decisions (25L to 28L; 35L to 39L; 54L to 66L).

In terms of collaboration, it is always Louis who initiates the issue to be decided. In the face of Alain's opposition, he launches into a long explanation, supported by gestures, of the movements of the tools concerned. Alain begins by expressing astonishment ("Ah"), then he interrupts his companion's long statement with mild impatience ("I knew that, I knew that") , and finally cuts him off by himself, completing the observation (60–61).

Let us return to the completion of this exchange.

68L:	(...) okay, the reference now, how much is it?
	Clicks on the REFERENCE SURFACE dialogue box and deletes the 0.
69A:	The problem is it has to be accurate, huh!
70L:	Ouf, accurate with a cutter like that, huh... it's ten (*he has left the screen and uses a ruler to measure an already machined part that provides him with a model*)
71A:	So, minus 10.
	Types in −10 for REFERENCE SURFACE.
72L:	Minus ten. No, wait, it's less... (*they poke each other*)
73A:	Hey, yes, you are underneath!
74L:	(*they touch each other*). Yes, but the machine, how does it know what to do?
	.... (*he does not continue; he looks at Alain, then he points toward the computer, and looks at the part in silence for several seconds*).
75A:	Because (*he takes the part in his hands and twiddles with it*) in the clamp (*a hand gesture*), the clamp, it knows it's at zero.
76L:	Ah! It knows? (*he picks up the part*)

77A: Why, yes//
78L: Ah, good.
79A: … if not, you could never know that you were at zero.
80L: Hey, yes, exactly, that's what I was asking myself; how was it making the machine know…
81A: Yes, it's in relation to…(?) to the clamp
82L: (*He has taken the mouse again*) **Clicks on OK.{\DIA}**

Their entries are as follows:

Safety depth: Z = 20	Rapid approach: Z = 2
Reference surface: Z = –10	Depth of cut: Z = –2
Number of movements: 1 CN code: linear	Depth of the movement: Constant

The subject of this last confrontation is the value to be given to the reference surface. In 70L ("…it's ten"), Louis announces this after having used a ruler to measure the difference between the surface of the part and the depth of the already machined hexagonal pocket. However, as soon as Alain types in -10 on the keyboard, Louis begins to have doubts (72L: "Minus ten, no, wait, it's less…") and then begins to pose a question but does not finish it. Alain, nonetheless, seems to understand it because he suggests an answer, of which Louis asks for confirmation (76). Alain then expands his answer into an argument (79), which apparently leads Louis to the (unfinished) question that he had asked (himself) in 74 (how does the machine know?), the circle is completed, and he accepts his companion's answer ("the clamp, it knows it's at zero"). The culmination of this exchange consists in Louis adopting the value proposed in 71A (–10).

Thus Alain provides the decision this time, within a phase in which it is still Louis who initiates the decision making and defines the objective (68L: "…okay, the reference now, how much is it?"). It is also he who measures, who opens up an issue for reflection (by casting doubt on his own suggestion: 72L: "Minus ten. No, wait, it's less…"), and who brings the exchange to an end. Thus he retains the dominant position in the management of the approach. He is always the master of communication with the program; even though the instructions are shared (Alain on the keyboard and Louis operating the mouse), most of the inputs given to the program are made via the mouse (and thus by Louis). From the point of view of the content of decisions, matters work differently, and here their approach, like their mode of collaboration, displays interesting characteristics.

Indeed, in contrast to the first sequence and to the approach adopted by other groups, we do not observe unilateral decision making here or in the attempt "to see"; on the contrary, each decision is a matter for thought and discussion until agreement is achieved. Nonetheless, we found one strikingly recurrent behavior and it raises several questions: the two students frequently cut across each other's speech and we are not always in a position to know whether this is a way of constructing a common discourse in which one is completing and pursuing the other's observations because he has understood the issue, or whether these interruptions indicate impatience, a difficulty in hearing the other out to the end, that ultimately leads to misunderstandings. Looking at this more closely, one observes that these two forms of interaction seem to coexist. For example, exchanges 60–67 appear to us to be consistent with the first hypothesis. In contrast, we will see that in the following exchanges (94–95), Alain's interruption clearly seems to damage elaboration of a shared understanding because it prevents Louis from explaining how he calculated the depth of the cut and denies Alain access to the other's point of view.

Phase 3: The Limitations of Discussion in the Face of an Error Message

83APS: **Displays a message: the reference surface must be equal to or less than the height of the cut.**

84L: What's that? REFERENCE SURFACE must be... (*We notice that at this moment Alain is operating the keyboard and Louis the mouse*).

85A: ...Equal to or less

86L: Go back!... Click! Click!

87L: **Clicks on OK.**

88APS: **Returns to the window dealing with the working depths of the tool (SPIRAL POCKET).**

89A: Minus 10, DEPTH OF CUT; but it's not minus two, it's minus twelve (*he points to the screen*), no?

90L: No!

91A: Then that doesn't work...

92L: That thing doesn't work, we have to change something else (*he plays with the part*)

93A: (*Pause, Looks elsewhere. But all of a sudden:*) No, put minus twelve! Because your REFERENCE SURFACE, it goes to minus ten, if you want to machine your little area, which is there (*he points to the part*), you have to go to minus twelve//

94L: Yep, but the depth of cut, it's always in relation to//

95A: Wait, no, but I'll explain to you, because there, you don't start your thingy (*he takes the part from Louis's hands and shows where [?] on the part*), that doesn't mean you put a zero for your thing.

96L: (*Accompanying his words with illustrative gestures of the hand simulating the tool*). No, if you displace the REFERENCE SURFACE every time you come down to something, it's like you had put zero before, all the times that you were putting in a negative number it went lower, if you put in a positive number it stays higher, which is to say in relation//

97A: Okay, I get it, I get it (*Pause*). But then that means their thing no longer works after their error message (*he fiddles with the part, striking his open hand with the part during the three following talking turns*)

98L: Something has to be done here, yes exactly//

99A: That no longer works when you have a situation like that.

100L: I think you have to change the zero on the machine, it's no longer this zero here (he takes the part back), you have to say somewhere, it's no longer this zero here, it's something else.

101A: But that there is getting complicated, that (*he leans back and folds his arms*)

102L: Yes, but you have to do it, because if not it's not worthwhile. Wait. SAFETY DEPTH, it's good. RAPID APPROACH, down to two, that there is okay, REFERENCE SURFACE, that's minus ten there.

(*A looks elsewhere, distracted by a noise*)

103L: Depth of cut, it's minus two (*pause*)

104A: **(with the mouse) selects DEPTH OF CUT**
(with the mouse) deletes −2
(*Waits 4 seconds*)
Types in −12 on the keyboard.
Clicks on OK with the mouse.

105APS: Go to the next window

106L: It's true, it accepts it like that

107A: Yes

108L: Like that it accepts it, but after you do the twelve thing, or it won't change the reference point (*showing all this on the part*)//

109A: No, because it knows that its reference point is at minus ten, it knows that it has to go to minus twelve, it starts from minus ten (he simulates this on his own hand)

110L: But that's stupid!

111A: Hey, that's the way it is!

112L: Wait, me I don't believe.... Yes, it's possible//

113A: Why, yes//

114L: ...but it's stupid!

115A: Why yes, yeah but if not it doesn't work, huh, you can't (?)

116L: But listen...

117A: Listen (*gestures with a flat hand toward the screen*), we only have to look at the simulation, and you'll see what it does.\DIA}

To recall, the values entered were the following:

Safety depth: Z = 20	Rapid approach: Z = 2
Reference surface: Z = 10	Depth of cut: Z = –2
Number of movements: 1 CN code: linear	Depth of the movement: constant

In 83APS, the software displays a rejection of these values, "the reference surface must be equal to or *less* than the height of the cut." As we know, this message contains a wording error: the program should in fact have displayed: "the reference surface must be equal to or *greater* than the height of the cut." The students are not aware of this problem with the program. Moreover, they do not discuss the content of the message, but Alain immediately suggests a change to the depth (–12 in place of 2). Louis's opposition (90L: "No") produces a long discussion (91–103) that is sometimes difficult to follow. Alain does not ask Louis to give his reasons for disagreeing but throws in a "that doesn't work," which Louis completes and approves (92) in a manner that is entirely obscure to the external observer. In exchanges 92–97, the mutual interruptions and use of terms such as "thing" and "thingamy" also interfere with our understanding of what is exchanged and developed. Nonetheless, we can grasp that the issue is the reference with respect to which it is appropriate to calculate the depth of cut (94L, for example). Alain gets to this point from the conclusion that the error message presents a problem "in this situation." In 98L, Louis seems to agree ("...yes, exactly") and suggests a new change, that of zero for the machine. Alain shows his disagreement both physically and verbally by leaning back, folding his arms, and judging this proposal to be "complicated." From this point onward, they no longer argue on the basis of reasoning or in terms of what is correct or wrong; instead, they advance judgments of value about the solutions considered: what is complicated, worthwhile or not (102L), or " stupid" (110L). So when Louis starts to go through all the values again (102L–103L), and faced with his continuing opposition, Alain grabs control of the computer and enters his own solution (depth of –12), which the program accepts. Louis acknowledges this but does not know how to be satisfied with this "success" and persists in finding this solution inadequate: "But it's stupid." Alain can only come up with the argument: "that's the way it is" and, confronted with the impossibility of bringing his companion around to this, brands the program as arbitrary and suggests using the simulation option (visualization on the screen of the machining operation concerned).

An important element, from the point of view of the approach to the work, resides in the way in which the two students define the problem. Having received an error message (83APS and 88APS), they do not deal with the latter's content but launch into a discussion (once again very difficult for an external observer to follow). If in the first phase they had referred to the information provided by the teacher and had read the message carefully, they would have been able to express doubts about the signal given by the program, which wrongly asked them to correct a relationship between values (–10 for the reference surface and –2 for the depth of cut). This was not the case, even when Alain's suggested solution (–12 for the depth of cut), which is in the opposite direction to that indicated by APS, is nonetheless accepted by the program!

We can advance the hypothesis that the essence of their discussion is that it reflects the existence of two divergent representations of the manner in which to calculate the depth of cut in relation to the reference surface: Alain calculates both the reference surface and the depth of cut on the basis of the machine's zero point (the vice); thus he suggests –10 for the one and –12 for the other. As for Louis, he calculates each level in relation to the preceding level: as the depth of the pocket is two millimeters greater than the reference surface, he suggests –2.

Alain, whose representation is actually the correct one, has to go to the trouble of providing a convincing picture and allows himself to be unsettled by his companion and in all probability by the error message as well. When Alain's solution is accepted, Louis casts doubt on it with a negative judgment, and we wonder whether in this he is drawing on his previous experience of digitally controlled machines, which he had mentioned previously. Additionally, Alain does not try to understand or reject the "argument" of the reality of the program (of which he seems to have the better grasp): "that's the way it is." Moreover, this can be generalized: their exchanges contain numerous assertions of their own respective points of view and few questions put to each other about the other's perspective, even though they did not always understand each other's perspective.

After a period of exchange of arguments and reasons of a hypothetico-deductive nature prior to taking action (their recourse to objects or to the computer serve at this particular moment only to illustrate or defend their argument), Alain breaks away from this way of doing things and, without consultation or agreement, enters his suggestion into the program. In sum, not being able to convince Louis, who is himself unable to suggest an alternative, Alain asserts himself and acts. The program's reaction, accepting this input, provides him with the ultimate argument. It thus establishes a more concrete "approach" centered on the act and the practical verification of its effects (the program's response and the simulation of the machining operation).

Phase 4: Solutions Derived but Unsatisfactory

The remainder of the sequence, which we return to deal with now, can be divided into three parts: observation of the simulation, a second part in which Louis is absent, having gone to find the teacher (during this time Alain answers questions put by the observer), and a final part in which Louis passes on to Alain the fruits of his discussion with the teacher, allowing them then to decide on the values that should be entered.

The two students are not explicit about what they are able to verify during the course of the simulation: "It simulates, and you watch!" They comment on what they see. Louis shows himself to be rather impatient with the program: "Get on with it, infernal what's-its-name." The two notice that the tool machines in thin air and consequently that they are going to lose time. At the end, Louis is irritated and exclaims, "That's it, we've seen nothing" and, without further explanation, gets up and leaves.

Waiting by himself, Alain has the screen display the drawing of the part in 2D and then responds to some questions from the observer. He knows implicitly that his companion has gone to look for the teacher. In his view, their problem is as follows: they would like to change the value for the reference surface in order to save time in the machining. But according to the message, it cannot do this, because they are right down to a depth equal to or less than the reference surface. "If we change the reference point, if the reference point is that there, we can change it and from there we can drill lower, but the problem is, it's that with the error message, which tells us we have to have a distance equal to or less than... (*illustrative gestures with the part*)" (153A). It is also necessary to know if they can nonetheless change this last value or if it has to remain 0, with the risk that the tool will however "...work in empty space" (159A). In what he says there is nothing to indicate that he thinks either that there are two different representations of the situation or that the program's message could be wrong.

Louis comes back with the teacher's answer: their solution is correct but too complicated to put into effect; they will have to re-enter the value presented for the reference surface right at the beginning of the sequence (that is to say, 0). The remainder of the explanation remains obscure to us, but Alain seems to understand and accept it, though not without recrimination: he persists in thinking their initial idea should be possible and that it is not really so complicated. So they change the reference surface (from −10 back to 0) and leave the depth of the cut at −2. We should emphasize here that they have not, after all that, clarified the procedure for calculating the reference surface or the depth of cut in relation to the machine's 0, and thus they have not seen that they have put into operation a different method of calculation!

With regard to their collaboration, we should note that it was Louis who took the initiative to go and seek out the help of the teacher, while Alain seems to have confidence in his own description and explanation of the problem. Louis then continues to establish the rhythm of work, canceling the machining operations that they had previously programmed to reset the work on the basis of the teacher's directions.

Overlapping Interactions

The sequence considered here is particularly interesting because it displays different aspects of the interactive process at play in the collaboration and problem-solving approach.

Concerning Forms of Collaboration

In the sequence analyzed, the form of collaboration that unfolds takes the following shape: Louis finds himself in control, both figuratively and in practice; he initiates and concludes the phases of work and the decision making, carries out one part of the exercise by himself without any appeal to discussion, states the immediate objectives, takes the initiative to go and find the teacher, etc. Moreover, the students are aware that between them there is a turnaround in the situation, as their comments reveal:

L: You see, me, I don't understand anything, but I know how to make it work!
        (...)
L: It's me that does it, it's me that controls the situation!
        Or, a little later:
A: You've understood how it works quickly!
L: But it's easy!

Even though he recognizes the progress Louis is making, Alain does not, however, desist from playing the expert (95A: "...I'll explain it to you...") and seems on a couple of occasions to be irritated to be on the receiving end of long explanations from Louis (59A and 97A: "I get it, I get it"). Regarding this latter interjection, as we have just seen, he is not in the least bit indifferent to the fact of no longer having control of the situation. In addition, during the machining and when the teacher comments on their work, the two students are brought back, in the manner of a game, to the responsibility for the problems encountered. Competence seems to be used to accord themselves value or as a source of power, even if the relationship proceeds amicably enough with, it is true, an abundance of joking and teasing.

In the sequence analyzed, there is more searching for a solution through discussion than previously. Decisions and actions are preceded by exchanges in the course of which the students are reminded of what they agree on (such as is the case when they state their aim of "gaining time on the machining"), but more often in which they argue contrary viewpoints up to the point at which an agreement is elaborated. The tentative groping, the trials "to see" what happens, have disappeared. This domination of reflection and of exchange about the action is also marked by nonverbal comments: instead of looking at the screen and taking action on the program, we see a number of exchanges of mutual glances to confirm contact, maintaining the communication or marking its end, and an abundance of illustrative gestures (indicative movements directed at the screen or the part, and mimics of the tool), as well as gestures involving self-touching during pauses and moments of confusion (for a presentation of these behaviors and a more detailed discussion of their function during interaction, see Plety, 1996).

Two elements, however, moderate this picture. When Alain does not manage to convince his companion, he abandons this approach and without consultation enters his preferred solution into the program, regarding this as a test of (or support for) his view. When Louis continues to oppose this solution, despite the positive feedback from the computer and without offering an acceptable alternative, he again describes the program as arbitrary and suggests using the simulation. In these two cases, discussion proves to be a limited solution, and recourse to action seems necessary.

Concerning Problem-Solving Strategies

While at the beginning of the exercise, the students moved straight to action and gave priority to attempts "to see" what would happen, in the sequence analyzed here, their approach has moved on. The choice of machining operation is made on the basis of a rational utilization of the tool, and there is a defined objective: save time in machining holes at the bottom of an existing pocket by beginning the cutting lower down, and doing this by giving the reference surface a value below 0. This objective is in response to one of the evaluation criteria announced by the teacher: speed of machining. Hence the students are taking this criterion into account, along with the other evidence available to them; they show themselves to be capable of checking the operations, and before moving to take action, they define an objective and the approach to be followed. It is worth noting that this is the only group to have demonstrated this kind of competence; in analogous situations, the other groups actually moved straight to action.

When it is a matter of choosing values for the depth of cut and the reference surface, each decision is preceded by an exchange in which two different points of view are expressed about the way to calculate the values. These exchanges are significant in allowing them to give voice to an important element of the situation: the machine's zero in relation to which all the values are calculated. Viewed from outside, their solution (−10 for the reference surface and −2 for the depth of cut) consists of an amalgam of two conceptions that we believe to be the following: a calculation of the reference surface and the depth of cut starting from the machine's zero and a calculation in which the value for the depth of cut is equivalent to the difference between this latter and the reference surface.

The error message is subject neither to close consideration nor to discussion. The students never comment that in this message the program issues a requirement that their values already match (this because of an error in the program). On the other hand, they are not led to try something at random and instead tackle the values mentioned in the message. This last encourages Alain to voice a solution that conforms to his method of calculation. Despite the arguments deployed, Louis's opposition and the discussion that ensues do not enable the two students to completely explain their respective approaches. Our hypothesis is that the manner in which the students cut across each other's observations contributed to this impasse.

Alain's reaction is then to change approach; he stops arguing and moves to action, entering his solution into the program from which he clearly expects positive feedback. Louis then displays a unique and interesting reaction: the fact that the program accepts the solution does not satisfy him, and he continues to regard Alain's proposal as inappropriate, probably on the basis of criteria derived from his work on digitally controlled machines but perhaps also because of the difficulty of sticking to his position. In all the other groups, whatever the computer says is accepted by the students, who get on with their work even if they do not entirely understand the situation.

Alain, who no longer seeks to understand his companion's viewpoint and seems to weary of the argument, suggests instead a screen simulation of the machining operation. But this does not allow them either to cut through or to resolve their disagreement. They are not explicit about what they expect it to verify. At the end of the day, Louis leaves to seek the teacher's help. From this he returns with a solution that goes against their initial goal and the information transmitted in the first sequence, namely to save time by entering a reference surface value lower than zero, but this will leave them dissatisfied.

What do the students learn in this situation? In an initial interaction with the teacher (at the beginning of the practical work session), the students have been told that the rapid approach must be above the reference surface, and Alain realized that the safety level could not be equal to this, for risk of scratching the part. They also understood that the depth of cut had to be indicated by a negative value. As the conversation proceeded, Louis learned from Alain that absolute zero is the level of the clamp. But they had not taken account of their respective ways of calculating nor had they understood the error contained in the program's message. Finally, it is not certain that they had seen why, in this case, it was not possible to specify a reference surface of less than zero.

COLLABORATION BETWEEN STUDENTS AND STEPS TOWARD SOLUTIONS: AN OVERVIEW OF OBSERVATIONS OF FOUR WORK GROUPS

What can be derived from observations of the other work groups? What tendencies are apparent? Do the four work groups display similar or totally different behaviors in the matter of collaboration and the approaches they adopt to the work?

Forms of Collaboration: Sharing the Work and Issues of Power

What have we been able to observe in general terms? At the start of these practical work sessions, in each group and without any preliminary negotiation or protest, one student is immediately seated at the computer, the others are seated by their sides and have picked up the instructions or an already machined part. In this way they start to work. The students have developed a notion of each other's competences, and this dictates their initial sharing out of the tasks and equipment available. The student on the computer could be the one who is most at ease on a keyboard, but also the one with the most experience of APS.[3] Neither this division nor other ways of acting on evaluations of their respective competences are explicitly negotiated.

Generally, most of the decisions concerning the major choices to be made about the machining (selection of contours, choice of values, etc.) are the subject of exchanges that can vary from a fairly minimal form in which the one who enters the input simply announces in a loud voice what he has done, through question-and-answer type exchanges, all the way to an extensive argument. Although unilateral decisions are made in all the groups, these involve one or another of the students alone, searching for a solution for a long period.

Beyond this general conclusion, what do we observe in terms of each individual's intensity of engagement and participation in their group? First of all, pairs and groups of three differ from each other in these respects. In the two groups of three, the exchanges between two of the members are intense while the third occupies a much quieter position. The two situations differ in other ways. In group 4, at the beginning, one of the students plays a major part in the debates while the others show confidence in his views. Later on, excluded by the too rapid rhythm of interactions between his two fellow group-members, he devotes himself instead to specialized tasks and plays the specific role of "checker" (Plety, 1996). In this way he

---

[3] Analysis of the sequences shows, however, that the student at the keyboard is not necessarily the master of operations. On the contrary, he often finds himself merely executing others' instructions. It can also happen that the students share the keyboard and the mouse (groups 2 and 4).

makes his own particular contribution to the work of the group. In the other group, the third student finds himself more clearly marginalized; his posture is one of withdrawal, his contributions are often ignored and he adopts a defensive attitude of distance or mockery. He is "the independent" (Plety, 1996). In other respects, the intensity of individual participation varies according to inter-individual dynamics and the current state of each participant (concentrating or tired, involved or bored). The opportunity that group work provides, across a set of practical work sessions, to vary the degree of engagement seems to be beneficial; when one student loses patience or gets tired, another takes over.

What is the division of roles and of power and how do these develop? At the beginning of the sequences analyzed, in three groups out of the four one student plays a dominant role. In group 3, installed at the controls, he initiates and concludes each phase of the work, he consults his colleagues and evaluates their suggestions. In group 2, he takes advantage of his position to enter the data without submitting decisions to any discussion or taking any account of his companion's advice. Finally, in group 1 he dictates the information to be entered to the partner seated at the keyboard. Group 4 displays a more complex mode of functioning, with one student in command of the rhythm of the work but needing the others to provide the contents. Over the course of the session, the roles change as does also the locus of influence, and this is particularly the case every time the students encounter a difficulty that the group or the leader of the moment is unable to resolve. Then we see, as in group 3, the position of the dominant student becoming destabilized and another student assuming a more significant place in the search for a solution. In the first group, the leader makes to consult his companion more and then, exasperated, withdraws and leaves the other to try out his own ideas. In group 2, we observe a turnaround in the situation: the student who is least up to date with things at the outset (he has not taken the course before) becomes more assured over the course of the practical work sessions and finds himself in the role of the one who moves the work forward, arguing as an equal with the others. Group 4 displays a particularly marked instability of roles and positions and a striking degree of turmoil. One of the students turned out to be particularly impulsive. But we have also interpreted these sometimes violent outbursts as responses to a major characteristic of these practical work sessions: the uncertainty, both cognitive and social, felt by all the students. They have, in effect, to make numerous decisions in the absence of much practice with this software; this depends on the more or less accurate memory students have retained of exercises presented in the previous year. In addition, they are unable to rely upon having an expert within the group. Finally, although they can depend on a degree of complementarity, they all find themselves at one moment or another relatively bereft in the face of the difficulties they encounter.

In all the groups, but in a particularly exaggerated manner in group 4, stress generally increases the tendency to interrupt one another and to throw orders and peremptory comments around, rather than to listen to one another and negotiate. Even in group 2, which in the sequences analyzed seems the most serene in the face of difficulty and which had the richest exchanges, the partners regularly cut each other off.

Corresponding to the division of roles and tasks is a distribution of power, and this is also a source of tension now and again. The students are not indifferent to these kinds of concerns and can sometimes be quite competitive. Thus one student, faced with a partner who wants to take the lead, will show his discontent either verbally ("no one ever listens to me") or by trying to interfere in the dialogue between the leader and the APS software. Another might seek to maintain his initial status as an expert, showing irritation with explanations provided by the other, cutting him off, and trying to protect his own role as the one who explains things. This competition is also apparent in the attitudes expressed when errors occur, although the students are supposed to tackle the practical work session tasks together, in group 3, the student at the computer controls is held responsible for any problems encountered. In the first group, the leader leaves his companion to conduct inquiries by himself and then accuses him of being the cause of a difficulty, and this upsets the latter. Finally, during the machining phase, when the errors become apparent, the students in group 2 played at mutually rejecting responsibility for these. We also saw occasions on which there was both help and competition among the groups, with students comparing performances, generating criticism and mockery, or playing at competition between professions (mechanics versus computer technicians).[4] The educational context they shared, together with the summative individual evaluation, caused each of them to measure themselves against others, something that without doubt in significant part explains this ambivalent attitude in their combined efforts of both exchange and competition.

What resources are available to students to manage their collaboration? We have seen that an implicit form of task and role division exists, and that this can evolve as a function of performance, as some groups displayed during the practical work sessions. In the heat of the action, students react to those behaviors that upset them (groups 1, 3, and 4), and in doing so reveal their notions of what constitutes good collaboration. Thus, in groups 1 and 4, we witnessed expressions of impatience and shouting sparked off by negative comments. This was also the case in groups 3 and 4 when one

---

[4] These behaviors seemed to be exacerbated by stress but particularly by the presence of the camera.

student, who had been only marginally involved up to that point, all of a sudden joined in and made inappropriate comments, and in group 3, when one member seemed too obviously uninterested or, again in group 3, when one student wanted to dominate the search for solutions and made decisions without communicating them. Here the implicit rule seems to be: Decisions and inquiries must be shared and each must participate. Let us not forget that the grade given for their work is collective and that the teacher exercises a certain surveillance. For example, he made a remark to a student in group 1 who had temporarily deserted his post. Thus we should recognize that without making them explicit, the students do nonetheless express in their reactions criteria for, and expectations about, collaboration, even if these expectations vary across groups and from one occasion to another.

We have been able to establish at what point the work of the group mobilizes its personnel at affective and relational levels and has an influence on the expression of individual knowledge and skill. A multiplicity of competences is required here, both social and cognitive, especially when those involved have not chosen their collaborators, as is often also the case in professional work environments. The development of these competences merits much greater attention. In what other contexts—scholarly, professional, or leisurely—have these student technicians received, or will they receive, coaching in these skills, and where are they likely to make progress in these respects? Here we might, for example, mention certain kinds of activities to be found in youth movements, such as those described by Heath (1999).

Approaches to Work, Representations of the Problem, and Forms of Problem Solving

Through the systematic observation of students confronted with difficulty in the course of planning a machining operation, we can describe how they approach this phase of the practical work, the manner in which they decide on the data to enter into the program, and what arguments they use. We also examine how they respond to the error messages with which they find themselves confronted, how they make a diagnosis on the basis of these, and how they use these to solve their problem. Finally, it is important for us to understand how they represent this problem and to what degree they relate the information presented on the screen to the machining situation with which they are dealing.

Forms of Decision Making

The observations reveal two types of decision making by the students. In the first scenario, they seem very confident of their answer, which is apparently based on their recollection of exercises carried out in the preceding year: Without consultation, the student on the keyboard enters a value, or suggests it, and there follows a brief exchange without either explanation or argument. This is the most frequent kind of behavior.

G: (*He reads.*) Rapid approach (*turns toward T*): Just to z 0? Is that right?

T: No, less…., no, more! +2!

G: Just to z 2. Yep, that's good (*He types in +2*).

When they find that they are unsure, they then adopt various behaviors, among which we observed the following:

- Ignoring the level when they have not been able to understand its definition:

G: (*He reads the screen and then says without turning his head toward his companions*): Safety level, Pfff. (*He moves to the next without entering anything.*){\DIA}

- Asking what the level in question corresponds to (groups 2, 3, and 4), suggesting a more or less complete answer:

C: Safety level, why z

M: Safety level, you know, it's uh//

C: But we don't know//

M: It's the approach like that (*he makes a gesture of the tool descending*)

- Leaving the question unanswered:

M: Because safety level, what does that mean?

R: I don't know that

M: Isn't it for the depth?

C: (*Who does not hear them*) Reference safety. No, reference surface, that's zero, that's right.

R: (*to himself*). Safety level…
       They move on to something else.

- Arguing and discussing up to the point at which a shared position is defined.{\BL}

Treatment of Error Messages

All of the groups entering one or more erroneous values receive an error message from the program. For setting up the cutting (groups 1, 2, and 4 in the first sequence), this message consists of an audible beep and information about the relation between the depths. At this point, they are confronted with information that contains a sign error. In the case of drilling (groups 3 and 4 in the second sequence) the program gives an audible signal and remains at the same window instead of moving on to the next one, but does not specify what has not worked or what they need to do. How do the students react to these messages and the information provided?

In the case of cutting, although all of them might have read the written information out loud more than once, none of them immediately compares this with the values that they have been[?] given. Generally, the students interpret the message as "Something is not working," and assume that the information provided by the program must be correct. It is not until after several displays of the message that, in two of the groups (1 and 2), one student expresses some doubt, but still without getting to the point of clearly identifying the error in the program.

In the case of drilling, the situation is more confusing. The program remains on the same window and emits the audible signal but without giving any information and while at the same time displaying a modification that is not an error message (the depth given for the full diameter is automatically recalculated for the tip of the tool). Because the students seldom remember this point (or have never had it explained), they immediately interpret this change of depth and option as a signal that there is a mistake, although the problem is actually elsewhere.

Then, the first reaction, characteristic of all the groups except group 2, consists immediately of moving to action and changing, with or without any preliminary discussion, the value of one of the parameters. A striking fact is that in certain cases this does not involve a parameter mentioned in the error message, but rather one relating to a point on which there remains doubt, and the change is made by way of an attempt "to see what happens."

Group 3:
G: (*looking at the screen*) What am I ch...! Depth of hole, what is this c...
T: (*In a mildly agitated tone and looking at him*) Because you haven't defined the depth of the part, we can't make a hole on a sheet of paper!
G: (*in a low voice and looking at the screen*): Yep, perhaps it's not like that...
Group 4:
P: The reference surface should be equal to or less than the height of the cut.
M: (*He reads*). The reference surface should be//
R: Should be equal to or less//

M: There we are!

        (…)

M: We put zero (*for the safety level*). That's it! Reference surface, did it say?

R: Yep

C: Yep

C: We have to see, try it.

M: (*types in 0 for security level, clicks on OK*)

What solutions do they end up finding? In groups 1 and 4, after several attempts and repeatedly reading the error message, one of the students suddenly recalls the right answer: It is necessary to attach a negative sign to the value for the depth of pocket to be machined.

R: (*reads the end of the message*) Equal to or less than the height of the cut. Ah, it can't be to –5, it's there that you put – (minus) for the depth?

Have they, for all that, understood the problem? No, because when these same two groups encounter a similar situation later on (completing the "depth" window, this time for drilling), they again have difficulties: The first group tries to use the same solutions that proved to be wrong in the first sequence and cast doubt on the direction of the sign. After various attempts, they turn to the teacher to get them out of their dilemma[?]. Although we did not have access to later observations to determine whether they understood this time how to proceed, we have nonetheless had indications that they do not interpret the values to be given to the program as stages in the tool's trajectory of descent nor do they understand the purpose of the reference surface.

Group 4 mentions the direction of the sign, but encounters other difficulties. In effect, its representation of the problem remains partly correct: although the students appropriately relate the values to be provided to the tool's descent trajectory, and although they know the impact of the answer, they have not integrated the need to give for the safety depth and the rapid approach, both rather vague concepts, values greater than the reference depth. Because one of the students does not understand the purpose of these concepts, their "solution" is to enter 0 for all three depths.

In group 2, the error message certainly prompts an immediate suggestion from one of the partners, a proposal concerning the correct parameter. This does not emerge from groping around for answers. The two students have a correct representation of the problem and think in terms of the machining situation. What divides them in the ensuing discussion is their different ways of calculating the relationships between absolute zero, reference surface, and depth of cut (one of them is wrong). They do not manage to explain their conceptions completely to one another, and finally call upon the assistance of the teacher because one of the students is not satisfied that the program accepts the solution advanced by his companion.

This behavior deserves emphasis because all the other technicians we observed reacted in the opposite fashion: If the program accepts an answer, as far as they were concerned that was because "it's right," and they were able to move on, even if the group had not come to an agreement and had not necessarily understood the ins and outs of the problem. In group 3, the direct consequence of such an attitude was that the part was scratched several times during the actual machining! In its approach to problem solving, this group fastened on to the definition of a parameter that had nothing to do with their problem. They were going to test the program to confirm a solution:

> T: Try to see where zeros have been entered into the field *<in the window dealing with the tool's working depths>* . You put in bogus values to see if it accepts them. If it accepts them that means we have forgotten to put in a value. *<there is one of the depths for which it is necessary to put in something other than 0>*.

This group is no more successful than groups 1 and 4 in forming a correct representation of the problem: its members do not make the link between the values to be entered and the steps in the tool's trajectory.

We again need to recall here two aspects of the work requested: The requirement, formulated by the teacher, to devise a rapid machining operation, and the possibility for checking, in particular via the simulation option, which allows various forms of visualization of the operations programmed. During this phase of their work, only groups 2 and 4 take explicit account of the temporal constraint. Given that the others do not make any allusion to this, it could be taken as confirmation that they do not make the link to the subsequent machining situation. Regarding simulation of the machining operation on the screen, group 2 is the only one to make use of it. But they did not notice anything in particular as a result, perhaps through a fault in how they defined what would deserve attention, perhaps through the fault of not having chosen the most appropriate visualization.

Computer and Students: What Interactions, What Influences?

By incorporating into our transcriptions the actions on the program and the reactions of the latter, we wished to give ourselves the means for observing the part played by the computer in the approaches to work and in the interactions. In effect, by virtue of the organization of its interface and the order of appearance of the windows in particular, the program structures the information on the basis of which the students work (Blaye et al., 1992). In the task observed, the action on the final object (the part) is in addition doubly mediated: The software is the instrument through which one acts on the machine, which in its turn acts upon the part. What types of mediation were we able to observe and how did the particular characteristics of the equipment shape the students' approaches and thinking? Before making any attempt to answer these questions, further comment is merited. In fact, it is awkward, and indeed of limited relevance, to take into account the interweaving of the individual factors involved, or to isolate one element in the situation—the equipment—and then try and observe its effects on these complex processes. The manner in which the students read the error messages, without paying any attention to the incoherence introduced by the error in the sign, is but one illustration of this: The information extracted from the program is mediated by the expectations, representations, and competences of the users. Despite this reservation, some observations do nonetheless seem to us worthy of being made and discussed.

The trajectory of the tool is represented in a discontinuous manner, without any visual reference to the movement in question. This is not without influence on the way the students tackle the work, and how they remember that among them are some having little familiarity with machining. It seems to discourage them from recognizing the nature of the action actually involved, namely a descending trajectory of the tool for which the values given for depths must be in descending order.

Next, a series of features of the software clearly favor blind groping and trial and error more than anticipation. Thus, once students have chosen an operation and the necessary tool, they can only follow the succession of steps imposed by the program. As with the majority of computing tools, operations can be cancelled. The option at the end of the programming of reorganizing the order of machining operations itself allows the user to work without a plan for machining or any effort of anticipation. Finally, the large number of choices and decisions required by the production of a machining program can only encourage students to feel their way forward and certainly accounts for the brevity of thought and of some of the discussions. As one of the students remarked, "We can't discuss everything; if we did, we'd never finish...." This is not specific to the software used for this particular task: In the eyes of the students, who, during their training come across a wide range of software without becoming specialists in any of them, but recalling their individual particularities and knowing all of the commands present difficulties that they sometimes try to resolve by laborious trial and error and exploration.

In this work, the students make use of equipment endowed with a certain autonomy: It carries out, in the place of the user, an entire series of mathematical operations and makes a number of the decisions on its own.

How do the students react to this? We sometimes see them trying to understand "what it wants," even indeed attributing intentions to it. Most often they just want the program to accept their inputs and, with the exception of one student, they are satisfied with this form of "acceptance." Also, they are regularly astonished by the reactions of the software, which they curse. They have not achieved what Rabardel (1995) calls "instrumentation," meaning they have not appropriated the tool for their own goals. The students instead experience the autonomy of the program as an irritating obstacle and a mark of "ill will" on the part of an instrument that is supposed to assist them (computer-*assisted* manufacture!). This reaction is undoubtedly exacerbated by the haste with which they wish to, and with which they must, complete their work by the end of the afternoon.

SOME COMMENTS ON THEIR OWN FUNCTIONING BY THOSE INVOLVED

What do the students themselves think about their ways of collaborating and working in groups? The opinions we heard in the course of interviews we conducted several days after these practical work sessions can be summarized as follows: The students emphasize how during these sessions they learn to work together and report that during their training they rely, on a daily basis, on sharing information among their peers and drawing on the competences peculiar to each course of study. For example, one student expressed this in the following terms: "I don't know everything and I often ask others about things, particularly those doing operations management because they have been here two years now, they are really aces at this stuff." This corroborates the observations gathered during visits to the workshops; exchanges between students are frequent in these places.

Finally, during a discussion with all of the student technicians, we played them extracts from the video recordings showing students at work, and asked them to watch and comment on their methods of collaboration and their approach to the work. It emerged from this that for them the effectiveness of collaboration depends on the personalities involved and also whether group work is profitable while at the same time "hellish." The students did not mention the possibility of improving the collaboration if it was working badly; it was just something one endured. This confirms the impression we formed during the practical work sessions, but also the results of other studies carried out in this area among students in compulsory schooling; it is not designed to be negative nor is this the objective of such a pedagogical arrangement, but group work is most often suffered as a difficult experience at the interpersonal level and is not always fruitful in terms of its results (Crook, 1995).

We also questioned the students and their teacher on the forms of problem solving they adopted and the way they handled the work. The students in group 3 referred to what was in their eyes a "normal situation, real," which they contrasted with these practical work sessions in which "we take the time to understand the philosophy of the program." "Here we are thrown in like that; you need time to adapt. And then, good, the time to adapt, this can generally be taken more calmly." They mentioned their lack of concentration, which had led to a poor reading of the information provided by the program. How do they do it "normally"? "That depends on the problem. We try to go as fast as possible without thinking, we try several times, and then we stop and look at things in a more structured fashion, we write. Here, the ideal solution, it's to ask oneself about the problem and what it involves for the part." They add again that it would be necessary to see what "safety depth" means and to envisage in concrete fashion the problem of the depth of cut. Thus they are capable of describing a more appropriate approach than the one they had actually adopted. We should recall that these particular students had established the consequences of their error only after the cutting was done, which is to say during the machining of the part. Thus, although they had been unproductive from an industrial point of view and in relation to the teacher's assessment criteria, we can nonetheless hypothesize that they learned more than the students in groups 1 and 4, who had retrieved a correct solution from memory, one without any unfortunate consequences, but without having understood the problem.

The teacher noted that the student technicians in these practical work sessions did not have a reliable method for tackling a problem. He added that having given computing classes to people of all ages, he had found that children often proceeded by trial and error, throwing themselves into it without any fear, while adults, and in particular professionals who need to train on an unfamiliar tool, take a lot of time studying the problem and thinking about what they want to do. These students have adopted a kind of intermediate attitude. The teacher seemed to think that the trial and error method is not bad in itself but that it carries the risk of not doing what is necessary to achieve the goal and not ensuring recall of the solution found if an analogous situation is encountered later. According to him, businesses lose a lot of money because, when faced with a breakdown or technical incident, their employees, instead of observing what happens and analyzing the elements of the situation, make hasty and often false diagnoses; we have to learn to observe to then be able to construct a hypothesis about the causes of the problem.

PEDAGOGICAL PROPOSITIONS

The pedagogical propositions that emerge from these observations were initially developed and discussed, in the course of the research, with the teacher responsible for these practical work sessions. They are based on a single principle: to integrate constraints into training activity, obligatory routes leading the students to articulate the decision criteria more explicitly and thus to improve their diagnoses of the causes of difficulties. The aim is to favor the relation between time for action and time for thinking about the activity pursued. From an analogous perspective, English research (Healy, Stefano & Hoyles, 1995) demonstrates the positive effect of alternating between periods of individual work on the computer and time spent coordinating perspectives on the overall goals.

This led us to reflect with the teacher on how to introduce periods of individual and shared reflection on the various objectives of the task and upon problems encountered, a reflection that took us far from the computer keyboard and from attempts at immediate action. But how can this be done? To stop working is as difficult as it is to report on one's method of working (Hennessy & McCormick, 1994). To encourage anticipation, it is, for example, helpful to ask students to work out, at the beginning of the exercise, a plan for the successive phases of machining. Students could then be led toward agreement about the points to be taken into consideration and about the objectives to be pursued; two conditions for productive group work as Mercer (1996) shows in his review of studies made of students in compulsory education. On the other hand, in case of difficulty, one way of encouraging students to develop their powers of observation and to structure their inquiries is to specify conditions under which they can ask for help: when they seek out the teacher, students must be invited to describe the difficulty encountered as well as the attempts already made to find a solution and the results of these attempts.

One other pedagogical path is suggested by the difficulty certain groups had in establishing a link between the numerical data to be given to the program and the concrete milling situation, and in appreciating the relevance of their solution in relation to this latter. Now, options in the software could allow them to compensate, at least in part, for these weaknesses; there are various options for simulating and visualizing the operations programmed. But they did not use these. Nonetheless, this means of anticipating and checking constitutes a significant skill; it is common to numerous computing tools that mediate direct action on the objects worked. It would be interesting, within the framework of a generalist technical education, to explore with teachers their thinking about the shared characteristics of different technologies and then to identify what similar general procedures it is essential to master. Confronted with numerous computing tools among which students seem mainly and with some anxiety to perceive variety and differences rather than common features, such identification would certainly help to provide a better overview of the technologies available and of their uses.

CHAPTER 6

ALTERNATIVE INTERPRETATIONS OF LEARNING ACTIVITIES[1]

In the practical work on automation examined up to this point, what perceptions do students have of the task to be carried out, and what meanings do they accord to this learning situation? This chapter seeks to answer these questions.

Our previous research, centered initially on the role of social interaction in the development of intelligence and knowledge, had led us to pay more and more attention to the meanings that actors in learning or test situations accord to these. Effectively, irrespective of the precision with which the goal of a task is communicated, learners reinterpret this as a function of various characteristics of the situation (nature of the task, time available, forms of assessment of the work carried out, etc.), of implicit expectations that they are able to detect, or even of their past experiences on similar tasks. We

[1] In this chapter, we draw closely on Daniele Golay Schilter (1997). Apprendre la fabrication assistée par ordinateur : sens, enjeux et rapport aux outils. Document de recherche. Séminaire de Psychologie, University of Neuchâtel.

Apprentice in a Changing Trade, pages 113–127

113

thus focused on analysis of the way in which sociocognitive interaction is marked by the meanings that the participants we questioned accord to the task and to the activity that is appropriately applied to it. The behavior of children observed in different interaction situations turns out to be strongly marked by their own interpretations of the situation (Perret-Clermont, 1992; Perret-Clermont & Nicolet, 2001; Light & Perret-Clermont, 1989; Perret-Clermont, Schubauer-Leoni, & Trognon, 1992; Grossen et al., 1997; Perret-Clermont et al., 2004; Tartas et al., 2010).

Even apparently simple conversational events (e.g., posing a question in a test situation) can turn out to be complex, polysemic situations (Rommetveit, 1979; Hundeide, 1985; Grossen, 1988; Saljo, 1991). In practice, students do not always confer upon the situation, the task, or the the meaning anticipated by the teacher (Donaldson, 1978: Perret, 1985; Schubauer-Leoni, 1986; Light & Perret-Clermont, 1986, 1989; Bell, Grossen, & Perret-Clermont, 1985; Perret-Clermont, Perret, & Bell, 1991; Carugati & Perret-Clermont, 2003). Observation of students in interaction reveals that they engage in an extensive cognitive activity to grasp not only what it is they should do, but also the meaning of the situation in order to be able to play a role in it that is to their advantage. In academic settings in particular, we know that the institutional framework is deeply implicated in structuring the images that teachers and students have of their roles and of the performances expected (see Gilly, 1980; Brossard & Wargnier, 1993; Schubauer-Leoni & Grossen, 1993; Iannaccone & Perret-Clermont, 1993; Säljö & Wyndhamm, 1993.

WHAT MEANINGS DO LEARNERS ACCORD TO A PRACTICAL WORK SITUATION?

How can this question be appropriately addressed with respect to young adults in professional training? Do we come across signs of interpretative work analogous to those observed in the research mentioned above? Or must we instead recognize that adults in professional training, more experienced and better informed than children could possibly be and similarly more aware from past experience of making mistakes, know how to readjust and renegotiate their understanding of the situation, thereby avoiding the occurrence of misunderstandings about the meaning of the tasks they are asked to undertake?

The task presented to technical students in the context of the practical work sessions we observed seems to be clearly defined. The students must use software to design the machining of an already drawn part, referring back to material learned several months earlier. In the first part of this exercise, devoted to planning the machining operations, they have to work in threes around the same computer, and then in the second part they must put the machining unit into operation to manufacture the part automatically. At any moment, they can go to the teacher to get his assistance in repairing a breakdown or for advice as needed. At the end of the afternoon, after four hours of practical work, students must provide a brief report on their activities and return this to the teacher along with the machined part. As we have seen in Chapter 4, the instructions provided seem to be comprehensive, the conditions of work well defined, and the goal to be pursued clearly designated. This apparent clarity nevertheless merits careful examination.

ATTITUDES ADOPTED AND MEANING
ACCORDED TO THE TASK

Consideration of the behavior displayed and the verbal exchange made during the course of the actors' activities allows us to uncover not only the meaning that they accord to their activity, but also their way of referring to and commenting on it both among themselves and for the researchers. This is the perspective taken in the work of researchers such as Woods (1990), Perrenoud (1994), Clot (1995), Sirota (1993), Filliettaz and Bronckart (2005), and Filliettaz (2008).

In our case, before making our observations of the practical work sessions, we carried out a series of interviews beginning with the teacher and the staff member responsible for the course on industrial computing. This allowed us to identify the objectives envisaged for the course and the corresponding practical sessions, to understand the way in which these related to the curriculum as a whole, and to achieve a better appreciation of their technical organization and related issues. We then worked with the audio and video recordings of the practical classes and in particular with verbal material of the following kinds:

- All comments made by students about the practical work
- Questions raised by students about the goals of the exercise
- References to work situations, both experienced and idealized
- All commentaries on the technical equipment, whether addressed to a classmate, the teacher, to no one in particular, or the machine itself
- Propositions referring to the machine (the computer) as sentient: "it thinks that...," "it hasn't seen that...," etc.

With respect to nonverbal behavior, we assessed each individual's intensity of engagement in the task, as well as displays of feeling, posture, sighs, expressions of concentration, gestures of impatience, etc.

The marked assessment of the groups' work gave rise to exchanges between students and teacher. These exchanges identified weak and strong points in the work, as well as providing explanations of how assessments were scored; students then asked questions or disputed various points in their assessments. These exchanges were recorded.

Finally, on completion of the practical work, we played back extracts to each group from the video recordings of their activities; here, students answered questions about their approach, their collaboration, their experience of the practical work sessions in general, the interest they found in this activity and in the use of this equipment, and finally the place these technologies occupied in their vision of their own professional future.

The status of the material obtained in these different contexts in one way or another prompts a methodological comment: expressing an opinion, suggesting an interpretation, displaying approval or rejection, etc., has a place in interaction. Because of this, the comments gathered form part of the many messages addressed to interlocutors in the situation. These allow individuals to locate themselves in relation to the subject, to demonstrate their identification with a group or person present, or instead to signal their differences (Schubauer-Leoni, 1991). These identity aspects of expression were often apparent to us in the course of the practical work sessions. It may be, for example, that as a mechanic a student might address a criticism of the unit to a computer technician. In addition, in each conversational encounter, students more or less consciously pursue different objectives. In fact, we have sometimes noted that students' comments can change as a function of context even though the subject is the same. Thus, for some of them, the interviews were opportunities to revise their representations of the practical work in the course of an interaction with the researchers.

To complete our inquiries, after having analyzed the tapes, we again presented our findings to the teacher and recorded his reactions. We also showed an extract of our recordings to two cohorts of younger technical students and questioned them about various aspects of these. Finally, in the course of preparing the text, various observations gathered from other teachers and apprentices in the college allowed us to put the facts described in perspective.

AMBIVALENT ATTITUDES IN THE COURSE OF ACTION

In the course of their activities, students often display an attitude colored by ambivalence. On the one hand, they are pushing themselves hard to produce a good outcome, to achieve what is asked and match the specified quality criteria. On the other hand, some of them reveal in their comments a certain unself-conscious mocking; they say they want to finish it faster and criticize the exercise and the program. More concretely, they do not always bother to read the instructions and may sometimes be ready to skip over unresolved problems.

The activity analyzed here occurs within an institutional and academic context, and even if it concerns a course of professional improvement and a population of young adults, the behaviors observed clearly involve performing the role of student as practiced in compulsory education (Sirota, 1993; Perrenoud, 1994). There is a realistic investment in the work, focused on concern with getting a good mark, an investment that goes along with a desire to finish quickly and, in reaction to feelings of constraint, caustic humor and more or less overt criticism (Perrenoud, 1994, p. 153). Wanting to finish as quickly as possible, while at the same time achieving a satisfactory result, moreover seems *a priori* obvious to the students as to their teacher. Furthermore, the latter does not expect that his students will have the same thirst for learning as his evening-class professionals, so it is by using marks and assessments, among other devices, that he will often try to motivate "average" students.[2] As we are going to see, this "school-based" attitude is not seamlessly monolithic among the students. On the contrary, it maintains a dialectic relationship with another discourse, one that places the reality of work in industry, such as they understand it, at the center of their preoccupations.

WHAT ARE THE LINKS BETWEEN COLLEGE AND WORK?

In the interviews, the groups sustained a discourse that shows the same ambivalence or complexity as their actions and comments while working. Sometimes they go so far as to contrast a caricature of the college with the world of work: In college we value marks and we try our best for them but we make errors without thinking because "breakdown" does not have the consequences, either technical or economic, that it has working for a business. Students believe that in order to learn and understand, they have to be able to try things out without worrying about waste or breakage, while they attribute a certain seriousness to industry, which, in their view, the practical work exercises do not have. This draws attention to a central question that preoccupies those responsible for training as much as the students themselves: how and to what degree does full-time education provide preparation for the world of work?

For the teachers the question is sensitive, because it concerns the apprentices as well as the technicians. In the course of reexamining all the opinions gathered, a particular pattern emerged that reflected a universally shared conclusion: Students must be prepared for the exercise of a trade and for industrial practice rather than for diploma exams, "That's the goal of our training here; it is to put them truly in contact with an industrial environment" and again "We shouldn't be training them for the CFC (Certificat Fédéral de Capacité) but for work."

---

[2] However, the students of engagement in personal projects, such as their diploma work, is very good.

But how is this to be done? Here the picture loses its sharpness. We quickly learn that daily pedagogical and technical realities are complex. Industrial demands (productivity, complicated and costly systems, constraints to be managed) are not readily compatible with some basic pedagogical objectives (to try things out, to understand, to come to grips with those aspects of the system most likely to be encountered in places of work and in other technologies), or with the exigencies of a training regime (timetables, assessment, etc.). Hence, according to the teacher in charge of the FMS course, even when they are not involved in responding to an order from a client, but "simply" in producing a series of parts (without even talking about flexible production, which is to say production modified in the course of manufacture in response to the demands of the moment), the difficulties and constraints involved exceed the possibilities of the practical work sessions and the knowledge of the learners, even though these latter may not always be aware of it. The full pedagogical utilization of such a system of production, technological maintenance of which alone requires considerable effort on the part of the trainer, requires radical rethinking of the timetable. The training schedule is probably appropriately organized in terms of a 2- or 3-week full-time course on the manufacturing unit, such as, for example, is the practice at the Ecole Technique du Centre Professionel du Littoral Neuchâtelois. In the absence of this kind of modification to the timetable, the ambitions for training in the practical knowledge of a computer-assisted production unit is going to be significantly impoverished.

Let us also note the development of courses located within business enterprises is a response to this need to understand more fully the processes of manufacture in a real-world production situation. The perspectives provided by models of training based on alternation are of particular interest to full-time professional training establishments. Nonetheless, the difficulties, both pedagogical and institutional, of setting up a fruitful alternation between time spent in college and time devoted to courses turns out to be significant, as two reviews of these issues clearly show (Amos, 2001a, 2001b; Perret, 2001).

INFORMATIVE VIEWS ON THE VALUE OF PRACTICAL WORK

Questioned about their interest in these practical work sessions, the students did not show any great enthusiasm overall,[3] and made various and indeed widely differing observations, organized around the issue of the value (or otherwise) of the training ("It provides good revision" versus "We've already covered all that") and its utility for professional practice

---

[3] The responses collected by the teacher in the evaluation questionnaire that he distributed to students at the end of the practical work sessions indicate this.

("It's concrete; we can see how it works, even if you need to spend more time and use the entire unit" versus "It's equipment not found elsewhere" or the equipment is only "semi-professional" and thus "it doesn't prepare you for anything"). Their lack of information on the industrial penetration of technologies partly explains what are *a priori* surprising variations of opinion. These also seem to depend on the training course students are following. Thus some of the information technology students say they are unable to find any interest in this technology because they see no advantages compared to conventional machines. Additionally, automated manufacture actually has no place in their occupational ambitions. In contrast, it is among the students who have had previous training in mechanics that we find those who have most thoroughly grasped the pedagogical objectives pursued by their teacher over the course of these practical work sessions. According to this teacher, it is a commonplace attitude among technicians to show they are selective in their interests as a function either of their earlier training or of their future goals.

These reactions concerning the "utility" of the practical work and of its relation to future employment allow us to reconsider through the "spectacles" of technical students the issue of the development of "transferable technical skills" that is so often debated by educationalists. In computing particularly, training has become very broad; it involves familiarity with many areas and numerous technological environments as well as specialization within the context of diploma work. Some students admit that they therefore learn to "get by" while others see their training as familiarization "with a little bit of everything," and do not expect to become "true professionals."[4] Now, faced with an uncertain future, these students have a desire to feel competent in some specific area or in the operation of particular equipment; at the same time they are conscious that they must be ready to learn continually and to adapt to novelty. As their teacher commented, some of them are anxious and would like the security of being trained precisely in what they are going to be doing subsequently. Teaching of flexible manufacturing provides a clear illustration of these problems: "They have not become specialists in FMS units doing this, but they now know about the functionalities of such a system," said one of the staff. However, the transmission and integration of such objectives is not achieved without difficulties; not all the students immediately recognize or appreciate the wider relevance of the practical work sessions, namely to practice the management of a complex system. These observations shed light on the difficulties inherent in the pursuit of objectives that are more abstract and less precise than the mastery of particular instruments. These difficulties bring us back to pedagogical questions but

---

[4] This perception may be rooted in their experience of their previous training: the CFC, in which "becoming professional" involves in large part mastery of specific machines and tools with a view to passing the relevant exam.

also to the dimensions of feeling and identity implicated in all occupational training: perception of one's competences, the need for self-confidence and sometimes the need for a clear professional identity, based on mastery of specific techniques and instruments.

MANAGING UNCERTAINTY IN THE FACE OF DIFFICULTY

Did the technical students derive any pleasure from managing to produce their part well? This was not apparent from the interviews. During the practical work sessions, positive comments occurred only when everything was going well, "It's nice, when it works!" or "That there, that's technology!" The technicians had shown themselves to be as favorably impressed and interested eight months earlier when the teacher, at the beginning of the FMS course, had given them a demonstration of the unit's functioning. In contrast, in the heat of the action and the difficulties encountered, uncertainty and stress predominates, producing a more negative experience. In effect, the students questioned emphasized that they were in the habit of coping with the difficulties and digressions linked to the learning of information technologies; here, they endured having to grope about time constraints with poorly understood equipment and stress. In the course of the practical work, some of them had even said they considered these demands to be "beyond the contract," too far removed from what was normally asked of them.

Is this way of experiencing things when they work well as normal and heartening, and the feeling that uncertainty and the unexpected are abnormal and contrary, a heritage of compulsory schooling and occupational apprenticeship in which lack of mastery and mistakes are punished? Might not this kind of attitude make it difficult to practice professions in which incidents of technical breakdown are on the increase and in which "perfecting techniques increases the power of individuals while the burden of responsibility is reduced by the power of tools" (Clot, 1995, p. 73)? How can students be prepared for entry into a work context in which, as the teacher put it, it will be necessary to cope with new equipment and objectives under time constraints and sometimes on one's own, without necessarily having access to all the relevant information? Such are the challenges facing students and teachers in technical training.

RELATIONSHIP TO COMPUTING TOOLS

Over the course of the practical work sessions, students use the APS software for computer-assisted design and manufacture. This type of tool possesses considerable autonomy; it automatically executes numerous operations and makes a number of decisions. Its substantial possibilities give it a relative complexity that the students never truly master. Frequently they find that something "doesn't work"; then the students, like the majority of computer users, take it out on the machine! Its autonomy becomes "ill will" and what does not work with it is frequently attributed to its "stupidity." As the teacher commented, this attitude is current among students but also among users in general: "The more computerized the equipment becomes the more one is going to consider it as intelligent or unintelligent." We may even accord it intentions in relation to ourselves (Pochon & Grossen, 1995). In contrast, during an interview and standing back from the issue a little, a student can recognize that the problem encountered also reflects his own lack of knowledge of the program, and he may then express a more balanced opinion about it.[5]

Compulsory schooling and even professional education has traditionally promoted the ideology of "talent"; if one succeeds it is because one is "talented," and if not it is because one is "hopeless." This way of thinking tends to be applied to the world of machinery; if software behaves in an incoherent fashion, this is because it is "stupid." Despite these spontaneous expressions of such a view, often in a humorous gesture, this way of thinking is, however, not necessarily profoundly convincing; the explanation seems very fragile and too simple. The possibility cannot be excluded that these new technologies and their complexity have the happy effect of rendering this obscurantist and disdainful ideology of "talent" obsolete, substituting instead a meta-reflexive attitude allowing a systematic approach to the analysis of difficulties of operation and a search for strategies of resolution or remediation.

Some students display an apparently paradoxical mixture of confidence and suspicion toward the computerized systems they use. Rapidly confronted with the need to make a lot of decisions and to introduce numerous parameters, they often go back to the program to judge the correctness of their choices, rather than relying on their own reflections on their reasoning and understanding of the problem at issue. In sum, they seem to act as if they think that "if the program accepts it, it is because it is correct." This behavior, based in the case of some students on earlier disappointments, can largely be explained in terms of the limited time available to them and of their lack of knowledge. In contrast, we come across suspicion of automated machines and programs, sometimes among the same students: they never seem to be reliable, they make errors, the computer does not "tell" or show everything. During the process of putting the unit into operation, some show considerable mistrust. Perhaps this is because it has been nec-

---

[5] Over the course of their training, students encounter a wide range of software and computing environments, and their judgments on these latter evolve with their growing competence and on the basis of the comparisons they are able to make between software packages. It emerged during the inquiry that they misunderstood the extent of industrial penetration of the software used in the practical work sessions.

essary for them to give a complex system a long series of instructions, the implications of which are not always known, and when the precise effects that will result are not foreseen… "Keep your finger over the stop button!" The teacher regards this attitude of mistrust as healthy, especially when an error can result in damage to the equipment. The apprentices we questioned on their initiation into CNC machining expressed these same fears, just like older mechanics when they have to make the transition from conventional machines to computerized systems (Léchevin, Le Joliff, & Lanoe, 1994). Delegating control is not easy. Learning to gauge the possibilities of a machine or a system, assessing what one can expect of it, and evaluating the limits of one's own knowledge are no less difficult and without doubt represent important learning objectives.

Do these students expect that one day they will work with a flexible manufacturing system (FMS)? Among the computer technicians questioned, this is not the case, but what about those taking the courses in construction and operations management? This prospect seems above all to have the connotation of "working on an automated machine," which immediately seems to arouse in them a fear of monotonous work. Some of them said it was precisely in order not to spend years "on" a single machine, however fine and beautiful it may be, that they chose the route of technical training. They are suspicious also of deskilled, "push-button" work and of solitary machine minding. Their representations of the operation of an FMS system and of the work undertaken by a technician do not always correspond to reality, according to their teacher. Thus, the management of a unit requires more competencies than they imagine, in particular the ability to resolve the frequent anomalies, breakdowns, and other incidents. Depending on their course of study, some students think that they will not work on an FMS unit as such, but rather on the design and construction of its parts, creating and looking after the application of a manufacturing program, or even optimizing its use.

AMBIVALENCE IN THE FACE OF AUTOMATION

Confronted with automation, the comments and reactions gathered from the apprentices and technical students revealed an interesting diversity of attitudes. Certainly, in the questionnaire-based inquiry that we present in the next chapter, students indicate that working on the computer is interesting and useful. Nonetheless, we are far from a position in which these young people seem at ease with information technology. Some consider this to be foreign to, and indeed in opposition to, their identity as mechanics. One of them might, during the practical work sessions, continually refer back to his experience in mechanics with conventional or directly programmed machines and then be reproached for his meanness of spirit by his classmate. Others evoke the experience of their fathers, who had found it difficult to come to grips with information technology or who had lost their jobs. The enthusiasts seemed to us motivated by the wide range of applications (in the medical sector, in the media, etc.) as much as or more than the equipment itself. Finally, during the course of a visit to one of the rare examples of a company in the region that had installed an FMS system, several showed a very lively interest in response to the system's performance, although one student wondered about the point of such a financial and technological investment, which he found futile. Two interview extracts complete our observations here. They reveal the ambivalence that can be felt by these students (C, N, and R) about the development of technical occupations:

Interviewer: And as constructors, information technology plays a part in your work?

N: Yes, okay, that. Unfortunately, we cannot be left behind!

Interviewer: Unfortunately?

N: No, it's not unfortunate. Me, I think it's great!

C: What are you saying?

N: Working with computers. Designing on the computer.

C: That depends. Designing on the computer, that's terrific, it's practical!

N: It's really much faster.

R: For us, but for someone, for an older person, who has never done it...

N: Then it's very hard.

Questioned about their machining practical using numerically controlled machines, two apprentices in their final year provided some interesting comments. One of them, the more expert of the two, liked computer control. He said that the more he did it, the more he liked it, and the more he found it to be "great." Why? "Because it is varied; it makes a change from more routine activities. We make more complicated parts, more varied, and we can see the result straight away." He noted that he had learned to enjoy it, sometimes by making nothing in particular, by trying things out, by trial and error. The other student said he did not like computer control. Why is that? we asked. He thought about it for a moment. In fact he had taken the trouble to memorize the codes and more specifically to translate the desired machining instructions into numeric codes. He did not like programming. "OK, a part comes out of the computer-controlled equipment, it's neat, OK ... but that doesn't grab me." He also thought that computer control had replaced jobs and referred to his parents (who had lost their own jobs?). What if he worked in an organization using computer control, as is often the case? "I would do it, but I wouldn't like it much." Finally, he spontaneously revealed that he was somewhat intrigued by this, that he liked information technology a lot, that he had a computer at home, and that he did programming. Apparently, he liked information technology except when it was applied to mechanics.

As regards the computing equipment and the training situation as a whole—the two were not always clearly distinguished from one another—the reactions (in both words and deeds) that we observed can be classified in terms of the three dimensions that de Montmollin (1984) describes with respect to attitudes: cognitive (knowledge, judgments, beliefs ...), affective (interest, attraction/rejection...), and conative (actions, intentions, plans...). Students judge the technologies used according to the potential they perceive in these and their supposed use in the world of work (they are not all, however, very well informed on this subject). Corresponding to these judgments are more affective reactions of attraction or rejection, which are characteristic reactions to all training activity. As with the activity, attraction to, or rejection of, equipment is also revealed by the actions and experiences arising during training; mastery engenders self-confidence and the satisfaction of seeing the equipment "obey." Difficulty and uncertainty can lead to personal doubts and a defensive attitude, the cost of which is borne in particular by the computer program. Here again action and feeling are combined. But these attitudes fluctuate; we have seen that judgments and "feelings" about this equipment can evolve with the development of their mastery and with the comparisons the students are able to make among different software packages. Finally, judgments, representations, and affective reactions vary as a function of the occupational intentions and plans of the students.

IMPLICATIONS FOR WIDER SOCIAL AND PSYCHOLOGICAL ISSUES

We again show the manner in which the meanings the apprentices give to the task reflect at this micro-level of analysis various psychological and social factors operating in the wider reality of the lives of the students and the school. Several authors have already shown how the "macro" is reflected in the "micro," in their detailed observations of pedagogical realities (see, e.g., Carugati, Emiliani, & Palmonari, 1981; Woods, 1990; Benavente, da Costa, Machado, & Neves, 1993; Garduna Rubio, 1996).

The comments of students introduce considerations that actually go well beyond the specifics of the training situation to embrace the wider social implications of technology, for example, employment, the perceived utility of the objects produced, and the types of work involved.

The arrival of automated production systems does not occur without creating disquiet and even anxiety in the social contexts affected. Just how far will the machine go in replacing human workers? How can we position ourselves in relation to these developments; is there a risk of human activity being subjugated to the machine or on the contrary will these tools lead to its enrichment? Who will really benefit from the changes taking place? What level of competence on the part of the worker, the technician, or the engineer must be expected if they are to participate in these changes rather than just bearing the costs? These questions can seem somewhat philosophical, but they are actually very concrete and everyday concerns, because everyone (in the aera of students, teachers, sometimes parents) is aware, within his own experience, of companies that have restructured as soon as they introduced computer technology, putting relatives, neighbors, or friends' parents out of work. Everyone also knows that other companies in the region have been able to develop by virtue of their knowledge base in computing and automation.

In the sessions observed as well as in the opinions that some of the students expressed to us on the subject of automated manufacture, we find still other traces of this ambivalence toward the technological change: The technical students do not always truly feel entitled to take control mentally of the technical equipment to which they are being introduced. They are attracted by the idea of mastering functioning at the level expected of them, but their relationship with this technology and the ambivalence it arouses are not displayed, reflected, or thematized as such.

The introduction of new technologies for computer-assisted manufacture and the perceptions those involved have of these technologies have repeatedly posed a question about the status of traditional industrial skills, those that we might describe as the skills of the craftsman: Are they still necessary? To what degree is mastery of conventional machine tools an indispensable requisite for technical training? Or can we learn automated manufacture without passing through this stage? These questions are not unique to the Ecole Technique de Ste-Croix: they arose with the introduction of the very first generation of computer numerically controlled machines (Martin, 1991). Thus, in the sessions we analyzed, we saw students vacillate between a concrete treatment of the problem (at certain moments, some of them drew on gestural language to make themselves understood), and on other occasions (e.g., just after using these gestures), trying in a more formal fashion to manage data that no longer seemed to have a close connection to reality. In this case, this second type of reaction predominated in the groups. This led some of them to "fill in" all the options presented by the software and to move their work forward in this way, but the completed part was spoiled by a lack of realism in the values specified on the screen. From a psychological point of view, we might thus conclude that concrete experience of the tools' operation and the reaction of materials are resources that would facilitate the programming of machining operations, but some other conditions remain to be addressed.

These considerations bring us to the question of effectiveness. What might this constitute in this context? Is it a matter of effectiveness in terms of completing as quickly as possible the work set by the teacher? Or does effectiveness reside rather in the quality achieved at the price of a greater investment of time to reduce the risk of errors? This is time that might be invested in visualization, in checking the work done or in anticipating the particular actions that the machine will perform. It is not certain that students consciously consider this question, either because their education has perhaps never required of them the competence to evaluate their own functioning in this way, or because this kind of competence is still too partially developed at the expense of a systematic bias toward achieving short-term academic gains. We can also talk in terms of the effectiveness of all the learning and knowledge acquired to overcome the difficulties encountered; but for the moment no one seems to think or see that this could constitute a pedagogical "advantage" in terms of new ways of evaluating achievement.

Other significant issues for the Ecole Technique are also reflected in the observations we have described here. Indeed, a study of the curriculum allowed us to identify an aspect that is at once highly symbolic for, and yet still marginal to, these practical work sessions. Although accorded value by the college every time its brand image is at stake, training on the FMS unit represents only a small part of the course and does not play any part in the final evaluation for the technician's diploma, this in particular because national regulations for professional training have not yet integrated these technological changes into the evaluation system. The relative marginality of this practical work is not solely due to its still precarious inclusion in the college but also reflects the subjectivity of students. They made us aware in their many comments of their doubts as to whether this is a real machine or a genuine industrial activity. The fact is that they use resin and not metal (for reasons of safety and so that the operations can be made visible) and the software used is not very widely available among companies in the region. Moreover, as no relevant standards exist and each automated system has its own specific characteristics, students do not know what value to accord to this learning situation. Some of them are interested in the possibility of being able to make such complex equipment work (this is particularly evident in the interest, and sometimes even excitement, that surrounds finally putting the automatic machining into operation). Other students who were not encouraged to think about the characteristics, either specific or general, of the machine and the software available retained doubts about the value of work undertaken with specific equipment that they were not certain to come across again in their future working lives.

This raises a problem of identity: We have seen students struggle to save face and try to establish relationships in which they occupy the superior position. This attitude is without doubt linked to feelings of insecurity that they experience in the face of a still fuzzy representation of their profession: Is it more important for a technician to know *how to* do things or to *understand?* The ethos of the occupation of precision mechanic anticipates that the student will acquire, during the course of years of apprenticeship, almost perfect mastery of classical machine tools. But this requirement cannot be transferred to new devices, sometimes still in development, and with respect to which the objective of the college can only be initiation. In this situation what does it mean to be a *good student* or a *good worker?* Thus we see that various issues recur across these learning situations.

CHAPTER 7

OCCUPATIONAL MOTIVATIONS AND THEIR RELATION TO LEARNING SITUATIONS

The activities involved in computer-assisted design and manufacture are demanding for future technicians. Chapters 4 and 5, devoted to a presentation of what goes on in the practical work sessions on automation, showed that in this situation students find themselves continually confronted with the need to make decisions and with difficulties and unforeseen conditions that are sources of uncertainty.

These observations confirm the general conclusions drawn by Zarifian (1999, 2003) on the importance that events assume in work. It should be understood here that "by an event" is "that which occurs in a partly unforeseen or surprising fashion, coming to disturb the normal operation of the production system, exceeding the capacity of the machine to guarantee its own self-regulation. These events are well known, they make up the daily life of an automated workshop. They are the breakdowns, the drifts in quality, the material shortages, the unforeseen changes in the manufacturing

Apprentice in a Changing Trade, pages 129–155

program, impromptu orders from clients, etc. In brief, they are everything that one could call hazards.... It is around these events that the most complex and essential human interventions are located. The individual must cope with the event, resolving the problems it reveals or creates" (p. 37).

This approach to work, in terms of the expert actions of a professional confronted with a factual situation, has profound consequences for the way in which we think about training. The ability to "cope" actually requires an understanding of the entire production procedure as well as continual mobilization of actors' cognitive and social capacities, without forgetting the socioemotional demands made by often distressing hitches. Now the development of these competences cannot easily be accommodated within an approach to learning that progresses from simple to complex.

In addition, these competences, which are always "situated" or "in action" (Le Boterf, 1994), cannot be acquired in a one-off or once-and-for-all fashion. We have seen the difficulties of seeking to achieve, over the course of initial training, definitive mastery of unanticipated situations that by their very nature require an inventive search for solutions. In addition to the acquisition of knowledge and the command of skills, initial training is also without a doubt increasingly expected to foster a state of mind that allows future professionals to exploit to the best advantage the resources to which they have access and to take an active part in their own continuing professional development.

However, favoring the autonomy and responsibility of apprentices, their feelings of personal control over events, over their environment, and over their own careers can be problematic for students whose academic and professional development has not always provided real choices. Certainly in this case, an aspiration to strengthen the capacity for self-improvement and the sense of personal responsibility of those concerned does not immediately connect with apprentices' habits of thought and action.

This promotion of individual initiative can similarly be illuminated by studies of the attribution of causes of behavior and explanations that individuals give for the consequences of their actions (for a review, see Deschamps & Clemence, 1987), as well as by studies on *Kontrollmeinung* or the subjective representations individuals have regarding control of their environments (Flammer, 1992, 1994). Two major categories of explanations can be identified, first those that refer to the origins, properly so called, of behavior, within which can be distinguished internal attributions (linked to the individual) and external attributions (to the environment); and second, explanations linked to an individual's degree of responsibility. Research reveals a social prioritization of explanations centered on the role of the actor with respect to outcomes or with respect to what is done. Dispositional explanations seem to reflect a social norm of "internality" (Beauvois, 1982; Le Poultier, 1986; Dubois, 1988, 2003).

What about students at a technical college? In what state of mind do they engage with their training? Are they aware that this should probably be pursued beyond the certificate or diploma that constitutes their present aim? What view do they have of their own capacities and resources or of the competences that are demanded in the world of employment? In particular, do they perceive themselves as future professionals capable of flexibility and adaptation? How do they construe their own identity at the intersection of profiles that describe "virtual" identities (corresponding to expectations of the world of work), identities based in the tradition of the trade, and finally "experienced trajectories," in which "real" identities (Dubar, 1995, 2000) are shaped? Over the course of the interviews we conducted with teaching staff at the college, they spoke to us of their students, their motivations, and their capacities, providing a very mixed picture that we briefly outline here.

The issue of students' motivation often comes up in their comments. For example, one teacher declared to us: *The students have little motivation; they lack interest.* For another teacher: *The students do not see the necessity of expanding their basic knowledge.* In addition: *The weakest students don't take the trouble to concentrate. Faced with a difficulty, they try for a minute and then it's finished, they "zap" on.* A similar observation was formulated in the following terms: *When they meet a difficulty in the completion of their work, they stop.*

But elsewhere, very positive comments are made about the manner in which students try to mobilize themselves to deal with quite substantial tasks. *Some students got very enthusiastically involved in building a motor. This collective product arose out of a personal project. Students demonstrated inventiveness and perseverance here.* A second remark attracts attention by virtue of the explicit link it makes between motivation and a pedagogical relationship that comes close to coaching: *Sometimes I put myself in their position, I study with them but often they become more specialist in the area than I am. But this motivates them; up to this point few of them have complained when one throws them in at the deep end like this.*

The need to provide close supervision of students' work is frequently invoked; assessment practices along with a focus on final exams seem to play a major role here. *For them to learn to work fast, efficiently, it's difficult. In the last year, they are hard pressed because there is a deadline.* One teacher underlines the importance of monitoring each individual's work very closely: *You need to be on top of the students, to make them work, to make sure that everyone has a chance.*

These individual interviews with the Ecole Technique de Sainte-Croix teachers provide us with a composite, but also not entirely consistent, image of the young people attending the college. They are sometimes described as difficult, unmotivated students, sometimes as future professionals deeply engaged in their training activities.

The weak academic level of some apprentices also occupies a significant place in the comments teachers gave us. Some of them revealed themselves to be somewhat cynical and discouraged: *They don't even know how to add 2/3 and 3/4.* The fault here is seen to lie with their former education and sometimes their parents. What is to be done in the face of such failures? What approach can be taken with those students who at school ended up convinced that academic knowledge is not for them? How can this dead end be reconciled with the requirements of occupations that expect more and more knowledge? The unhappy relationship with knowledge that so many young people develop over the course of their compulsory schooling is too often ignored. Although it bears upon a different training context, Wiel's (1992) analysis is applicable to the situation studied here: "For want of recognising the repercussions of the feeling of educational failure, which is to say of recognising what is called here the syndrome of educational failure, and freeing students from this, training in the professional high school is severely crippled by problems of educational rejection which are not sufficiently taken into account" (p. 35).

A QUESTIONNAIRE-BASED INQUIRY

In this complex picture, conceived to make sense of the way in which the students locate and describe themselves, we devised a questionnaire intended to identify various general principles that structure opinions, images, and attitudes with respect to the following:

- Their previous education and their current training
- Reasons for choices and the motivations leading them to undertake this training
- Representations of the learning process
- Competences currently expected of professionals{\BL}

Of the 143 students in training at the college, 129 completed our questionnaire, effectively 90% of the population. These included 43 apprentices in mechanics, 38 apprentices in electronics, and 37 future technicians.

The mechanics and electronics apprentices had a mean age of 18 years, the technicians a mean age of 22 years.

Three-quarters of the electronics apprentices and two-thirds of the mechanics apprentices at the Ecole Technique had entered directly from compulsory education. The others had started either a course of post-compulsory education or another apprenticeship before registering at the Ecole Technique. As for the technicians, more than three-quarters of them had previously obtained a *Certificat Fédéral de Capacité* (CFC).

ATTITUDE TOWARD THEIR PREVIOUS EDUCATION[1]

A large majority of the students (71%) had not repeated any years of compulsory education. However, there was a difference in pattern as a function of course. The technicians were less likely to have repeated (16% had done so) than the mechanics apprentices (31%) or the electronics apprentices (40%).

In response to a question concerning their experience of their previous schooling, the mean response on a 6-point scale (from 1 = very good to 6 = very bad) was 2.82. The distribution of responses, also expressed in percentages, was as follows:

Q: *In general what was your experience of your compulsory education?*

	Very good	Good	Somewhat good	Somewhat bad	Bad	Very bad
Mechanics	5%	23%	37%	21%	0%	14%
Electronics	16%	37%	24%	21%	0%	3%
Technicians	8%	43%	35%	5%	3%	3%

Overall, the attitudes expressed with respect to their previous schooling cannot be regarded as negative, even if we cannot rule out the possibility that the responses obtained here reflect a social desirability effect. It is more gratifying to say that, all in all, one's schooling passed without any particular problems. However, our objective is not to make a survey of opinions. For our purposes it is more interesting to analyze the dynamics of responses in relation to the course of training pursued, and to compare across courses. Thus, the differences of interpretation of previous schooling appear to be linked to whether or not that education had been completed "without problems." The technicians were less likely to have repeated a year than the electronics or mechanics apprentices. Thus, the memories these latter had of their education were less positive.

ATTITUDES TOWARD CURRENT TRAINING

In response to a question asking whether they would do the same training if they could start over, we again found a division of opinion according to the course of training they were following.

If I could start over…

---

[1] We report here in large part an analysis of the results carried out by Claude Kaiser and reported in the research paper: Kaiser, C., Perret-Clermont, A.-N., Perret, J.-F. & Golay-Schilter, D. (1997). Apprendre un metier technique aujourd'hui: Représentations des apprenants. Séminaire de Psychologie, University of Neuchâtel.

	Combined N = 114	Mech N = 42	Elec N = 37	Mech+Elec N = 79	Tech N = 35
I would do the same again	39%	40%	30%	35%	46%
I would do another kind of training	39%	29%	40%	34%	51%
I have no views on the matter	22%	31%	30%	31%	3%

Although the distribution of responses across the categories is more or less equal for those on the apprenticeship courses, the technicians are rather more definite; we find there is only a very small percentage without a clear opinion. There is no statistically significant difference between the responses of the electronics and the mechanics students.

Two interpretations can be advanced to explain this greater lack of certainty among those on the apprenticeship courses. The first relates to the relative status of the different kinds of training. It would certainly be reasonable to expect that the older technicians, involved in a course to improve skills, would be guided more strongly by the logic of voluntary choice. But it is surprising that half of them would now pursue a different course of training if it were possible. Is there a certain kind of adherence by individuals to their initial decisions here, as commitment theories have shown (Kiesler, 1971), or this a reaction by a group of people particularly open to a change in occupational orientation?

We might consider that the greater indecision of the mechanics and electronics students, who are in the process of learning, is a result of their progressive discovery of an occupation and that their views about this are as yet unformed. Perhaps the information they have at this stage does not allow them to form a sufficiently clear idea of the training they have chosen. If so, on what was this choice based? Was it really an explicit choice or was it determined by circumstances? The next question sheds some light on this.

REASONS FOR OCCUPATIONAL CHOICES

This question was intended to distinguish the principal dimensions underlying choice of training. It was formulated as follows:

Here are different reasons we often hear for choosing a particular kind of training. Indicate the seven reasons that seem to you to correspond most closely to your own choice (by putting +) and the seven reasons that correspond the least (by putting −).

I opted for the training that I am currently pursuing because:

- It allows me to acquire a trade
- It allows me to take other kinds of training afterward
- It's an area in which you need to learn new things all the time
- It matches my abilities and my personality

- I like searching for solutions to problems
- It gives me access to a well-paid occupation
- It allows me to work in an autonomous fashion, to work as I wish
- It's the thing that bores me the least so far
- I like anything technical
- It allows me to rise to a high position
- It's an area in which one is continually confronted with new situations
- It allows you to get to know lots of people
- I like working on a team
- My academic results did not allow me to choose what I wanted
- It is what I was advised to do
- I like constructing things, producing things
- The training provides access to the occupations of the future
- It is what my parents want
- It makes it easy to find a job
- Quite simply, I enjoy it
- It's near where I live

To process the responses, a hierarchical analysis was executed on the basis of nominations and rejections that were linked. The results are presented in Figure 1.[2] The reasons are grouped according to decreasing degrees of similarity starting from the left.

A reading of the dendrogram points to a first major division (the first two blocks) between reasons referring to circumstances (which could also be described as external attributions) and reasons relating more to personality or to one's own interests (internal attributions). Within the first subdivision we can make an additional distinction between reasons relating, for example, to the advice of others or to educational attainment, and those relating to attractive employment or pay.

The second large subdivision (the latter two blocks) groups together reasons that refer to more personal characteristics. It also can be divided into two categories, the first embracing two perspectives on personality, the second bearing on personal tastes or on career aspects of the profession chosen.

In order to determine the importance for choice of the principal categories revealed by the hierarchical analysis, we calculated for each major subdivision an index that combined the "positive" choices and the "negative" choices, recalling that students were asked to select reasons that best corresponded to their own choices, and reasons that corresponded least.

---

[2] For a review of the method, see Doise, Clémence, and Lorenzi-Cioldi (1992).

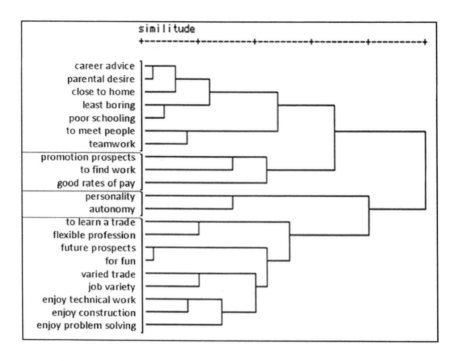

FIGURE 1.   Graphic representation of the hierarchical classification of reasons for choice of training.
Simple matching indicator; aggregation method: mean interclass distance.

For the students as a whole, internal reasons (2nd subdivision) were much more often positive than negative selections.[3] External reasons (the 1st subdivision) were for their part much more often rejected than accepted.

However, this general pattern did vary across the subsamples. If we subtract negative choices from positive choices to derive an index comparing these two kinds of choices (and thus producing a balance of choice in which a positive sign indicates a greater number of positive than negative choices), two observations emerge: Although internal reasons are chosen positively by all respondents, they are chosen more by the technicians (M = 3.54) than by the mechanics and electronics apprentices (M = 2.38); in a complementary fashion, we also found a differentiated effect for external reasons, rejected more by the technicians (M = 3.57) than by the apprentices (M = 2.33).

---

[3] Of 11 items, a mean of 4.59 were positive selections, as against 1.88 negative.

In addition, probably for reasons of social desirability, a majority of students opted for items indicating that their choice arose from their own wishes. Internality, which represents a valued and image-enhancing norm, is thus well recognized by our respondents. However, it can be said that there are differences in degree of investment in this general approach. The apprentices, whose uncertainty with respect to the previous question we have already pointed out and whose previous education had been a little more problematic, are also those for whom external factors weigh more heavily in the choice of training.

FEELINGS OF CONTROL

The differentiating considerations surrounding choice of training can be related to representations of the future, and how it will subsequently unfold, as well as the ways in which learning situations are conceived. On the basis of Rotter's (1966) work, it is possible to show that some individuals are inclined to give internal explanations for the determinants of their behavior (relating to individual responsibility) while others tend to give external explanations (relating to environmental factors that are seldom particularly under individual control).

Broadly, the responses to the questions presented below indicate the extent of control that individuals think they have over their current and future environments. Based on a questionnaire developed by Flammer (see Grob, Bodmer, & Flammer, 1993; Flammer, 1994), within the framework of comparative studies on *Kontrollmeinung* (an expression translated here as "feeling of control"), three situations were presented to the students, who were asked to imagine themselves in each situation. The first refers to a situation involving employment search, the second is based on an academic learning situation, while the third has a more general character. In relation to each of these, students first indicated the degree to which they had the feeling that they would be able to do something. They responded on a 10-point scale from 1 = "I am not certain of having any influence" to 10 = "I am certain of having a decisive influence."

Do you think you would be able to do something here?

	Total	Mech	Elect	M+E	Tech
	N = 118	43	38	81	37
Situation 1: At the end of your training, you go to look for a job. There are certainly some opportunities and places of work that interest you more than others.					
Indicate the extent to which you think you would be able to do something now to find an attractive job. (10-point scale: 10 = decisive influence)	6.41	6.78	5.50	6.16	6.95

	Total	Mech	Elect	M+E	Tech
And in 3–5 years' time? In relation to your last response, to what degree do you think you would be able to have some influence in finding an attractive job?	7.34	7.70	6.82	7.28	7.46
How important is it for you to be able to exercise influence in finding a job? (4-point scale: 4 = very important)	3.28	3.42	3.11	3.27	3.30
Situation 2: At school it happens that you must learn something that does not interest you at all and that you regard as useless.					
Indicate the degree to which you think you would have influence over what you must learn. (10-point scale)	5.43	5.48	5.48	5.47	5.32
And in 3–5 years? In relation to your last response, to what degree do you think you would be able to have influence over what you have to learn? (10-point scale)	6.08	6.23	6.11	5.97	6.00
How important is it for you to have influence over what you learn? (4-point scale)	3.03	2.98	2.96	2.95	3.19
Situation 3: There are times in life when we need to take stock. We begin to ask questions like: why am I as I am; why do I behave and act in such a fashion?					
Indicate the degree to which you think you have influence on the way you are and the way you conduct yourself. (10-point scale)	7.75	7.70	7.70	7.71	7.86
And in 3–5 years? In relation to the response you have just given, to what degree do you think you would have influence on the way you are and the way you conduct yourself? (10-point scale)	7.97	7.90	8.06	8.24	7.78
How important is it to you to have influence on the way you are and the way you conduct yourself? (4-point scale)	3.41	3.30	3.36	3.42	3.51

Overall and if one does not take into account the time frame (thus combining the current situation with that anticipated in 3–5 years), it turns out that influence is seen as weakest in the context of formal education (Situation 2: M = 5.74). Next comes influence in the context of finding employment (Situation 1: M = 6.87), while the strongest influence is expected at the more general level of personal life (Situation 3: M = 7.86). We might also note that although influence is judged to be least in the educational context, this is also the situation in which such influence is seen to be least important.

These views about influence are broadly shared by all the respondents, with the exception of the matter of finding employment. The electronics specialists see themselves as having less influence (M = 6.16) than the mechanics (M = 7.20). An internal analysis shows that this difference is largely due to perceptions of the present; the difference is less marked when a more distant future of 3–5 years is invoked.

Note also that although the electronics students' responses differ for the employment search situation, where they anticipate that their influence is weaker, they also accord less importance to this (M = 3.31), particularly compared to the mechanics (M = 3.42).

We have seen that the educational careers of apprentices have often been more problematic than those of the technical students. A greater number of external factors have also had an influence on their occupational choices (even if the general tendency is toward internality), and there is greater uncertainty about beginning the same training again if the possibility were to arise. We might in consequence expect weaker feelings of control among the apprentices. However, the above results do not support this expectation: We do not find any systematic differentiation between the groups of students considered in terms of their feelings of control.

SUCCESS AND FAILURE AT SCHOOL

Another way of making sense of the apprentices' representations concerning the feelings of control they have over their environment is provided by analyzing the attributions they make for their own success or failure in school. Studies on this subject show that in general terms there is a tendency to attribute success to causes over which the individual has control (e.g., conscious effort). Failure is in contrast imputed more to uncontrollable causes (such as personal capacity) (Luginbuhl, Crowe, & Kahan, 1990; Rotter, 1966; Weiner, 1979, 1986).

In our questionnaire, we included two sets of reasons relating respectively to success and failure in school. For each set, respondents were asked to choose the three reasons that most closely corresponded to them. Each set included the same themes, but adapted respectively to the scenarios of success and failure. The general instruction to select only three reasons was almost entirely followed. In fact, there were 352 responses (out of 354 expected) in the case of success, and 347 responses in the case of failure. The distribution of responses is given below.

When things go well for me at school it is mainly because... (three options to be selected)

	Total	Mech	Elect	M+E	Tech
	N = 118	43	38	81	37
I like the subject or the activity involved	74%	69%	76%	73%	76%
It is well explained and therefore easy to follow	62%	60%	61%	60%	68%

	Total	Mech	Elect	M+E	Tech
I decide to give it a go	47%	38%	47%	43%	57%
The level of demand is manageable	35%	38%	32%	35%	35%
I have the ability	35%	43%	32%	38%	30%
The class atmosphere is stimulating	17%	19%	16%	18%	16%
I've been lucky	14%	17%	18%	18%	5%
I had a friend's help	10%	7%	13%	10%	11%
I like the teacher	7%	7%	5%	6%	8%

The most frequently chosen reasons can be seen to be directly linked to the content taught, including the appeal of the subject, the explanation provided, and the conscious effort of the student. These choices contrast with more situational reasons that are less linked to content such as chance, a companion's help, or whether the teacher is likeable. These views are shared by the students as a whole. There is in fact no statistically significant difference among courses of study. Note finally that among the three most frequently chosen reasons effort is the only controllable factor.

When things do not go well for me in school it is mainly because… (three options to be selected)

	Total	Mech	Elect	M+E	Tech
	N = 118	43	38	81	37
I have not done enough work on the subject or I haven't had enough practice	61%	56%	49%	53%	78%
It hasn't been explained well enough	57%	42%	78%	59%	51%
I do not like the subject or the activity involved	54%	46%	51%	49%	65%
Some days are just like that	31%	42%	22%	32%	30%
I have a lot of difficulty with this subject or this activity	27%	24%	32%	28%	24%
I don't like the teacher	26%	32%	41%	36%	5%
The level required is too high	24%	29%	11%	21%	32%
The atmosphere in the classroom does not favor work	16%	22%	14%	18%	11%
I did not have any help	6%	10%	3%	6%	5%

As regards reasons linked to failure, we find a very similar response profile. Lack of effort, poor explanations, and lack of appeal of the subject seem to be the principal causes given for failure.

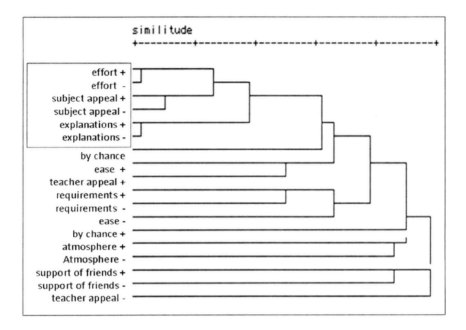

FIGURE 2. Graphic representation of the hierarchical classification analysis of reasons for success and failure at school. Plus signs indicate items selected for success, minus signs for failure.
Jaccard index; aggregation method: mean interclass distance

A hierarchical classification analysis, executed with the aim of identifying common response profiles, confirms the above-mentioned tendencies in explanations for success and failure. Respondents tend to associate both success and failure at school primarily with effort, adequacy of explanation, and appeal of the material.

Comparing the different courses, the electronics students place more emphasis on level of explanation (78%) than the mechanics (42%), while the latter stress the fact that the level of demand can be too high (Mech: 29%; Elec: 53%).

As regards the technicians, they attach more importance to lack of conscious effort (78%, compared to Mech + Elec: 53%) and acknowledge less impact of the likeability of the teacher (Tech: 5% versus Mech + Elec: 36%).

Overall, success and failure are interpreted mainly in terms of factors linked to the content of the material taught. Although effort, a controllable factor, assumes considerable importance in explanations of success and even more so of failure (and this particularly among the technicians), the two other most frequently selected reasons (quality of explanation, particularly among the electronics students, and appeal of the material) are beyond the respondents' control. Finally, the likeability of the teacher, a relatively uncontrollable factor, assumes relatively more importance for the apprentices than for the technicians.

REPRESENTATIONS OF LEARNING METHODS

Training institutions have as their objectives the transmission of general knowledge and occupation-specific knowledge, the acquisition of skills and ways of reasoning, and even induction of certain social norms. They also aspire to develop within the learner a certain state of mind that could be defined as creative, communicative, critical, and constructive. The model of the learner contained within these different visions is necessarily of a composite nature. It appeals both to processes of knowledge transmission and to active processes in the construction of competences.

What kinds of models are technical college students spontaneously disposed to mobilize in their learning practices?

A series of questions were asked that bear upon the activities undertaken and the most appropriate attitudes to adopt when faced with difficulties in each of two settings, namely within the context of a theoretical course and within that of workshop exercises. Our analysis here has three aims: (1) to examine patterns of response and to attempt to identify the dimensions underlying learning methods (achieved by means of a principal components factor analysis); (2) to establish what kinds of responses are judged most effective at different levels (accomplished by analysis of means for sets of items representing the dimensions identified through the factor analysis); and (3) to analyze the position on each of the factors of groups of individuals representing the different courses (based on mean factor scores).

In the event of difficulties in a theoretical course, what seems to be the most effective thing to do?

(6-point scale; 1 = not at all effective; 6 = totally effective)

	Total	Mech	Elect	M+E	Tech
	N = 118	43	38	81	37
In general, in a theoretical course, when you encounter difficulties, what do you think is the most effective thing to do?					
Return to basics, things, or chapters poorly understood	5.10	4.93	5.11	5.01	5.30
Do additional exercises outside the course	4.79	4.51	4.74	4.62	5.16
Ask the teacher for an explanation	4.68	4.72	4.5	4.62	4.81
Repeat the exercise or activity a number of times	4.60	4.56	4.37	4.47	4.89

	Total	Mech	Elect	M+E	Tech
Work with more successful classmates	4.59	4.70	4.45	4.58	4.62
Ask a classmate for an explanation	4.27	4.14	4.22	4.18	4.49
Do similar things, the same kinds of things	4.16	4.05	3.97	4.01	4.49
Watch teachers doing a demonstration	3.90	4.16	4.16	4.16	3.32
Relax and don't force it; things will go better next time	2.95	3.12	2.82	2.98	2.89
Work with classmates having similar difficulties	2.86	3.26	2.47	2.89	2.78

The factor analysis identified four factors accounting for 64% of the variance[4] (factor 1: 21%; factor 2: 17%; factor 3: 15%; factor 4: 11%).

The first factor is defined by items referring to repetition or to demonstration of a correct solution as a model for learning. These are the items that refer to undertaking exercises, going back to basics, and redoing the activity several times.

The second factor is of a more interactional nature, making reference to peer collaboration. Items important for this factor include asking a classmate for an explanation, working with more successful classmates or with those experiencing similar difficulties.

The third factor can be interpreted as based on decentration. It is defined by attitudes recommending doing related things or the same kinds of things, relaxing and expecting things to go better next time.

The fourth factor is organized around the idea of confrontation with a correct model, as in the first factor, but this time in terms of a request addressed to the teacher. This factor can also be understood in terms of its contrast with the second factor (with its focus on interaction, but on the basis of symmetrical relations with others), because in this case, the interactional dimension is rather more asymmetric. This factor is defined by two items, one referring to the observation of a demonstration by the teacher and one referring to a request to teachers for an explanation.

Aggregating the items defining each of the factors, those relating to confrontation with a correct solution (factor 1) describe responses regarded as the most effective (M = 4.85). Those defining factor 4, also involving exposure to a correct solution but provided by the teacher, are in aggregate judged the next most effective (M = 4.29). Less effective are those relating to cooperation with others (M = 3.91), and least those related to decentration (M = 3.56).

A comparison of mean factor scores of the different subpopulations indicates a difference on factor 1 (repetition or exposure to a correct solution).

---

[4] Kaiser's criterion; varimax rotation.

The technicians place more emphasis on the effectiveness of this learning method than those taking the other courses. There was no difference among the subpopulations with respect to the other factors, nor among the different kinds of apprenticeships.

Next, the same questions were posed but in the context of workshop activities.

When difficulties arise during workshop activities, what seems to be the most effective thing to do?

(6-point scale; 1 = not at all effective; 6 = totally effective)

	Total	Mech	Elect	M+E	Tech
	N = 118	43	38	81	37
In general, when you encounter difficulties in the workshop, what do you think is the most effective thing to do?					
Ask the teacher for an explanation	4.72	4.93	4.61	4.78	4.59
Return to basics, things, or chapters poorly understood	4.58	4.56	4.63	4.59	4.57
Work with more successful classmates	4.45	4.3	4.58	4.43	4.49
Ask a classmate for an explanation	4.37	4.14	4.34	4.23	4.68
Watch teachers doing a demonstration	4.2	4.26	4.29	4.27	4.03
Do similar things, the same kinds of things	4.2	4.23	4.11	4.17	4.27
Repeat the exercise or activity a number of times	4.11	3.98	4.37	4.16	4.00
Do additional exercises outside the course	3.77	3.48	3.84	3.65	4.03
Relax and don't force it; things will go better next time	3.29	3.42	3.11	3.27	3.32
Work with classmates having similar difficulties	2.92	2.79	2.87	2.83	3.11

Factor analysis this time revealed a different structure for learning methods. Four factors were extracted, together accounting for 65.7% of the variance.

The first factor is again oriented toward learning based on the correct solution, but this time with the emphasis on imitation (it included the option of relying on classmates but only if they were successful), or on repeating the exercise numerous times.

The second factor is based on repetition. It is defined by those items describing going back to basics and doing additional exercises outside the course.

The third factor is defined by ideas of learning based on teacher support—asking for explanations and observing demonstrations.

The fourth factor is defined by the same items as in factor 3 in the preceding analysis but in addition to the items describing relaxing and doing similar things, it includes the item that describes working with classmates having similar difficulties. Thus we might regard this factor as defined by responses regarded as irrelevant or inappropriate.

Here, when the items defining each factor are combined, no marked differences are found between alternative learning models. Only the responses described in the factor 4 items are judged less effective than others.

It is interesting to note that although working with classmates, whether they are more successful or whether they are having similar problems, has similar implications in the context of a theory course, matters are quite different in the workshop context. Concepts of learning based on exposure to correct solutions seem to be regarded as particularly relevant here. In their view, turning to classmates experiencing similar difficulties is not an appropriate response.

Overall, social interaction among peers is considered only marginally relevant as a means of improving performance. Additionally, we can conclude that students judge repetition and confrontation with correct solutions as generally the most effective strategies.

EVALUATION OF DIFFERENT LEARNING TASKS

We examined students' judgments of four types of activities. These were finding the cause of a fault in a machine or a circuit, solving mathematical equations, constructing a part or a circuit on the basis of a diagram provided, and working with a computer. These activities were chosen because they appeared to be representative of the range of tasks undertaken by these students.

What do you think of the following activities ... ?
(6-point scale; 1 = disagree strongly; 6 = agree strongly)

	Find the cause of a breakdown	Solve math equations	Construct part or circuit	Work with a computer	Activities combined
Interesting	4.91	3.72	4.98	4.98	4.65
Easy	2.78	3.34	3.91	3.8	3.46
Useful	5.21	3.67	4.78	5.3	4.74
Motivating	4.38	3.21	4.66	4.71	4.24

Across activities and independent of courses, the students were in agreement in their views of these activities as useful, interesting, and motivating. The question about easiness produced the only responses at variance with those to the other questions; there was less unanimity in their views about how easy each of the activities was.

Considering the general picture, the activities involving constructing a part and, particularly, working on a computer still attracted the highest agreement as to interest, utility, ease, and motivation. Judgments about solving a breakdown and constructing a part (or circuit) are somewhat similar to one another except for the matter of ease or simplicity; searching for the cause of a breakdown or fault is judged as less easy.

Although interest in general is quite high, it is somewhat less for an activity involving the solution of mathematical equations. This activity is also judged the least motivating and the least useful.

Performing the different activities presented successfully would require the following:

(6-point scale; 1 = disagree strongly; 6 = agree strongly)

	Combined	Breakdown	Equations	Construction	Computer
Having a good working method	5.07	5.22	5.09	5.21	4.66
Time and effort	4.96	5.14	4.98	5.00	4.70
A good stock of knowledge	4.93	5.06	5.18	4.65	4.85
Resourcefulness	4.55	5.23	2.53	4.84	4.61
Having been taught well	4.54	4.22	5.05	4.47	4.42
Intelligence	4.49	4.49	4.83	4.14	4.50
Having good reference manuals	4.28	4.52	3.95	3.94	4.75
Being able to count on someone's assistance	4.08	4.20	3.84	3.84	4.45
Working on it in twos or threes	3.16	3.47	2.70	2.96	3.49

Considering all activities together, having a good working method and time and effort, together with secure knowledge, are judged to be the most necessary elements. In decreasing order, the next element is resourcefulness, then having benefited from a good education, and intelligence. Reference manuals, another's help, and working in a group were regarded as the least helpful.

Regarding differences among the activities, it is primarily with respect to finding the cause of a breakdown and solving mathematical equations, and to a lesser extent manufacturing a part, that having a good working method, effort, and sound knowledge seem to be the most appropriate, while these are regarded as less relevant for working on a computer.

Resourcefulness is particularly helpful in finding the cause of a break-down and also, though to a lesser extent, in constructing a part or a circuit. It seems to be regarded as less relevant for solving mathematical equations, for which having benefited from a good education and intelligence are apparently more useful. In contrast, their responses indicate that intelligence is the least relevant requirement for constructing a part. Good reference works, benefiting from another's help, and working in a group are particularly valued when the task is to find the cause of a breakdown or working on a computer.

Another interesting finding concerns the importance accorded to working on a team and another's help as a function of type of task. Although overall these resources are judged to be the least relevant, something that probably corresponds to an underestimation of the role of social interaction, this seems to be less true when it is a matter of finding the cause of a breakdown or working on a computer. These effects seem on the one hand to reflect the ideology and academic approach that classically emphasized the individual relation to knowledge and on the other hand the informal daily workshop practice of students sharing information and frequently helping one another to solve the problems encountered.

THE IMAGE OF THE PROFESSIONAL

We have now reached the point at which we need to ask about the image students have of their futures, and in particular of the demands confronting professionals in their chosen careers. The rationale for choice of items to explore this is empirical; it takes elements from a number of previous enquiries. A principal source of ideas is work on gender orientations (Parsons & Bales, 1955),[5] work that draws a distinction between expressive orientations granting importance to relationships and communication (and more common among girls), and instrumental orientations aimed at more individualist self-realization and directed toward productive task completion (more common among boys). One of our number had already been involved in testing various items, drawn from questionnaires on gender orientation, with a mixed, male–female adolescent population at the end of compulsory schooling (Kaiser & Rastoldo, 1995); these young people were asked to describe various areas of employment. The research also included items on educational attainment. This work indicated that technical occupations were specifically distinguished from other areas of employment in being described essentially in terms of instrumental items. In this earlier

---

[5] For a review of this issue, see in particular Lorenzi-Cioldi (1988) and Ashmore and Del Boca (1986).

study, it emerged that to be audacious, to know how to make decisions, to be self-confident, and to have a logical mind were particularly relevant descriptions for technical occupations, while knowing how to express oneself well, liking languages and literature, and generally having been a good student were judged to be the least appropriate.

Thus, we first chose items reflecting dimensions of gender orientation and then added some items that seemed to us especially relevant to tasks intrinsic to technical professions and others inspired by a list of traits derived from studies of schoolchildren's vocational orientations (Kaufman, 1975). These gave us an *a priori* classification of items as follows:

Instrumental characteristics
> Having a logical mind
> Being autonomous, having a spirit of initiative
> Being able to assert oneself, having authority
> Being self-confident
> Knowing how to make decisions

Expressive characteristics
> Having intuition
> Being at ease meeting people
> Being careful, meticulous
> Knowing how to come to agreement with others
> Knowing how to present oneself in a good light

Educational characteristics
> Having a good knowledge of German
> Having a good knowledge of English
> Having a good knowledge of mathematics
> Having a good academic record
> Being in good physical condition
> Knowing how to draw well
> Knowing how to write well
> Knowing how to express oneself well

Vocational orientation
> Having a practical mind
> Being able to execute instructions rapidly
> Being able to understand rapidly what is being asked
> Being able to meet deadlines
> Being good with one's hands
> Being punctual, a good time-keeper
> Knowing how to adapt rapidly to a computing environment

Having a sense of responsibility
Being ambitious
Being resourceful
Being ordered, methodical
Having perseverance, even in the face of failure

It should be understood that this *a priori* categorization is merely a provisional point of departure. It goes without saying that the groupings we may identify on the basis of an analysis of response patterns will determine whether or not this *a priori* classification also has psychological meaning.

As with the study of representations of learning methods, three types of analysis were undertaken. The first examined general tendencies; here, the aim is to determine what, in the eyes of the students, corresponds most and least directly to their various specialties. For this, the mean scores for each of the scales are compared. The second type of analysis concerned the structure of interindividual variations. What general dimensions defining the occupational universe can be distinguished in the responses? To determine this we performed a principal components factor analysis. The third analysis aims to examine the institutional anchoring of the dimensions defining the occupational universe (based on mean factor scores across the courses of study).

General Tendencies

Two options can be distinguished for providing a general view of the 30 characteristics that we presented to respondents to define occupations. One focuses on the relative importance of these different characteristics in defining a typical member of the occupation. The other compares the differences found among the subgroups of students. Let us begin by examining the characteristics seen to be the most relevant.

What is in the future going to be increasingly required of a professional in your chosen area of work?

(6-point scale; 1 = does not correspond at all, 6 = corresponds completely)

	Total	Mech	Elect	M+E	Tech
	N = 118	43	38	81	37
Being able to meet deadlines	5.24	5.23	5.11	5.17	5.38
Being autonomous, having a spirit of initiative	5.22	5	5.18	5.07	5.54
Being able to execute instructions rapidly	5.22	5.28	5.08	5.19	5.3
Having a practical mind	5.19	5.23	4.89	5.07	5.46
Having a sense of responsibility	5.18	5.21	5.13	5.17	5.19

	Total	Mech	Elect	M+E	Tech
Being able to understand rapidly what is being asked	5.17	5.05	5.21	5.12	5.27
Knowing how to make decisions	5.16	4.95	5.13	5.04	5.43
Being punctual, a good time-keeper	5.14	5.23	4.95	5.1	5.22
Having a logical mind	5.11	5.09	5.05	5.07	5.19
Being careful, meticulous	5.07	5.42	4.82	5.14	4.92
Being resourceful	5.07	5.02	4.89	4.96	5.3
Being ordered, methodical	5.03	4.07	4.78	4.94	5.24
Being self-confident	5.01	5.12	4.71	4.93	5.19
Having perseverance, even in the face of failure	4.89	4.77	4.87	4.81	5.05
Being good with one's hands	4.89	5.3	5.03	5.17	4.25
Knowing how to express oneself well	4.84	4.67	4.92	4.79	4.95
Being at ease meeting people	4.79	4.56	4.76	4.65	5.08
Knowing how to come to agreement with others	4.79	4.67	4.84	4.75	4.86
Having a good knowledge of mathematics	4.76	4.72	5.18	4.94	4.38
Knowing how to adapt rapidly to a computing environment	4.75	4.51	4.63	4.57	5.16
Being ambitious	4.69	4.53	4.63	4.58	4.95
Having a good knowledge of English	4.63	4.3	4.68	4.48	4.95
Being able to assert oneself, having authority	4.51	4.44	4.55	4.49	4.54
Having intuition	4.49	4.21	4.32	4.26	5
Having a good academic record	4.47	4.44	4.66	4.54	4.32
Knowing how to present oneself in a good light	4.35	4.49	4.32	4.41	4.22
Having a good knowledge of German	4.28	4.26	4.08	4.17	4.51
Knowing how to draw well	4.09	4.86	3.68	4.31	3.62
Knowing how to write well	4.03	4.02	3.97	4	4.11
Being in good physical condition	3.73	4.33	3.97	3.88	3.41

Overall, students judge that all the characteristics presented relate to what will be expected of a professional in the future. Thus we cannot say that any characteristics are seen to be irrelevant, only that some are judged to be even more important than others.

Personal qualities and attitudes linked in some way to following instructions are seen to be the most relevant. This contrasts with characteristics referring to the expressive domain such as languages and writing.

Turning to a comparison of the subpopulations, the technicians consider autonomy and a practical mind as particularly important. Being self-confident, knowing how to adapt rapidly to a computing environment, having a good knowledge of English, and having intuition are also valued more by the future technicians than by the others. The mechanics stress the importance of the quality of performance in their emphasis on a practical mind, careful work, being good with one's hands, speed, and personal confidence. Knowing how to draw and being in good physical condition are also qualities to which more importance is attached by this occupational group than by the others, while recognizing that they all consider these to be of relatively little importance. The electronics specialists, for their part, attach particular importance to mathematical ability. Aptitude for manual work and to a lesser degree a good command of English are also seen as desirable qualities for their futures.

The factor analysis extracted eight factors,[6] accounting for 67.4% of the variance.

The first factor was the most general, combining several types of characteristics. These included more personal attributes, such as a sense of responsibility, perseverance, good expressive skills, a logical mind, ability to make decisions and to work with one's hands. These also included characteristics related to sociability such as meeting people, knowing how to come to agreement with others, and also performance-related attributes such as ability to meet deadlines.

This first factor might be regarded as a general notion of occupations built on a contrast between an entire set of personal and social qualities and characteristics referring to the academic domain; moreover, these latter were seen to be the least directly linked to work in a future occupation. The strongest contrasts were in fact found for items such as having a good academic record, knowing how to draw well, command of German, and to a lesser degree English, as against such items as rapid execution of task requirements and ambition. Only knowledge of mathematics seemed to lie outside this effect, further underlining the link to expression of the academic characteristics referred to above.

The second factor was more specifically defined by academic characteristics related to expression. The most strongly important items were knowledge of English and German, knowing how to write well, knowing how to present oneself in a good light, and having a good academic record. Also weighted on this factor are capacity for expression and capacity for coming to agreement with others, which further underlines the expressive nature of this factor. It also confirmed the strongest contrasts, setting "expressive academic" attributes against a practical mind, perseverance, ability to meet deadlines, being good with one's hands, and a logical mind.

The third factor is primarily organized around a set of personal attributes focusing on individualized action. It includes qualities such as intu-

---

[6] Kaiser criterion; varimax rotation.

ition, autonomy, rapidity of adaptation to a computing environment, ambition, perseverance and, to complete the list, a rapid understanding of task requirements and having a practical mind. These characteristics are contrasted with those that bear more upon self-presentation, such as physical condition, knowing how to present oneself in a good light, being good with one's hands, being careful, and knowing how to draw well.

The fourth factor includes characteristics related to quality and rapidity of performance such as being careful and meticulous, being ordered, as well as understanding and knowing how to execute task demands rapidly. The strongest contrasts here are with physical condition, knowledge of mathematics, and being intuitive.

The fifth factor gives more emphasis to those personal characteristics not included in the third factor, but in combination with qualities more closely based on resourcefulness. Thus it includes resourcefulness itself but also self-confidence and having a practical and logical mind, contrasting these with qualities such as ambition, facility for manual work, a good previous academic record, good time-keeping, and good mathematical knowledge.

The sixth factor embraces gestural abilities such as knowing how to draw, being in good physical condition, and being good with one's hands.

We did not interpret the final two factors, each of which were effectively defined only by single items: having authority and good time-keeping, respectively.

The Factor Hierarchy

In order to give some further meaning to preferences between factors, we took the items defining each of the factors and calculated mean preferences. The items defining factors 4 (related to performance; M = 5.09) and 5 (related to resourcefulness; M = 5.12) summarize qualities that are perceived to be particularly called for in the future in each occupational sector. Next come the attributes related to factor 1 (primarily those relating to attitudes and competences; M = 4.98), followed by the qualities represented in factor 3 (linked to individual action; M = 4.49). Academic attributes related to expression (factor 2; M = 4.36) and then those related to gestural capacities (factor 6, M = 3.91) are the qualities regarded as least important.

To summarize, the competencies of a future professional are conceived less in terms of academic attainments (and even less so those attainments related to expressive characteristics) than in terms of general capacities related to quality of performance, resourcefulness and above all traits of personality. A certain inclination to follow instructions is also deemed appropriate. There were, nonetheless, differences among our subpopulations. The technical students put a bit more emphasis on personal qualities while the apprentice mechanics and electronics specialists attached more importance to gestural capacities. Finally, the mechanics, more than the others, were inclined to stress performance quality and resourcefulness, and also perhaps compliance with various rules.

COMPARISONS BETWEEN THE IMAGE OF THE OCCUPATION AND SELF-IMAGE

The same items that made up the questionnaire on the image of the occupation were also presented to the students as a basis for self-description. This allowed us to examine the distance perceived between what these young people thought about their future occupations and what they believed about themselves. For the items defining each of the factors, we aggregated the differences, in terms of absolute values, between self-image and occupational image.

Overall, proximity was most pronounced for resourcefulness (factor 5: $M = 0.88$[7]), individual action (factor 3: $M = 0.92$), and personal attitudes (factor 1: $M = 0.99$). The disparity between occupation and self-image was most marked for performance-related characteristics (factor 4: $M = 1.03$), the academic domain (factor 2: $M = 1.08$), and finally, gestural aspects (factor 6: $M = 1.16$).

Those on the technician course saw themselves as closest to the occupation with respect to both individual action (factor 3, technical students: $M = 0.78$; apprentices: $M = 0.98$) and resourcefulness (factor 5: technical students: $M = 0.67$; apprentices: $M = 0.96$). With respect to the other characteristics, no statistically significant differences were apparent.

Among those on the apprenticeship courses there were course-related differences with respect to performance capacity (factor 4: mechanics: $M = 0.94$; electronics: $M = 1.26$), but particularly for gestural capacity (factor 6: mechanics: $M = 0.95$; electronics, $M = 1.34$). Compared to the electronics apprentices, the apprentices in mechanics saw themselves as closer to professionals in these qualities.

IMAGES AND REALITIES OF TRAINING

In this chapter, we have examined the issue of the value attached to the occupation and the issue of autonomy from the perspective of students' motivations for their career choices. We were ourselves immediately struck by the fact that such a high number of students were not certain they would make the same choice of training if they could start again. This observation is all the more surprising in the case of the student technicians.

To be independent and employed were values generally shared by the respondents. Nonetheless, there were differences of intensity across the training courses. The apprentices in mechanics and electronics were more likely

---

[7] The higher the value, the greater the self-occupation distance.

than the technicians to say that their choice of training was determined by circumstances. This could reflect influences particular to the students questioned (in the sense that their particular course of training had been chosen as a last resort because they had no other options), but may also reflect hierarchical differences among the courses (thus, it is less costly to self-esteem to suggest that if one is pursuing a training that is comparatively undervalued, this is by force of circumstance and not because of anything to do with one's personality). Although these two levels of explanation are linked, in the first case it would primarily be a problem relating to the range of options available, while in the second it is a problem relating to the value attributed to different occupations.

Another striking result concerns representations of learning methods. An active role for the learner does not seem to be valued. These young people display a very traditional concept of learning, founded above all on practice and imitation and in which social interaction and relational skills carry little weight. In a way this is also reflected in the image they have of the employee; academic attainments, particularly expressive capacities related to communication, are perceived as having little relevance.

We must, however, draw attention to the gap that can exist between discourse and the facts. It should be noted that autonomy and mastery of one's destiny are values the respondents acknowledge while also attributing a greater effectiveness to imitative learning at the expense of anything they might derive from their classmates, yet they rely upon one another continually. No doubt these conceptions reflect a kind of "traditional official discourse" that the students believe is desirable to employ in response to investigators like us. Their teachers display a different view about the desirable approach to training. But what is the practice? Is the traditional discourse founded upon an implicit pedagogical reference? What we observed in the context of the practical work sessions seems to contradict the views the student technicians hold (or have learned to hold), without their being aware of this contradiction. In reality, relying on classmates, even when these classmates are themselves having difficulties, occurs all the time, and the availability of a third party allows valuable decentrations; examples of simple repetition and imitation were in the event quite rare, a paradoxical tension between practice and consciousness of what is developed and avowed here.

This mismatch deserves much greater attention. In a technical college, the ambitions of promoting apprentices' autonomy, their engagement in their own training, and their ability to work on a team are probably achieved through reflexive work with students on their effective practices and learning strategies. The college context is quite possibly more conducive than any other to undertaking this kind of work. This would be all the more straightforward to the extent that teachers could provide a systematic examination of the implicit and explicit didactic contracts established within each training situation. This would undoubtedly result in a change of views (on the students' side about the "traditional" class hour, and on the teachers' side about their sometimes "idealist" image) and a revision of the pedagogical models underpinning the institutional functioning of a training establishment.

CHAPTER 8

FACING UP TO THE INTRODUCTION OF NEW TECHNOLOGIES

Identifying the Dimensions Involved

As we have been able to observe at the Ecole Technique de Sainte-Croix, the introduction of new technical apparatus into a training setting and more particularly the arrival of new systems of automated manufacture trail in their wake a whole set of adaptations. These include reorganization of training programs, redefinition of teachers' job requirements, and development of new course materials, without forgetting the new budgetary resources that must be found to accommodate increasingly costly investments. Certain arrangements are relatively easy to identify and anticipate. For example, there is the need to adapt physical settings, to find a room spacious enough to accommodate the bulky equipment. The necessity of finding such a location is of course just one aspect of the problem; numerous other aspects of the institution are also affected. The majority of them are not obvious in advance; it seems to be very difficult to anticipate all the

Apprentice in a Changing Trade, pages 157–166

consequences a technological innovation will have for an institution's operation. It is only in the course of the process that the numerous questions are negotiated, that solutions are devised, and that sometimes provisional arrangements are worked out, more or less successfully.

Industrial enterprises that launch into the automation of their production are familiar enough with these kinds of organizational difficulties. What goes on within a training establishment is not so very different. They have to cope with the constraints of new technical devices that are not necessarily readily integrated into habitual practices and operations. In this respect a college is probably no more disrupted than a business but there is a significant difference in the fact that the pressure for an innovation to succeed is not felt with the same intensity as is imposed by the demands of productivity in a highly competitive industrial context.

Identifying the various parameters of the training situation that turn out to be affected by an innovation proves to be complex, in particular because new technical facilities of different kinds do not all produce the same upheavals. For example, the introduction of new software for management of computer-assisted production, like that of computer-assisted design, involved no particular problems within the college. It was as if some of these tools possessed a certain complicity with the training context, and it was possible to integrate them without any disruption. In particular, these rather flexible facilities were capable of supporting individual work as well as opportunities for more exploratory and tentative approaches that carried no significant risk. Additionally, they were often sold in combination with immediately accessible teaching materials (tutorials) and also with a maintenance contract and updating provided by suppliers who commercialize this form of software.

When the assimilation of new technology is more problematic, as was the case with the introduction of an automated production system at the college, it is important to identify the parameters affected, to analyze the more profound effects on established operating practices and the resistance inherent in this kind of a system to being "educationalized." These are the resulting disruptions that we have been able to identify in the course of our study, and we shall discuss them further in this chapter. Our view is that their identification and their anticipation to a large degree underpin the capacity of an institution to cope with them, to manage the changes introduced, and to overcome the difficulties encountered. In other terms, effective management of a technological innovation benefits from drawing upon a deep knowledge of the landscape of disruptions that it can bring in its wake and upon identification of the most appropriate responses.

Understanding this landscape leads us to a better appreciation of the mismatches that can arise between initial intentions and subsequent realization. For example, we were able to establish the value that the Ecole

Technique de Sainte-Croix attached to the installation of a flexible manufacturing system and a robotic assembly unit as training tools for the initiation of students into automated manufacture. In numerous ways it was clear to us that this was a "plus" for the college, a significant asset that helped the Ecole Technique to cement its reputation as a forward-looking establishment in the training field. And yet ultimately the training provided on this equipment came to occupy only a very modest and relatively marginal place in the courses for technicians and apprentices who for their part had only a glimpse of the process.

The causes of this kind of mismatch are assuredly numerous. Between the first outline of a project and its eventual realization, a whole set of pedagogical, organizational, regulatory, and even financial constraints come to bear upon the initial intentions. Additionally, technological innovations do not assume exactly the same meanings for all of those involved. The wide range of issues, both institutional and personal, is a source of tension and disagreement leading progressively to a reconfiguration and redefinition of the original project.

Here we describe the matters affected by the introduction of new technical facilities, drawing directly upon and synthesizing the observations made in the course of this research. We then complete this chapter with some thoughts on the effectiveness of an establishment in transforming the disruptions encountered into opportunities for social–pedagogical–technical development.

DIMENSIONS AFFECTED

Mastering Complex New Tasks or Attempting Only a First Introduction?

Traditionally, training in precision mechanics aims to develop in the apprentice a complete, assured, and very precise mastery of the machine tools with which he works, and to achieve this over a period of years. These days, this objective changes in nature when automated production equipment is involved. These complex and not necessarily completed systems consist of "open-ended" facilities that are often still in development.

Under these circumstances, the operation of such a system cannot be mastered by everyone in the same way as conventional machines. Here the technician is called upon to cope with the unforeseen, with frequent breakdowns and the diagnoses of their natures; in effect, he is required to manage uncertainty. Aiming at complete mastery of a system of this type, according to a traditional perspective, is not a realistic training objective (considerable time would have to be devoted to this end and it is not the purpose of the college to train specialists in automated production). It is nevertheless appropriate to provide the trainees with an introduction to basic principles and an initiation in the general operation of a flexible manufacturing system. The intention is thus no longer to lead students to a command of well-defined techniques, but to have them appreciate how to explore, elaborate, and anticipate manufacturing solutions by grasping the nature of the unanticipated difficulties that arise in the course of a system's operation. This transformation of learning objectives calls for the acquisition of new technical competences oriented more toward the logic of operation than toward the logic of use. It also requires adoption of a different "posture" or attitude with respect to the technical tasks to be accomplished, one more concerned with *understanding* than with error-free *success*.

The Growing Complexity of Equipment and of the Competences Required: A Threat

The complexity of the technologies involved is not just perceived in terms of a need to develop new competences. It also poses a threat. The arrival of automated production systems does raise some anxiety among those affected. New technologies can enrich the professional activity of the technician, it is true, but they can also impoverish this activity, and the fear may be expressed that one's job will become a push-button activity, which is to say a responsibility limited to supervising an entirely automated system. Is there a risk that human activity will become subordinated to the machine, or on the contrary do these tools lead to its enrichment? What level of competence does a person need to acquire to take part in this development and avoid being one of its victims? These issues are evident in some of the comments made by teachers, as well as in the ambivalent attitudes that the technical students show toward automation. Although it is difficult to anticipate the exact nature of the tasks that mechanics and technicians could be assigned in the future, it is nonetheless already possible to identify the competences and attitudes that today allow the student to get involved in and contribute to technically complex products. Principal among these are knowing how to collaborate, how to plan, simplify, or model an action or procedure, how to formulate hypotheses, consult resources, and question colleagues, and even how to join forces with another to develop a solution. To this list we could also add how to grapple with the difficulties encountered!

From an Individual to a Collective Learning Situation

An FMS unit involves more than an individual work post. It demands teamwork. Thus students find themselves needing to collaborate when working around computers and machine tools. Nonetheless, the size of these groups is greater than would be functionally required of a work team responsible for a manufacturing unit. Neither the education system nor professional training as yet possesses genuine traditions of collective learning.

Working in a group turns out to be imposed by circumstances. It does not flow from any analysis at the organizational level of the various possibilities for coordinating and distributing tasks among team members, or at the pedagogical level of the measures that might be taken to provide the relevant educational experience. Consequently, there is hardly any meta-reflection by students on the way they work, on the division of roles, or on the need to take different points of view into account. These are certainly training objectives that technical colleges could consider, not to mention opportunities to develop innovative educational approaches. Mastery of complex production facilities, probably more than any other learning context, calls for concrete organization of the deployment of collective competencies around substantial tasks and projects.

Rethinking the Didactic Sequence

The habitual approach to preparing a new course involves anticipating the class hours that need to be devoted to theoretical teaching in order to present all the elements of a system. These classroom sessions are then combined with scheduled exercises and with practical or laboratory work in the course of which students put into practice the knowledge they have acquired.

Note that this particular approach to course construction is actually to be found in several different areas of instruction.[1] It coincides with the fundamentally analytic perspective that classically underpins the organization of academic programs (Perret & Perrenoud, 1990). Its principle is to draw up a list of everything that must (or ought to) be known, and then to deal with the knowledge step by step, one bit at a time, so as to arrive finally at an understanding of the whole and an integrated command of the area concerned. In the instance where the subject matter of the training is a complex system, such as an FMS unit, this model of training has significant limitations. In particular, we have observed that it leads to the expectation that at the end of a long period of teaching students will finally possess the knowledge needed for overall management of the system. The amount of work undertaken with the general functions of the system, in contrast to exercises linked to each of its components, tends to be reduced to a minor part of the training and thus the meaning of this learning becomes obscured.

---

[1] For example, a high school course on fashion classically aims at the learning of all the different kinds of stitching, hems, and fashion, as well as exercises on trial pieces in order to achieve at the end of the year production of a small item of clothing.

Temporal Frameworks

It is additionally difficult to put a complete manufacturing system into operation, dealing with any difficulties that may be encountered and coping with unforeseen eventualities, if only a small amount of time is made available for these matters. These require substantial time slots. The temporal framework for learning activities effectively influences the way students are taught and ultimately the quality of their learning. With too little time and without allowing for externally imposed limitations such as delivery delays, but also because the college timetable is constructed that way, leads students to perceive the task as academic. What then preoccupies them is to complete it as quickly as possible and get it behind them.

Role of the Teacher

Let us now examine the teacher's role or more precisely the different roles that he[2] is led to fill in a training situation as a function of circumstances. The best-established role (at the Ecole Technique, as in all colleges in the world) is that of a scholar called upon to transmit his knowledge. For this, he looks for opportunities to "demonstrate knowledge," which in the present context means a demonstration related to the operation of automated manufacture. But computerized systems, with their share of hitches and breakdowns, constantly generate uncertainty, and in this way create situations experienced as educationally uncomfortable, as much by the teachers as by the students. Therefore, the instructor must at times cope with situations he finds challenging to his image as an experienced teacher. Now, if he were more clearly aware of the possibility, he could turn these into opportunities to demonstrate an image of a "competent professional" who, in real situations and in the pressure of the here and now, takes the risk of making shrewd guesses to identify a solution.

The exercise is then no longer a demonstration from "the front of the class," but an occasion for exploratory activity in which he will often draw upon the help of several students, thus taking on the role of the team's chief engineer rather than that of the teacher. It is often on these occasions that, quite informally, he transmits knowledge. The nature of the equipment itself, with its own complexity and limits, can occasionally lead the instructor to abandon the role of teacher and take on that of professional in the field or expert in the area. The consequence for the students is that they find they too are engaged in another role, one closer to the traditional role of the apprentice who lends a hand to the master and in return receives guidance in his own actions. We sought to identify the conditions likely to

---

[2] We use the masculine pronouns as all teachers of the Ecole Technique of Sainte-Croix were male. The only exception was a female professor teaching English.

facilitate these role changes. It turned out that in one way or another they involve a clarification of the different levels of activity involved. When the machining operation hits a difficulty, the activity momentarily changes objective; at this juncture, the difficulty becomes the focus of attention until pursuit of the initial objective can be resumed. Students must be led not only to identify these changes of level that characterize all problem-solving approaches but to clarify their nature and recognize the logic of action that inheres within them.

Cutting-Edge Equipment and the Professional Identities Involved

Keeping up-to-date with technological facilities is a constant preoccupation in professional training establishments. However, acquiring new equipment is not always possible, not just for financial reasons but also by virtue of organizational problems. It then becomes a matter of establishing what equipment is the most appropriate for teaching needs.

For initiation in the use of computer numerically controlled machines, the college chose so-called teaching equipment that machines resin rather than metal. The anticipated advantage of this type of machine is that it allows greater visibility of the operations and a reduced risk of dangers entailed in any programming errors. The teacher running the theory course stressed the educational interest these machines have for learning and doing exercises. But from the point of view of the workshop heads, responsible for the practical training of mechanics, these machines are by virtue of these same properties seen as limited compared to those used in industry; they are "unfortunately only for teaching."

The students express the same ambivalence in their own fashion; they are not convinced that their college's FMS machining unit is a "true machine" or that it prepares them for the "realities" of the industrial world. Certainly some of them are very attracted by the opportunity to make such a complex facility work, but others remain skeptical about the value of working with equipment that they will not encounter in this form in their future working lives. Perhaps this is due to the fact that they are not encouraged by the pedagogical approaches adopted to think about what they may or may not be able to transfer of their experience acquired on this technical teaching equipment to "true machines." Obviously the students do not understand why simulations are used in vocational training. This is a paradox because vocational trainers tend increasingly to rely on simulations (Pastré, 2005).

Generalist or Specialized Training?

Whatever their specific professional orientation, all the students are introduced to the operation of automated manufacturing and assembly units. The intention is to provide them, through coursework and practical exercises, a broadly based general training that for a while supersedes preoccupation with the specific occupational focus they each have along with any forms of professional competence each may previously have acquired (these competences were most likely to be in precision mechanics or electronics). We see that among the students this temporary suspension of already constructed professional identities in exchange for one that is more open, characterized by Dubar (1995) as "virtual" because it corresponds to an idealized projection rather than a reality, is a source of uncertainty and tension. The emphasis that those responsible for the various forms of training put upon "transferable" skills effectively comes into conflict with their students' desire for a recognized professional identity. This latter is the kind of identity these young people are in a hurry to adopt, one they believe is based on command of techniques and tools particular to an area of specialized activity. This need for professional recognition is probably all the stronger to the extent that these young people came to this view on the basis of a previous academic career in which they had been judged incapable of successfully pursuing a broader education.

The student-technicians seem to have little investment in these periods of general training on an FMS machining unit, without a doubt because they see this as far removed from those things that make up the central core of their specialized training. This core is the source of a relatively well-established professional identity, that of technician in mechanical construction (specialist in tools for computer-assisted design such as AUTOCAD), of computer technician (specialist in computer networks), or of production manager (specialist in software for management of computer-assisted production), reflecting the three training courses offered by the college. They tend to identify themselves as "good" professionals in whom the essential ingredient is a rigorous and precise command of the tools for a specific kind of work. Now the image of the multipurpose professional that seems to be offered appears to them artificial, indeed fraudulent. In this respect, technological development does not offer young people an attractive or encouraging prospect. On the contrary, it adversely affects the self-image and motivation of students because it makes it more difficult for them to construct the professional identity to which they aspire and through which they hope to find their place in a challenging industrial labor market.

Institutional Framework

The introduction of new equipment into a college also affects the management of both human and material resources. We have seen just how crucial is the issue of the burden placed upon teachers who are charged with a pioneer project. The investment that they need to make at particular stages in the process, especially in the installation and setting up of new devices and in their subsequent development, is in every case considerable.

The hours allowed to the teachers concerned seldom correspond to the time they effectively devote to driving the project forward, sustained at the beginning by enthusiasm or a sense of responsibility but in the end at a personal cost in terms of fatigue and weariness. This underestimation of the time budget for innovations risks holding back the pursuit of major projects, to the detriment of the quality of the training that students can ultimately be offered.

Undertaking large-scale projects involving technological facilities also raises problems of financial management. These relate both to the costs of purchasing and of technical development, but also to the budget for maintenance and operation. Innovating at the technological level thus requires that new sources of financing are sought out, often through a partnership between college and business, and this requires considerable initiative on the part of the institution's senior management. Can the leeway for local maneuver, traditionally accorded to trade schools, be maintained? Typically, it has had to be redefined and renegotiated in an intercantonal and confederal context that has led to a repositioning of the process of planning and restructuring in the area of occupational training. Paradoxical tensions are apparent in the growing responsibilities of college managements alongside an awareness on the part of the federal state that the successful introduction of technological innovations is an issue at the national level requiring coordination and indeed centralization of expertise. The current pressures for internationally recognized training qualifications are also strongly felt here.

TURNING A PROBLEM INTO A DEVELOPMENT OPPORTUNITY

As we have seen, innovation, whether on the technological or on the educational level, introduces uncertainty and disruption of various kinds. How are these consequences, so difficult to anticipate, experienced and dealt with in the context of a training establishment? Some of these effects are quickly recognized by those involved, who are then able to discuss and classify them, but others can remain unrecognized. Some problems become the focus of debates and proposals (e.g., about the need to adapt the job specifications of teachers working on a project), while others seem simply to remain hidden or else they elicit only clichéd responses (e.g., concerning the value of teaching machines).

A large-scale, technological innovation, such as introduction of a manufacturing unit into a technical college, brings with it new expectations and ideas about training. It seems that the various stakeholders involved—management, teaching staff, students—each develop their own understanding of the changes that ensue, at the risk of mismatches that may then become established between the meaning that teachers accord to a particular activity and the meaning it ultimately assumes for the students.

Under these conditions of potential mismatch, what seems to determine the effectiveness of the institution is the capacity of those involved in the training to identify the different issues involved, to make an effort to clarify the mismatches that emerge and then to reconsider aims and approaches adopted and also the meanings of the changes introduced. More generally, the effectiveness of a college resides in its capacity to achieve its objectives, central among which will be the training of its students in the use of new technologies, by readjusting strategies in response to the new internal and external conditions that arise.

Adjustments of these kinds cannot be planned in the abstract, but must be embedded in the way the college operates, with its own specific constraints, negative as well as positive. Its mode of operation can facilitate, or indeed it can obstruct, renovation within the school of its organization, its facilities, and its teaching programs. What is required in particular is taking advantage of experience, keeping informed about technological changes, developing links with industry and other partners, and identifying sources of financing. Renovation also contributes to the standing of the college, its attraction to students but also to teaching staff, and the reputation of the training that it provides.

Let us again note that the adaptive dynamic of an institution appears caught up within the interplay of various constraints, including the previous experience of students and teachers; the complex history of the evolution and recognition of occupations and professions within the context of a restructuring of professional training as a whole; and also the image, whether inviting or alarming, of the technological, industrial, and economic future towards which the present is heading. It is in this evolving and sometimes puzzling "landscape" that a technical college has to come to grips with the disruptions and tensions encountered and treat them as opportunities to keep improving the quality of its training.

CHAPTER 9

GENERAL CONCLUSIONS

Learning Spaces for Creative Initiative and the Taking of Responsibility

---

The task we gave ourselves at the outset was to observe the way in which a setting for occupational training is, in concrete terms, affected by the evolution of occupations in response to technological changes. We have focused in particular upon the introduction of new equipment for computer-assisted production.

We began this study to understand the wider landscape within which these changes occur and which shapes them. It is a complex reality that requires we take into account several levels of analysis. Our approach has involved, first of all, setting the college studied in its geographical context, the Jura Mountains, so as to describe its development and its functioning. This descriptive work allowed us to identify a set of issues as well as to pinpoint supports and obstacles related to the pursuit of training objectives. Then we chose to observe some prototypical training situations, paying attention to what was going on at the psychological level (the abilities engaged, perceptions of tasks, meanings attributed to the activities undertaken, relationship with computing tools, self-image, image of the occupation, actors' expecta-

Apprentice in a Changing Trade, pages 167–183
Copyright © 2011 by Information Age Publishing
All rights of reproduction in any form reserved.

tions) as well as on the educational level (teaching approaches, teachers' roles, management of teaching time and of teamwork, assessment practices, etc.), without forgetting the institutional dimension (organization, financing, etc.).

This investigation has required the collection of many different kinds of data, including analysis of documentary evidence on the history and organization of training techniques; interviews with senior management, teaching staff, and students; observation of exercises carried out in the workshop; video recordings of practical work sessions on automation; and a questionnaire enquiry conducted with all of the Ecole Technique de Sainte-Croix students. The analyses carried out and the results to emerge from these have formed the subject matter of the different chapters making up this book. This led, in Chapter 8, to a presentation of an overview of the various difficulties that accompany the introduction of new technologies into a place of training.

In this final chapter we concentrate on what it is that makes a technical college the setting for the emergence of innovative practices in a context of technological and occupational change. The capacities of such a setting for innovation and adaptation seem to us to be closely linked to two dimensions. One of these relates to the diversity of training situations and approaches that a technical college offers its students (learning by listening to presentations, as well as through practical work and exercises, but also by observation of someone more expert at work, the helping hand of an engineer teacher engaged in a technological development task, progressively taking over the task and responsibility for its execution while supervised by the teacher, joint work with classmates, collaborative learning, etc.). The second dimension bears on the plurality of issues that link each of these situations (the act of learning—and thus of training—aiming for cognitive but also social competence, challenging the student's self-image and his representation of the future, and the adoption of a particular identity). Let us explain these two dimensions and the manner in which they constitute resources for innovation.

THE TECHNICAL COLLEGE OFFERS A RANGE OF LEARNING SITUATIONS

Our observations reveal that the college actually offers many varied forms of training that cannot be reduced to one prevalent, if implicit, educational model. The study plans certainly distinguish between theory classes and practical sessions and embody these in the timetable. But the theory classes on occupational knowledge and the timetabled practical sessions frequently overlap, particularly when the same teacher is responsible for these two aspects of training.

"Practical training" is, moreover, not a form of teaching that should be thought of as homogeneous. It takes a variety of forms according to whether it involves classes in the workshop (where each individual moves at his own pace through the series of tasks and exercises to be completed), the execution of an individual project, collective production of a technical device, repairing or rebuilding a machine, or indeed participating in the design and development of technical facilities, either for the college itself or in response to an external order. These "practical hours" should be distinguished from the classes labeled as "practical work sessions" (or "laboratory" work) that tend to provide the opportunity to illustrate or experiment with elements that have been taught. Finally, another occasion for practical training that facilitates the integration of knowledge and skills is the "diploma work" to which the technicians devote the final semester of their training.

Corresponding to each of these forms of training is a "framing" specific to the learning activity concerned, based in particular upon the nature of the task involved (exercise, individual or collective project, development work), the type of educational support that is established, the implicit "teaching contract" that structures exchange, the individual or collective form of the work, the time frame (work to be completed in a few hours or over a course of several weeks, with or without a fixed deadline), and finally the forms of educational assessment made of the completed work.

When a new technique or new subject matter needs to be taught, the first question that arises is "where and when" within the existing curriculum and timetable. Can it be included without too much disruption to the existing landscape or does it require a rethinking of the training structure? Let us note that this process of institutional and educational assimilation takes on a form that varies according to whether the technologies to be integrated possess a certain resonance with the world of training (such as tools allowing individual learning and being sufficiently flexible and robust to tolerate the students' trials and errors without significant danger to the users), or whether they tend to be antithetical to the habitual academic game plan, for example, by imposing group activity or in requiring major maintenance and development work (e.g., with an FMS unit).

The numerous scenarios presented and the diversity of learning situations operating make it possible to identify the major educational variables and to determine on a comparative basis the most adaptive and dynamic solutions.

MULTIPLE ISSUES

Our investigation has also shown us the close overlap that exists between cognitive factors and socioemotional dimensions (relationship to technology, self-image, personal interests and aspirations, etc.), as well as with issues of identity (linked to course of study, academic orientation, occupational choice, image of the profession, area of specialization entered, etc.).

In the analysis of interactions between students presented in Chapter 5, the point at which our study reached its most "micro" level, namely the close analysis of forms of cooperation between students, we were struck by how often traces or reflections of more general issues were to be found. At the very heart of a joint problem-solving activity students sometimes embarked upon critical commentaries on the meaning of the task they were in the process of undertaking, on the conditions of its realization, on its utility for their future professional activity, or on the relevance and capabilities of the college's technical facilities compared to those they anticipated would be available in industrial enterprises.

Their observations and attitudes also convey, as we have seen, a certain ambivalence about automation; these future technicians, it is true, aspire to be associated with the design and development of facilities of fascinating complexity, but they also fear that technological innovations, developed in a world of engineers, will relegate them to machine-minding and "push-button" responsibilities. A technical device is thus not solely located within the domain of training practices; teachers and students also attribute to these new technologies meanings linked to the occupational and industrial practices that they support. The ambivalence aroused by automation along with the meanings attached to it provide opportunities to work with students on the representations that they may construct of their competences as future technicians and to explore with them the nature of the professional activities that they will in the future be able to deploy in the area of mechanical construction.

THE TECHNICAL COLLEGE MUST REMAIN A CROSSROADS

The plurality of training situations and the social and psychological dynamics played out in these are reflections of the particular kind of position occupied by a technical college, namely at the interface of two cultures, those, respectively, of the world of schooling and of the world of work. It is striking how many of the educational situations brought together in a college are marked by traditions and models of pedagogy with heterogeneous roots. Training practices derive their foundations in part from the traditions of occupations and of occupational apprenticeships, and in part from the academic model (where, for example, the aim is to aquire more general knowledge intended for subsequent application in a variety of concrete situations). In addition, the academic model of reference is periodically combined with other pedagogical standards that, depending on the occasion, encourage actors to focus their attention on one or another aspect of a training facility. For example, this is how the definition of learning objectives, working methods or even capacities for self-directed learning come by turns to grab the attention and momentarily inspire (albeit sometimes in a rather ephemeral fashion) particular practices.

The range of practices and reference models are also consequences of the different backgrounds of the teaching staff employed by the technical college. Some of them have extensive experience of professional and technical teaching and have themselves been technical college students; others come from engineering schools or polytechnics; while yet others have had university training. The role and place accorded, for example, to practical activities is not the same in each of these courses of training. In addition, there are among them wide differences in their respective experiences of the world of work.

The machinery also has a diversity of history and provenance. Different machines belong to different technological generations and arouse reactions that relate to the particular interface position each occupies between the world of "learning" machines and that of "true" industrial machines. For want of an adequate pedagogical framework to account for the particular functions of the machines the college possesses, its students lack an adequate appreciation of how training on a machine or with software that does not correspond to facilities currently available in industry can nonetheless be valuable. They aspire to familiarity with the work tools that they will find (or imagine they will find) in the industrial world. So the current practical work in the College does not help them to make appropriate comparisons, they do not actually see the "serious" purpose of what can be learned on equipment (such as an FMS teaching unit) conceived specifically for purposes of initiation and practice.[1] Courses located in commercial enterprises, currently recommended in the course of training, can certainly address the need for some contact with the reality of facilities and work in industry. But this kind of course will not on its own provide a better understanding of what does and does not need to be learned, in what manner, or on what kind of machine. The setting provided by a college that shelters under the same roof both practical and theoretical training probably remains the optimal setting for relating action to thinking about practice within a meta-cognitive perspective.

Management of the college also turns out to be at the sometimes paradoxical intersection of academic culture and business culture. When we examine the history of a technical college like that at Sainte-Croix, it is striking to observe the extent to which a business frame of mind has presided over each major step in the institution's development. The college becomes involved in large-scale projects to acquire and develop new technological

---

[1] We should note that they do, however, know that airlines train their pilots with the aid of flight simulators, and this does not undermine the seriousness of their training. Yet, although we could draw an entirely reasonable analogy between learning to pilot a plane and "piloting" a manufacturing unit, this does not cross their minds.

facilities, with the aim of expanding the training that it can offer and in this way assuring its own future. In the current climate, technical colleges such as this are now finding they have to locate themselves more and more within an academic culture. The effects of this " academization" are not entirely happy; the lack of financial resources of their own, the standardization of training curricula, the lack of flexibility in the responsibilities and time commitments of engineer-teachers, and increases in the cost of technology risk holding this type of college back in its capacity to undertake, on its own initiative, ambitious technological developments. The result of this is that purchasing devices and machines that are ready to run seems increasingly to be the most realistic approach to re-equipping. Now this is not without consequence for the quality of the training provided because it compromises the opportunities to involve students in projects of technological development, and thus deprives them of the chance to experience the highly motivating and effective learning situations that have previously been available to students.

A LABORATORY FOR OCCUPATIONAL TRAINING THAT COULD BE MORE EFFECTIVELY EXPLOITED

As we have just observed, a technical college combines under the same roof training practices that derive from several learning models, provided by people with diverse professional backgrounds, using both teaching machines and industrial machinery, and employing the latest technology as well as more conventional machine tools. This cohabitation is inevitably a source of tension and sometimes even of contradictions. The arrangements arrived at remain often precarious and provisional. Thus, for example, although training in automated production based on an FMS unit may be valued by the college management, it has ultimately been accorded only a modest place in the curriculum. Some tensions are explicit and recognized as such within the college (e.g., on the occasion of its renovation, the mechanics workshop became the focus of many debates to decide whether its reorganization should be founded on the requirements of training or on those of production). Other issues ritually receive the expected responses, while yet others remain apparently neglected (such as, for example, that of deciding if the development of simulators and teaching machines, an area in which the Ecole Technique has extensive experience, should be a project for the college to continue pursuing, whether it should be restarted on new foundations, or whether it should be abandoned).

The thesis we wish to develop here is that the plural reality of a vocational college by very reason of its heterogeneity and the tensions this can produce constitute a particularly dynamic arena for experimentation, a veritable cauldron in which tomorrow's training practices can be invented, forged, and tested. How do we take advantage of this natural "laboratory"?

It is not in reality sufficient to label a space as a laboratory to derive good advantage from it or to move forward our understanding of what goes on within it. On the basis of our experience, the principal conditions that seem to us to underpin the success of this enterprise are of two orders.

On the one hand, it is necessary to refine one's description of training situations so as to capture their true diversity and richness. The effect of the current restructuring of routes through professional training is above all to highlight organizational and institutional dimensions; thus there is discussion about the future of the dual system, about the role of full-time training, and about the provision of training according to an alternation model, together with its benefits. The weight and urgency of questions involving reexamination of the models and structures of training may, paradoxically, draw attention away from a more detailed and differentiated understanding of the learning situations actually experienced by young people. This understanding, as the current study shows, is nonetheless fundamental to a proper grasp of how high quality training operates. It is important to pursue the development of fine-grained descriptive categories that will allow us to identify the different stages of learning experienced by students attending a vocational college. A precise knowledge of the training practices employed could also ultimately contribute in its turn to the current debate surrounding the new structures of the Ecoles Professionnelles Spécialisées (specialized professional schools) that will be set up in particular in the technology, commerce and health areas.

On the other hand, our study has also revealed the need to abandon simple causal models that might otherwise allow us to suppose that, in a quasi-mechanical fashion, one approach to teaching or one form of learning is in itself sufficient. These simple causal models are unable to account for the facts observed. Educational reality is more complex than this; it is a setting in which social actors (teachers and students), with their knowledge and skills and also with their own representations of the act of learning, and their own expectations of the world of work, come together for the acquisition of competences. The backgrounds of those involved are numerous, as are their concerns and their strategies. All these elements, both objective and subjective, deserve attention because in one way or another they influence the dynamics of training situations and shape their effectiveness, whatever teaching approach happens to be adopted.

MARKERS FOR ACTION

In this "laboratory" that is a technical college, several paths of action emerged in our research. Here we outline four thematic axes with a view to deepening our understanding of both the goals of learning situations and the means of action that strengthen the effectiveness of these training settings.

Axis 1: Encouraging Student Reflection on Ways of Learning Insofar as These Might Vary According to the Knowledge (or Skills) Targeted

Technical college students have the opportunity to learn their trade with teachers, pursuing different professional routes and doing so, as we have seen, in various learning situations. Reflecting upon the plurality of practices and ideas about training that they encounter should, in our view, form an integral part of their curriculum. The goal should be to help them to identify what can and cannot be learned, on the basis of what approach, with whom, and at what stage.

The life of the college itself is in this sense a privileged setting for socialization into the situations that young people will encounter, in one form or another, beyond their initial training. It is for them an opportunity to become acquainted with ideas about training that are current in the professional world and that vary with the traditions of different work settings. The place accorded to on-the-job training, to resourcefulness, to allowing for mistakes, to the explanations of an elder, to documentary resources, or to collaboration between learners in fact varies from one setting to another. It is also a matter of appreciating the particular character of learning tools and work tools, the basis for the organization of a college workshop, the role of a period of training spent in a commercial enterprise, etc., in order that these young people can better understand their learning environment and so that they can better exploit the different resources available in a training situation and at work (Perret-Clermont & Perret, 2006).

Of course, this kind of reflection cannot be conducted with students in an abstract fashion. It needs to draw upon situations they have experienced. In this respect, a technical college has significant assets on which it can draw to introduce young people to the realities of both training and work, based on concrete and varied experiences. All the opportunities that arise in the daily life of the college are available. Critical incidents such as, for example, tasks judged to be too difficult by the students, a piece of software criticized for being too old, or the final assessment of work can all provide starting points for productive discussion. Individual interviews can also, in some cases, encourage a clarification of aims, expectations, and recommended approaches (Vermersch, 1994; Perraudeau, 1998). Across these various situations of dialogue, the goal is to gain a sufficient grasp of the aims pursued and the means employed by constructing effective and conscious knowledge and competences, which is to say abilities that are more readily adjusted, adaptable, socializable, and transmissible.

The interviews conducted with small groups of students following the practical work sessions in which they had been filmed showed us the extent to which they are ready and willing to talk about their practices, to discuss the benefits and limitations of particular technical facilities, and to cast a critical eye upon their own approaches to work in any situation, These positive reactions lead us to think that there should be no major obstacle to the development of this kind of activity. The approach could draw upon the "report-evaluation" procedure recommended by Wiel (1992) in the context of French professional high schools, a procedure that allows students to analyze their own learning situations and to suggest improvements in these.

Axis 2: Paying Attention to the Construction of Professional Identities as Well as the Competences to Be Acquired

We have established the presence among these young people of a need to assert the specificity of their vocational orientation and their professional specialization. In fact, these students strongly value the knowledge and skills, as well as the working tools, that they regard as belonging to the core of their future occupation. Other technical knowledge that might be taught, perhaps less specialized or else common to different occupations, seems to them peripheral and consequently less engaging.

This inclination among these young people to seek out confirmation of their identity by signaling a choice of occupation turns out to contradict the preoccupations of their elders, those responsible for their training who talk to them about multitasking and flexibility! Certainly the future technicians know that more than half of them, either by choice or by force of circumstance, will ultimately enter into forms of employment for which their training will not specifically have prepared them. However, this relatively open occupational horizon does not for the time being seem to lessen their need to assert a specific identity. For these young people, multipurpose employment is a given, more of an imposition than a choice, and not a constituent element of a revitalized professional identity and nor is it thought of as such.

Thus, if we wish to promote training contexts that guarantee the development of general and transferable competences, or of multipurpose skills that allow flexibility, then a better understanding of the role of a well-defined professional identity is desirable. It is not certain that young people in training can, as readily as others may think, abandon the markers that provide professions with their traditional points of reference. A working hypothesis is that the reactions observed are signs of a transitional situation in which the tradition of circumscribed occupations (with their particular specializations) coexist with the emergence of new professional identities responding to a logic of competence (Zarifian, 1996). Obviously, this question of the relation to occupations, in the developing context of vocational colleges that are in the process of becoming the professional "écoles supérieures" of the future, merits deeper investigation.

We might also ask how young people who embark on new training paths and thus paths by definition without tradition, such as, for example, training for the role of media technician, construct their professional identities. With whom do such young people identify? How are they going to manage the development (or survival?) of their profession? Is it instead the case that the idea of a "profession" itself is in the process of evolution toward a different kind of relationship with competence, is more individualistic and based less on identification with an occupational group, but centered more on promoting the value of a portfolio of personal experience?

Axis 3: Taking into Account Students' Academic Backgrounds and Their Relationship to Knowledge

To reinvest vocational learning with value, the training arena in Switzerland today is drawing attention to the possibility that has just opened up for young people to progress, via the route of vocational baccalaureate, to tertiary-level training in a specialized further education college or university of applied sciences.[2] The current evolution of the terminology is in this respect significant. For example, a recent campaign to promote careers in mechanics addressed itself to *students* in mechanics whereas previously they had been referred to as *apprentices*.

Sadly, it is not certain that the prospect of extended studies is appealing to young people. We cannot ignore the large number of students who were convinced by the school that academic knowledge was "not for them" (Perret-Clermont & Bell, 1985; Gosling, 1992; Charlot, 1999; Lamamra & Masdonati, 2009). Too many young people who have had hammered into them at various stages throughout their compulsory education (through the influence of assessments, discouraging comments, and finally through streaming and selection from the age of 12 and up) that they were not fit for extended studies. Therefore, how can this academically derived image of a degraded self be reconciled with the requirements of occupations that require ever more extended training and a capacity to acquire new knowledge? Can these young people really be motivated by the prospect of undertaking extended professional training all the way through to a university of applied sciences? What psychological or educational conditions would allow it?

As Wiel (1992) established in a book devoted to the French professional high school, "for want of recognising the consequences of a feeling of academic failure, which is to say of recognising what is called here the syndrome of academic failure, and freeing students from it, training in the

---

[2] In fact, it was already possible for the best apprentices to enter a "Technicum" and then the Ecole Polytechnique Fédérale or a university science faculty, but this remains the exception. Currently, however, the doors are open wider and encouragement is more explicit.

professional high school is severely hampered by problems of academic rejection which are not sufficiently taken into account." We have established that in the technical college many teachers and instructors are conscious of the key role that they can play in restoring the confidence of their students in their own capacity to learn. However, this support task is burdensome; it requires daily vigilance to guide and assist, step by step, each progression and convince the learner of his capacities. This training task, which becomes an educational task, has become the object of particular attention in the context of pre-apprenticeship classes (Zittoun, 2006). But much is still to be done to pin down the social and psychological conditions that allow young people to reengage with their development free from the syndrome of academic failure (Perret-Clermont, Resnick, Zittoun, & Burge, 2004).

Axis 4: Reconsidering the Classic Master–Apprentice Relationship in a Context of Technological Development

We have seen how information technologies, at once both complex and liable to breakdown, in some way disturb the classical master–apprentice or teacher-taught relationships. From time to time it happens that, faced with a problem, the teacher—who does not necessarily at first sight have access to the right answer—joins with the students in the search for a solution. In our view these changes in the role of the teacher right in the middle of the activity deserve careful attention; these are not just mishaps along the trail but special opportunities ripe for pedagogical exploitation. Certainly they do not correspond to the classic and often rather simplified forms we have inherited from the tradition of occupational learning. These are distinct formative moments in which the pedagogical relationship is experienced not simply as a process of instruction and practice but also as a number of exploratory episodes underpinned by coaching or collaboration. Our hypothesis is that these sometimes very rapid transitions (micro-alternations) from one role to another, far from being periods of incoherence in the process of training, perform instead a facilitative function in the passage of young people from the status of *student* (in relation to a knowledgeable master) to that of responsible *professional* (entering into the company of experts undertaking projects and searching for solutions). To the outside observer the young person becomes, little by little, a fully qualified participant in a professional activity (Lave, 1991).

The introduction of increasingly computerized technical devices, along with the changes in professional practice that arise from these, locates the issue of training, today more than ever, in the capacity to provide young people with opportunities to tackle real problems, to get involved in substantial projects, to cope with technical and organizational difficulties, to manage conflicts and to exercise responsibility. This learning of an occupation does require the presence of older experts, professionals ready to adopt the posture of a team leader or project director whose aim is not so much to make others learn (in the abstract academic sense) but to initiate them into the art of the occupation by progressive participation in its realization. It is necessary for this art to be presented so that it can be seen in all its complexity and totality, both in the urgency of action and in more reflective moments of consideration and planning. Placements in companies, within the framework of an alternation model of training, can certainly also provide this kind of opportunity. But a college that knows how to involve such professionals is without doubt a potent setting for providing learners in the course of action ("just in time") to think about the activity being undertaken, voicing these thoughts, comparing problems and answers found, honing diagnostic approaches, and evaluating solutions tried.

Several times we observed these kinds of situations in which teachers and students, side by side, dealt with a task that had turned out to be more complex than anticipated. Unfortunately, these opportunities for training seemed to us to occupy only a more or less fortuitous place on the margins of the curriculum rather than being deliberately placed at its heart. It was sometimes even entirely outside the teaching program that these situations unfolded, when, for example, teachers and students worked to install or develop new technical equipment for subsequent use in practical work. These collaborative activities are thus often located in transitional periods devoted to bringing into operation equipment around which a classical teaching relationship can subsequently be reestablished.

We also need to mention another period of training that brings into play a truly supportive educational relationship. This relates to the final weeks at the end of their studies, when the technicians devote themselves to the preparation of their diploma work. A great deal is invested in this individually executed work, in the tradition of a masterpiece that at the end of a course of training displays in an overt fashion the competences that have been acquired. The work undertaken is diverse and often creative. This can present problems of supervision. In some areas, technicians at the end of their training have effectively become better informed than their teachers. New, more horizontal pedagogical relationships are then likely to be established.

The question that presents itself is the following: how can one favor the deployment of those significant training opportunities that we have been able to identify? How can they be assigned a less peripheral status? Note that questions of these kinds are not exclusive to the technical college sector. The specialized high schools, which now find themselves accorded an applied research mission, are likewise expected to devise training approaches that are integrated with research and development activities. In all these cases it is a matter of perfecting the "shape" of training in which both the product envisaged and the learning it occasions are accorded importance.

The experience that has been accumulated over a period of many years by schools of engineering deserves to be observed and documented more systematically so that we may identify the basic conditions under which it is both possible and desirable to combine the activities of training and research. We should also examine the degree to which "junior enterprise" experiences do or do not serve the same ends and, if they do, under what conditions.

THE CONTRIBUTIONS OF PROFESSIONAL TRAINING TO GENERAL AND UNIVERSITY TEACHING

In conclusion, we advocate the thesis that the future of vocational colleges does not reside in their capacity to reproduce the traditional academic model but in the affirmation and development of their specificity, something that, given the current tensions in the world of training, risks being neglected. It is in fact a substantial asset to be able, with a degree of flexibility that is not possible in a commercial work setting, to manage periods and forms of training that bring together, around complex tasks and machinery, teachers and students engaged sometimes in conventional teaching situations, sometimes in situations of imitation (modeling), coaching, support, or collaboration. Moreover, each of these situations offers opportunities for reflexive analysis of the experience for both explanation and adaptation.

It is interesting to note that in college this variety of the "faces" that teaching assumes does not in the first place arise from an educational or ideological choice, but from constraints imposed by the technical facilities themselves. These do, it is true, form part of the subject matter of the teaching, entities whose logic and functions are matters to be covered in the course of teaching, but these are also devices to be mastered, devices that cannot always be left to operate on their own. In the area of technical knowledge, the teacher is at the same time also a professional in the sense that he may be called upon to demonstrate his skills, not just his knowledge. The presence of the machine, in a four-way teaching relationship that has normally been thought of as only three-way—teacher–student–knowledge—plays a decisive role here. It provides students with the sight of a professional in action, someone who is able to bring all his competence, his understanding of the situation, and his decision-making and planning capacities to bear.

Our study enabled us to enlarge our understanding of the processes by which technical skills are transmitted, appropriated, and acquired. It also allowed us to explore different learning contexts in which imitation, support for action, explanation, confrontation of viewpoints, collaboration, resourcefulness, and trial and error learning may all be at work. While not neglecting the strictly cognitive dimension to these skills, we were particularly interested in the characteristics of social interactions, in the weft and weave of these interactions into the daily life of a college and their role in knitting together all the competences acquired. A particular technical skill, probably more visible than any piece of knowledge, is not learned in isolation. Post-Piagetian research in social psychology on the construction of knowledge, research on the didactics of different disciplines, and also work inspired by Vygotsky's sociohistorical psychology, focusing on the asymmetrical relationships of guidance, tutoring, and mediation (Dumas & Weil-Barais, 1998), have all encouraged us to pay greater attention to the social situation in which knowledge and skills are deployed.

We have been struck by the degree to which the life of a technical college would quite simply not be possible without continual "horizontal" collaboration at every level. These include teachers taking on responsibility for the fulfillment of technological and educational innovation projects, technical help exchanged among adults and among young people, joint activity of teachers and several students to prepare, in advance of practical classes, the technical equipment on which they will later hold classes. Latour (1996) has taught us the extent to which the production of knowledge occurs through ajustments of technical mediation that enable successive movements of transformations. Technical teaching cannot avoid providing its students with an experience of these technical transformations and adjustments, compared to general or university teaching, which too often are content merely to present the finished product, issued out of abstractions that claim to be knowledge, while the learners do not necessarily have access to the source or production of this knowledge. In our opinion, it is a great shame that technical teaching, by becoming more scholarly and academic, will lose this quality. On the contrary, we should pay particular attention to it and ensure that it is even more deeply rooted in reflexive activities on the technological changes. Even universities could take inspiration from this.

The issue of skills and their transmission arises in numerous training situations. Here we undertook an inquiry into the skills that a technician in mechanical construction needs to acquire these days, but the issue certainly reaches well beyond this particular area of activity. It is posed in any training domain that seeks to equip learners for action, something that also happens to be true for numerous kinds of training found in the university arena (Mandl, Gruber, & Renkl, 1996). This is because understanding and action are so interdependent (Piaget, 1974a, 1974b). "Our theoreticians are thus vis à vis their theory in exactly the same position as our worker searching for a way to make his part by operating his lathe. Both are situated, both have a practice, both have a physical location, both need to talk, need documents, advice, colleagues, and instruments. The proof is that mathematicians in Cambridge, not managing to solve equations, are obliged to go and find Einstein in Germany, to learn from him directly the tricks necessary to make the calculations. From this point of view they conduct themselves exactly as journeymen learning their manual skills from a master. Likewise to produce a theory one needs a trained body, adapted locations, discussion groups and habits embedded in the body by long training"[3] (Latour, 1996, p. 136). All intellectual work, even that regarded as the most theoretical, turns out to be inseparable from command of know-hows and skills, a point that Hutmacher (1996) also makes: "Most intellectual workers know that they are artisans who read, think, analyse, formulate, write, take time, contemplate the method, expend effort. But there is in our heritage a curious tendency to hide this laborious dimension…" (p. 18).

General teaching requires from its students mastery of a set of practices (reading, writing, problem solving) but provides little indication of the approaches and actions that underlie this mastery. In a high school context, for example, how many students have seen their French teacher at work writing a text, or their mathematics teacher solving a real mathematical problem? In the context of university teaching, at what point in the course do students (finally) become involved in the thinking and work of their teachers who are also (and primarily) researchers?

Recommending the acquisition not just of knowledge but also of competences does not signify here a "vocationalization" of university training. It is to recognize that all intellectual activity, and particularly the research activity that is characteristic of the world of high schools and advanced teaching, is inseparable from often very concrete skills. These skills are partly concerned on the one hand with the activity of learning (taking advantage of others' experience, that of earlier generations, the innovations of peers or one's juniors) and on the other with professional or scientific activity (focusing, adjusting, transforming, observing, transcribing, evaluating, etc.). The skills that belong to the occupation of "student" (Coulon, 1997) are often explicit, notably in the form of guidebooks intended for students. "How to Prepare a Dissertation" by Fragnière (2009) is an excellent example. Most often students acquire this knowledge by following someone more expert than themselves, by seeking out the advice of professors (or more often their assistants and more junior colleagues) about scientific skills.

In conclusion, what we derive from these latter more general considerations about the transmission of knowledge in different contexts can be summarized as follows:

- In the first place, the educational models that underlie on the one hand academic teaching (in principle, general) and on the other hand occupational learning (based on an alternation between theory and practice) do not derive from realities that are so distinct and segregated that they could justifiably be represented in any simple

---
[3] Our translation.

educational model. Training practices are more tangled. In fact, just as teaching sessions in a sometimes very classic form are very much present in a vocational college, so can learning with a master-craftsman, sometimes as supporter, sometimes as guide, also be observed in those universities with the highest academic reputations.

- Several authors draw their inspiration from the traditional model of occupational learning (apprenticeship) in thinking about academic training situations (learning). Collins, Brown, and Newman's (1989) concept of *cognitive apprenticeship*, in particular, finds an important echo in the field of sciences and education and has inspired numerous works. The risk in this kind of borrowing is to see it frozen in a model of functions that is more prescriptive than descriptive, and yet the contribution of professional training to teaching in general can extend well beyond the importation of a few pedagogical principles.

- In Switzerland, the settings for occupational training that are provided by the vocational colleges (Ecoles de métiers) and the Universities of Applied Sciences find themselves, in terms of educational supervision and technological facilities, in a particularly favorable position to provide high-quality training. We can see in this a reflection of the social and political attention from which this sector has benefited, most particularly during periods of crisis and adaptation imposed by socioeconomic developments. The conditions now seem to be established for the deployment of innovative training practices and for experimenting with educational strategies capable of developing the competences that will allow young people not merely to cope with the changes already in motion but also that they become agents of the changes taking place in the working world.

- As "open-air" educational laboratories, the vocational colleges potentially represent a resource, a fertile ground for reflection, for educational innovations and for seeing what could be of value across all educational sectors. But this will not happen unless real scope for thought about professional action, about pedagogical action, about the existential quests of young people and their fundamental need to learn is developed in these places.

In the different sectors of our training system but also of our society we will come to understand in greater depth the reciprocal interdependence between technological development and scientific advances. We will also need to rediscover that neither one nor the other is possible outside the human relationships that support them. Here also the interdependence is considerable. It is in addition a matter of dynamic processes. Technology evolves, but so do interpersonal and social relations, and—need it be mentioned?—authentic science does not produce static knowledge (this kind of reified knowledge is always rapidly outdated); it produces methods of observation and transcription, of experimentation, analysis and interpretation, which is to say forms of knowledge that are processes. To know is a dynamic, multidimensional act. It is both an act of memory (the present is related to transformations of past experience) and an act of sharing in the lessons learned in the trials and tribulations of human activity. Knowledge is created and transmitted in the relational networks that link us to the past (the current state of our knowledge is the fruit of experience of those who came before us) and locate us in the present (my knowledge only exists socially if my contemporaries acknowledge it in me). Learning is an activity that takes place at the heart of human relations. Colleges and universities will always gain from the rediscovery within themselves of new constellations creating the triple development of society, science, and technology. These places of training can then understand anew each time that their first responsibility is to create spaces that can support in safety the exercise of both action and thought. Such spaces, if they offer interpersonal relationships open to debate, to questioning, to constructive criticism, to argument action and joint work then become settings for creative initiative and the taking of responsibility. When the door to imagination is open within the protective cocoon of a safe place, technology enchants and becomes art.

REFERENCES

Achtenhagen, F. (2003). Problems of authentic instruction and learning. *Technology, Instruction, Cognition, and Learning, 1,* 253–273.

Amos, J. (2001a). De nouveaux souffles pour l'alternance? *Panorama, 1,* 14–15.

Amos, J. (2001b). La question de l'alternance en France. *Panorama, 1,* 16–17.

Ashmore, R.-D., & Del Broca, F.-K. (1986). *The social psychology of female–male relations. a critical analysis of central concepts.* New York: Academic Press.

ASM. (1996). *Réforme des apprentissages.* Winterthur: Association patronale suisse de l'industrie des machines.

Aumont, B., & Mesnier, P.-M. (1992). *L'acte d'apprendre.* Paris : Presses Universitaires de France.

Aussenac, A. (1987). Des erreurs significatives dans les pratiques des machines-outils à commande numérique et des dessins spontanés. In P. Rabardel & A. Weill-Fassina (Eds.), *Le dessin technique: apprentissage, utilisation, évolutions.* Paris: Hermès.

Bailey, T. R., Hugues, K. L. Moore, D. T. (2004). *Working knowledge: Work-based learning and education reform.* New York: RoutledgeFalmer.

Barbot, M.-J., & Camatarri, G. (1999). *Autonomie et apprentissage. L'innovation dans la formation.* Paris: Presses Universitaires de France.

Barcet, A., Le Bas, C., & Mercier, C. (1983). Dynamique du changement technique et transformation des savoir-faire de production. *La Documentation Française* (8), 51–75.

Barth, B.-M. (1994). *Le savoir en construction : former à une pédagogie de la compréhension*. Paris: Retz.

Bearison, D. J. (1991). *Interactional contexts of cognitive developpement: Piagetian approaches to sociogenesis*. Norwood, NJ: Ablex.

Beauvois, J.-L. (1982). Théories implicites de la personnalité, évaluation et reproduction idéologique. *L'année psychologique, 82*, 513–536.

Bell, N., Grossen, M., & Perret-Clermont, A. N. (1985). Sociocognitive conflict and intellectual growth. In M. W. Berkowitz (Ed.), *Peer conflict and psychological growth*. San Francisco: Jossey-Bass.

Benavente, A., da Costa, A. F., Machado, F. L., & Neves, M. C. (1993). *De l'autre côté de l'école*. Berne: Peter Lang.

Billett, S. (2002). Critiquing workplace learning discourses: Participation and continuity at work *Studies in the Education of Adults, 34*(1), 56–67.

Billett, S. Fenwick, T., & Somerville, M. (2006). *Work, subjectivity and learning: Understanding learning through working life*. Dordrecht: Springer.

Blanc, C., Michel, D., Villard, I., & Perret-Clermont, A. N. (1994). *Interactions sociales et transmission des savoirs techniques* (Documents de recherche No 1). Séminaire de psychologie, Université de Neuchâtel.

Blatti, S. (1992). *La dimension humaine dans la mise en place d'un système CIM. Les pratiques méthodologiques d'autres pays d'Europe* (Document du Centre CIM de Suisse Occidentale, Givisiez).

Blatti, S., Mezghiche, H., Neuvecelle, D. (1992). *Formation et gestion des ressources humaines dans les entreprises en mutation technologique* (Rapport final du projet CERS No2356.1).

Blaye, A. (1989). Nature et effets des opposition dans des situations de corésolution de problèmes entre pairs. In N. Bednarz & C. Garnier (Eds.), *Construction des savoirs. Obstacles et Conflits*. Québec: Les Editions Agence d'Arc.

Blaye, A., Light, P., & Rubstov, V. (1992). Collaborative learning at the computer; how social processes "interface" with human–computer interaction. *European Journal of Psychology of Education, 7*(4), 257–268.

Brossard, M., & Wargnier, P. (1993). Rôle de certaines variables contextuelles sur le fonctionnement cognitif des élèves en situation scolaire. *Bulletin de Psychologie, XLVI*(412), 703–709.

Brucy, G., & Troger, V. (2000). Un siècle de formation professionnelle en France : la parenthèse scolaire? *Revue Française de Pédagogie, 131*, 9-21.

Bruner, J. S. (1983). *Le développement de l'enfant: savoir faire, savoir dire*. Paris: Presses Universitaires de France.

Carré, P. (2006). *L'apprenance: vers un nouveau rapport au savoir*. Paris: Dunod.

Carré, P., Moisan, A., & Poisson, D. (1997). *L'autoformation*. Paris: Presses Universitaires de France.

Carugati, F., Emiliani, F., & Palmonari, A. (1981). *Tenter le possible. Une expérience de socialisation d'adolescents*. Berne: Peter Lang.

Carugati, F., & Perret-Clermont, A. N. (2003). La perspectiva psicosocial: intersubjectividad y contrato didáctico. In C. Pontecorvo (Ed.), *Manual de psicología de la educación* (pp. 43–65). Madrid: Editorial Popular.

Cassagnes-Brouquet, S. (2010). *Le monde des métiers au Moyen Age: Artisans et marchands*. Rennes: Éditeur Ouest-France.

Charlot, B. (1999). *Le rapport au savoir en milieu populaire. Une recherche dans les lycées professionnels de banlieue.* Paris: Anthropos.

CIM/CCSO. (1993). Présentation des Centres d'appui CIM. *Document de travail.*

Clot, Y. (1995). *Le travail sans l'homme.* Paris: La Découverte.

Clot, Y. (1999). *La fonction psychologique du travail.* Paris: Presses Universitaires de France.

Cole, M. (1995). Cultural-historical psychology : a meso-genetic approach. In L. M. W. Martin, M. Nelson, & E. Tobach (Eds.), *Sociocultural psychology. Theory and practice of doing and knowing.* Cambridge, UK: Cambridge University Press.

Collins, A., Brown, J. S., & Newman, S. (1989). Cognitive apprenticeship : Teaching the crafts of reading, writing and mathematics. In L. B. Resnick (Ed.), *Knowing, learning, and instruction.* Hillsdale, NJ: Erlbaum.

Coulon, A. (1997). *Le métier d'étudiant.* Paris: Presses Universitaires de France.

Crevoisier, O. (1993). *Industrie et région: les milieux innovateurs de l'Arc jurassien.* Neuchâtel: EDES, Division économique et sociale. Université de Neuchâtel.

Crevoisier, O., Fragomichelakis, M., Hainard, F., & Maillat, D. (1996). *La dynamique des savoir-faire industriels.* Zürich: Editions Seismo.

Crook, C. (1995). On resourcing a concern for collaboration within weer interaction. *Cognition and Instruction [Special Issue: Processes and products of collaborative problem solving : some interdisciplinary perspectives], 13*(4), 541–547.

Darnon, C., Butera, F., & Mugny, G. (2008). *Des conflits pour apprendre.* Grenoble: Presses Universitaires de Grenoble.

De Castéra, B. (1988). *Le compagnonnage.* Paris: Presses Universitaires de France.

Deschamps, J.-C., & Clémence, A. (1987). *L'explication quotidienne.* Fribourg: DelVal.

Dewey, J. (1938). *Experience and education.* New York: Macmillan.

Dillenbourg, P., Baker, M., Blay, A., & O'Malley, C. (1996). The evolution of research on collaborative learning. In S. P. Reinmann (Ed.), *Learning in humans and machines* (pp. 189–211). London: Pergamon.

Doise, W., Clémence, A., & Lorenzi-Cioldi, F. (1992). *Représentations sociales et analyses de données.* Grenoble: Presses universitaires de Grenoble.

Doise, W., & Mugny, G. (1981). *Le développement social de l'intelligence dans l'interaction sociale.* Paris: Interéditions.

Donaldson, M. (1978). *Children's minds.* New York: W.W. Norton.

Dubar, C. (1995). *La socialisation. Construction des identités sociales et professionnelles.* Paris: Armand Colin.

Dubar, C. (2000). *La crise des identités. L'interprétation d'une mutation.* Paris: Presses Universitaires de France.

Dubois, N. (1988). *La psychologie du contrôle.* Grenoble: Presses Universitaires de Grenoble.

Dubois, N. (2003). *Sociocognitive approach to social norms.* London: Routledge.

Dubs, R (2007). Rapport d'expertise sur les questions concernant la formation professionnelle en Suisse. Berne: HEP Verlag.

Dugon, A. (1993). *Le concept GPAO à l'Ecole Technique de Sainte-Croix. Document interne.* Sainte-Croix: Ecole Technique de Sainte-Croix.

Dumas, A., & Weil-Barais, A. (Eds.). (1998). *Tutelle et médiation dans l'éducation scientifique.* Berne: Peter Lang.

Durand, M. & Fabre, M. (Eds.). (2007). Les *situations de formation entre savoirs, problèmes et activités.* Paris: L'Harmattan.

Durant, M., & Filliettaz, L. (Eds.). (2009). *Travail et formation des adultes.* Paris: PUF.

Ebel, K. H. (1989). L'usine automatisée a besoin de la main de l'homme. *Revue internationale du Travail, 128*(5).

Emler, N., & Valiant, G. (1982). Social interaction and cognitive conflict in the development of spatial coordination. *British Journal of Psychology, 73,* 295–303.

Engeström, Y., & Middleton, D. (Eds.). (1996). *Cognition and communication at work.* Cambridge, UK: Cambridge University Press.

Ferrand, J.-L., Le Goff, J.-P., Malglaive, G., & Orofiamma, R. (1987). *Quelle pédagogie pour les nouvelles technologies?* Paris: La Documentation Française.

Filliettaz, L. (2008). Compétences professionnelles et compétences langagières en situation de risque: La régulation langagière d'un « événement » en milieu industriel. *Langage et Société, 125,* 11–34.

Filliettaz, L. (2009a). Les discours de consignes en formation professionnelle initiale: une approche linguistique et interactionnelle. *Education & Didactique, 3*(1), 91–119.

Filliettaz, L. (2009b). Les formes de didactisation des instruments de travail en formation professionnelle initiale. *Travail et Apprentissages: Revue de didactique professionnelle, 4,* 26–56.

Filliettaz, L., & Bronckart, J.-P. (Eds.). (2005). *L'analyse des actions et des discours en situation de travail. Concepts, méthodes et applications.* Louvain-La-Neuve: Peeters, Coll. Bibliothèque des Cahiers de l'Institut de Linguistique de Louvain.

Filliettaz, L., de Saint-Georges, I. & Duc, B. (2008). Vos mains sont intelligentes!: Interactions en formation professionnelle initiale. *Université de Genève: Cahiers de la Section des Sciences de l'Education,* 117.

Flahaut, F. (1978). *La parole intermédiaire.* Paris: Le Seuil.

Flammer, A. (1992). Secondary control in an individual-centered and in a group-centered culture. In W. Meeus & M. D. Goode (Eds.), *Adolescence, careers and cultures* (pp. 134–141). Berlin: De Gruyter.

Flammer, A. (1994). Developmental analysis of control beliefs. In A. Bandura (Ed.), *Self-efficacy in changing societies.* Cambridge, UK: Cambridge University Press.

Flammer, A., & Grob, A. (1994). Kontrollmeinung, ihre Begründungen und autobiographisches Errinern. *Zeitschrift für experimentelle und angewandte Psychologie, 41,* 17–38.

Forman, E. A., & McPhail, J. (1993). Vygotskian perspective on children›s collaborative problem-solving activities. In E. A. Forman & N. Minick & C. A. Stone (Eds.), *Contexts for learning: Sociocultural dynamics in chidren's development.* New York: Oxford University Press.

Fragnière, J. P. (2009). *Comment réussir un mémoire.* Paris: Dunod.

Fragomichelakis, M. (1994). Culture technique et développement régional. Les savoir-faire dans l'Arc jurassien. *Cahiers de l'Institut de Sociologie et de Science Politique* (15), Université de Neuchâtel.

Garduno Rubio, T. (1996). *Action interaction et réflexion dans la conception et la réalisation d'une expérience pédagogique: l'Ecole Paidos à Mexico.* Neuchâtel: Editions EDES, Dossiers de Psychologie, Université de Neuchâtel.

Gilly, M. (1980). *Maître-élève. Rôles et représentations sociales.* Paris: Presses Universitaires de France.

Gilly, M., Fraisse, J., & Roux, J.-P. (1988). Résolutions de problèmes en dyades et progrès cognitifs chez des enfants de 11 à 13 ans: dynamiques interactives et socio-cognitives. In A.-N. Perret-Clermont & M. Nicolet (Eds.), *Interagir et connaître* (pp. 73–92). Cousset: Editions Delval (en réédition chez L'Harmattan).

Gindroz, J.-P. (2009). *Introduction aux problématiques de la formation professionnelle.* Dossiers de psychologie et éducation. Université de Neuchâtel, No. 64.

Girod, R. (Ed.). (1990). *Problèmes actuels de la formation professionnelle en Suisse.* Lausanne: Cahiers du Centre d'Etudes de la Politique Sociale.

Golay Schilter, D. (1995). *Le système Suisse de formation professionnelle: Repères généraux* (Documents de recherche No. 3). Séminaire de psychologie, Université de Neuchâtel.

Golay Schilter, D. (1995). *Regards sur l'organisation et les enjeux de l'enseignement à l'école technique de Ste-Croix* (Documents de recherche No. 4). Séminaire de psychologie, Université de Neuchâtel.

Golay Schilter, D. (1997). *Apprendre la fabrication assistée par ordinateur. Sens, enjeux et rapport aux outils* (Documents de recherche No. 13). Séminaire de psychologie, Université de Neuchâtel.

Golay Schilter, D., Perret-Clermont, A. N., Perret, J.-F., De Guglielmo, F., & Chavey, J.-P. (1997). *Aux prises avec l'informatique industrielle : collaboration et démarches de travail chez des élèves techniciens* (Documents de recherche No. 7). Séminaire de psychologie, Université de Neuchâtel.

Gosling, P. (1992). *Qui est responsable de l'échec scolaire?: Représentations sociales, attributions et rôle d'enseignant.* Paris: Presses Universitaires de France.

Greenfield, P. (1993). Representational competence in shared symbol systems : electronic media from radio to video games. In R. R. Cocking & K. A. Renninger (Eds.), *The development and meaning of psychological distance* (pp. 161–183). New York:Erlbaum.

Greenfield, P. (1994). Effects of interactive entertainment technologies on development. *Journal of Applied Developmental Psychology, 15*(1).

Grossen, M. (1988). *La construction de l'intersubjectivité en situation de test.* Neuchâtel: Dossiers de psychologie. Université de Neuchâtel.

Grossen, M., Liengme Bessire, M. J., & Perret-Clermont, A. N. (1997). Construction de l'interaction et dynamiques socio-cognitives. In M. Grossen & B. Py (Eds.), *Pratiques sociales et médiations symboliques* (pp. 221–247). Berne: Peter Lang.

Hakkarainen, K., Palonen, T., Paavola, S., & Lethinen, E. (2004). *Communities of networked expertise: Professional and educational perspectives.* Amsterdam: Elsevier.

Hamilton, S. F. (1987). Apprenticeship as a transition to adulthood in West Germany. *American Journal of Education, 95*(2), 314–345.

Hamilton, S. F. (1994). Social roles for youth: Interventions in unemployment. In A. C. Peterson & J. T. Mortimer (Eds.), *Youth unemployment and society.* Cambridge, UK: Cambridge University Press.

Hamilton, S. F., & Hamilton, M. A. (1994). Schools and workplaces: Partners in the transition. *Theory into Practice, 33*(4), 242–248.

Hatchuel, A., & Molet, H. (1992). Les obscurs sentiers de l'efficacité. In D. Linhart & J. Perriault & A. Fouquet (Eds.), *Le travail en puces*. Paris: Presses Universitaires de France.

Hanhart, S., & Schultz, H. R. (1998). *La formation des apprentis en Suisse. Coûts et financement*. Lausanne-Paris: Delachaux et Niestlé.

Haüschen, H., Kueng, P., & Wismer, D. (1998). *Informationstechnologien in Schweizer Unternehmen* (Vol. 5, Series in Computer Science). Fribourg: Institut d'Informatique de l'Université de Fribourg.

Healy, L., Stefano, P., & Hoyles, C. (1995). Making sense of groups, computers, and mathematics. *Cognition and Instruction [Special issue: Processes and products of collaborative problem solving : some interdisciplinary perspectives], 13*(4), 505–523.

Heath, S. B. (1999). Rethinking youth transition. Essay review of *Everyday Courage: The Lives and Stories of Urban Teenagers. Human Development, 42,* 376–382.

Hennesy, S., & McCormick, R. (1994). The general problem-solving process in technology education. In F. Banks (Ed.), *Teaching technology* (pp. 94–108). New York: Routledge.

Hoc, J. M. (1987). *Psychologie de la planification*. Grenoble: Presses Universitaires de Grenoble.

Howe, C., & Tolmie, A. (1999). Productive interaction in the context of computer-supported. In K. Littleton & P. Light (Eds.), *Learning with computers: Analysing productive interaction* (pp. 24–45). London: Routledge.

Howe, C., Tolmie, A., Green, K., & Mackenzie, M. (1995). Peer collaboration and conceptual growth in physic : task influences on children's understanding of heating and cooling. *Cognition and Instruction, 13*(4), 483–503.

Hoyles, C., Healy, L., & Pozzi, S. (1992). Interdependance and autonomy : aspects of groupwork with computers. *Learning and Instruction, 2,* 239–257.

Hoyles, C., Healy, L., & Sutherland, R. (1990). *The role of peer group discussion in mathematical environments*. London: University of London, Institute of Education, Departement of Mathematics, Statistics and Computing.

Hundeide, K. (1985). The tacit background of children's jugements. In J. V. Wertsch (Ed.), *Cuture, communication and cognition: Vygotskian perspectives*. Cambridge, UK: Cambridge University Press.

Hutmacher, W. (1996). *Compétences-clés pour l'Europe. Rapport général d'un Symposium du Conseil de l'Europe, Berne 1996*. Berne: Conférence des Directeurs de l'Instruction Publique.

Iannaccone, A., & Perret-Clermont, A. N. (1993). Qu'est-ce qui s'apprend? Qu'est-ce qui se développe? In J. Wassmann & P. R. Dasen (Eds.), *Les savoirs quotidiens. Les approches cognitives dans le dialogue interdisciplinaire* (pp. 235–258). Fribourg (Suisse): Presses Universitaires de Fribourg.

Jackson, A. C., Fletscher, B., & Messer, D. J. (1992). When talking doesn't help: An investigation of microcomputer-based group problem solving. *Learning and Instruction, 2,* 185–197.

Järvelä, S. (1995). The cognitive apprenticeship model in a technologically rich learning environment: Interpreting the learning interaction. *Learning and Instruction, 5,* 237–259.

Kaiser, C., Perret-Clermont, A.-N., & Perret, J.-F. (2000). Do I choose?: Attribution and control in students of a technical school. In J. Perrig & A. Grob (Eds.),

Control of human behavior, mental processes, and consciousness (pp. 427–442). Mahwah, NJ: Erlbaum.

Kaiser, C., Perret-Clermont, A.-N., Perret, J.-F., & Golay Schilter, D. (1997). *Apprendre un métier technique aujourd'hui : représentation des apprenants* (Documents de recherche No. 10). Séminaire de psychologie, Université de Neuchâtel.

Kaiser, C., & Rastoldo, F. (1995). Adolescents et adolescentes face au monde du travail. *Education et Recheches* (1), 70–88.

Kaufman, J. (1975). L'observation des élèves par leurs professeurs. *L'orientation scolaire et professionnelle, 4,* 51–76.

Kiesler, C.-A. (1971). *The psychology of commitment : Experiments linking behavior to belief.* New York: Academic Press.

Lamamra, N., & Masdonati, J. (2009) *Arrêter une formation professionnelle: Mots et maux d'apprenti·e·s.* Lausanne: Editions Antipodes.

Latour, B. (1996). Sur la pratique des théoriciens. In J.-M. Barbier (Ed.), *Savoirs théoriques et savoirs d'action.* Paris: Presses Universitaires de France.

Lattard, A. (2000). Permanence et mutations du système dual. Où va le modèle allemand? *Revue Française de Pédagogie, 131,* 75–85.

Lave, J. (1991). Situated learning in communities of practice. In J. M. Levine & S. D. Teasley (Eds.), *Perspectives on socially shared cognition* (pp. 63–82). Washington, DC: American Psychological Association.

Le Boterf, G. (1994). *De la compétence. Essai sur un attracteur étrange.* Paris: Les Editions d'Organisations.

Le Poultier, F. (1986). *La norme d'internalité dans le travail social.* Paris: Presses Universitaires de France.

Lebahar, J.-C. (1987). L'influence de l'apprentissage des machines-outils à commandes numériques sur la représentation de l'usinage et ses niveaux de formalisation. *Le travail Humain, 50*(3), 237–249.

Lebahar, J.-C. (2007). Graphisme technique et automatismes. Entre le naturel et l'artificiel, l'analyse du travail cognitif. In P. Rabardel & A. Weill-Fassina (Eds.), *Le dessin technique: apprentissage, utilisation, évolutions.* Paris: Hermès.

Léchevin, J. P., Le Joliff, G., & Lanoé, D. (1994). *Vivre les «nouvelles technologies»: perception et vécu de la «charge de travail»: une évaluation au travers d'une série d'entretiens avec les utilisateurs.* Paris: La Documentation française.

Leplat, J. (1993). Ergonomie et activités collectives. *Revue roumaine de Psychologie, 37*(2), 103–118.

Light, P., & Blaye, A. (1989). Computer-based learning: The social dimension. In H. Foot & M. Morgan & R. Shute (Eds.), *Children helping children.* Chichester, UK: Wiley.

Light, P., & Perret-Clermont, A.-N. (1986). Social construction of logical structures or social construction of meaning. *Dossiers de Psychologie, 27,* Université de Neuchâtel.

Light, P., & Perret-Clermont, A. N. (1989). Social context effects in learning and testing. In D. Gellatly, D. Rogers, & J. A. Sloboda (Eds.), *Cognition and social worlds* (pp. 99–112). Oxford, UK: Oxford University Press.

Linhart, D., Perriault, J., & Fouquet, A. (Eds.). (1992). *Le travail en puces.* Paris: Presses Universitaires de France.

Littleton, K., & Light, P. (Eds.). (1999). *Learning with computers: Analysing productive interaction.* London: Routledge.

Lorenzi-Cioldi, F. (1988). *Individus dominants et groupes dominés; images masculines et féminines.* Grenoble: Presses Universitaires de Grenoble.

Ludvigsten, S. R., Havnes, A., & Lahn, L. C. (2003). Workplace learning across activity systems: a case study of sales engineers. In T. Tuomi-Gröhn & Y. Engeström (Eds.), *Between school and work: New perspectives on transfer and boundary-crossing* (pp. 291–310). Amsterdam: Pergamon.

Luginbuhl, J. E. R., Crowe, D. H., & Kahan, J. P. (1990). Attributions causales de la réussite et de l'échec. In J.-C. Deschamps & A. Clémence (Eds.), *L'attribution: causalité et explication au quotidien* (pp. 163–184). Neuchâtel: Delachaux & Niestlé.

Mandl, H., Gruber, H., & Renkl, A. (1996). Communities of practice toward expertise : social foundation of university instruction. In P. B. Baltes & U. M. Staudinger (Eds.), *Interactive minds, life-span perspectives on the social foundation of cognition* (pp. 394–411). Cambridge, UK: Cambridge University Press.

Marro-Clément, P. (1997). *Résoudre à deux un problème de fabrication assistée par ordinateur: analyse interlocutoire d'une séquence de travail* (Documents de recherche No. 11). Séminaire de psychologie, Université de Neuchâtel.

Martin, L. M. W. (1992). *Technical and symbolic Knoledge in CNC Machining : a study of technical workers of different backgrounds.* Berkeley: National Center for Research in Vocational Education, University of California.

Martin, L. M. W. (1995). Linking thought and setting in the study of work place learning. In L. M. W. Martin & M. Nelson & E. Tobach (Eds.), *Sociocultural psychology. Theory and practice of doing and knowing.* Cambridge, UK: Cambridge University Press.

Martin, L. M. W., & Scribner, S. (1991). Laboratory for cognitive studies of work: A case study of the intellectual implications of a new technology. *Teachers College Record, 92*(4).

Mayen, P. (2000). Interactions tutorales au travail et négociations formatives. *Recherche et Formation, 35,* 59–73.

McLane, J. B., & Wertsch, J. V. (1986). Child-child and adult-child interaction : a vygotskian study of dyadic problem solving. *Quarterly Newsletter of the Laboratory of Comparative Human Cognition, 8*(3), 98–105.

Meirieu, P., & Develay, M. (1996). *Le transfert de connaisances en formation initiale et en formation continue.* Lyon: Centre Régional de Documentation Pédagogique.

Mellana, J. (1883). *Il était une fois une école ...* Sainte-Croix: Ecole Technique.

Mercer, N., & Sams, C. (2006). Teaching children how to use language to solve maths problems. *Language and Education, 20*(6), 507–528.

Mercer, N. (1995). *The guided construction of knowledge.* London: Multilingual Matters.

Mercer, N. (1996). The quality of talk in children's collaborative activity in the classroom. *Learning and Instruction, 6*(4), 359–377.

Mercer, N., & Wegerif, R. (1999). Is exploratory talk productive talk? In K. Littleton & P. Light (Eds.), *Learning with computers: Analysing productive Interaction* (pp. 79–101). London: Routledge.

Mercer, N., Wegerif, R., et al. (1999). Children's talk and the development of reasoning in the classroom. *British Educational Research Journal, 25*(1), 95–111.

Mercer, N. F. E. (1992). How do teachers help children to learn?: An analysis of teachers interventions in computer-based activities. *Learning and Instruction, 2,* 339–355.

Merri, M. (Ed). (2007). *Activité humaine et conceptualisation: questions à Gérard Vergnaud.* Toulouse: Presses Universitaires du Mirail.

Merrill, D. C. (1995). Tutoring: Guided learning by doing. *Cognition and Instruction, 13*(3), 315–372.

Miyake, N., & Norman, D. A. (1979). To ask a question one must know enough to know what is not known. *Journal of Verbal Learning and Verbal Behavior, 18,* 357–364.

Monteil, J.-M. (1989). *Éduquer et former. Perspectives psycho-sociales.* Grenoble: Presses Universitaires de Grenoble.

de Montmollin, M. (1984). *L'intelligence de la tâche.* Berne: P. Lang.

Moscovici, S., & Paicheler, G. (1973). Travail, individu et groupe. In S. Moscovici (Ed.), *Introduction à la psychologie sociale.* Paris: Larousse.

Moyne, A. (1982). *Le travail autonome. Vers une autre pédagogie.* Paris: Fleurus.

Muller, N. (1996). *Transmission de savoirs techniques: La relation maître-élève-savoir dans la perspective d'une psychologie socio-culturelle* (Documents de recherche No. 8). Séminaire de psychologie, Université de Neuchâtel.

Muller, N., & Perret-Clermont, A.-N. (1999). Negotiating identities and meanings in the transmission of knowledge : analysis of interactions in the context of a knowledge exchange network. In J. Bliss & R. Säljö & P. Light (Eds.), *Learning sites, social and technological resources for learning* (pp. 47–60). London: Pergamon.

Muller Mirza, N., & Perret-Clermont, A.-N. (Eds.). (2009). *Argumentation and Education. Theoretical Foundations and Practices.* Dordrecht: Springer.

Nelson-Le Gall, S. (1985). *Help seeking in learning.* Pittsburgh, PA: Learning Research and Development Center, University of Pittsburg.

Parmentier, C., & Vivet, M. (1992). Nouvelles technologies : production, gestion ou formation ? Le cas de la robotique pédagogique. *Education permanente, 111,* 71–86.

Pastré, P. (2005). *Apprendre par la simulation. De l'analyse du travail aux apprentissages professionnels.* Toulouse: Octares.

Pastré, P. (2007) Activité et apprentissage en didactique professionnelle. In M. Durand & M. Fabre (Eds.), *Les situations de formation entre savoirs, problèmes et activités.* Paris: L'harmattan.

Pastré, P., Mayen, P., & Vergnaud, G. (2006): La didactique professionnelle. *Revue Française de Pédagogie, 154,* 145–198.

Pelpel, P., & Troger, V. (1993). *Histoire de l'enseignement technique.* Paris: Hachette Education.

Perraudeau, M. (1998). *Echanger pour apprendre. L'entretien critique.* Paris : Armand Colin.

Perrenoud, P. (1994). *Métier d'élève et sens du travail scolaire.* Paris: ESF éditeur.

Perret, J.-F. (1978). Une expérience de «travail indépendant» : quelques réflexions psychopédagogiques. *Cahiers de la section des Sciences de l'Education. Université de Genève* (6), 1–18.

Perret, J.-F. (1985). *Comprendre l'écriture des nombres.* Berne: Peter Lang.

Perret, J.-F. (1995). *Les élèves de l'école technique de Sainte-Croix : données quantitatives à la recherche d'éléments de description et de comparaison signifiants* (Documents de recherche No. 5). Séminaire de psychologie, Université de Neuchâtel.

Perret, J.-F. (1997a). *Aperçu des travaux du séminaire de recherche : interactions sociales et acquisition de savoir-faire techniques* (Documents de recherche No. 14). Séminaire de psychologie, Université de Neuchâtel.

Perret, J.-F. (1997b). *Nouvelles technologies dans une Ecole Technique : logique d'équipement et logique de formation* (Documents de recherche No. 6). Séminaire de psychologie, Université de Neuchâtel.

Perret, J.-F. (2001). Concevoir une formation par alternance: points de repère. *Dossiers de psychologie. Université de Neuchâtel* (No. 57).

Perret, J.-F., & Perrenoud, P. (1990). *Qui définit le curriculum pour qui?* Cousset, Fribourg: IRDP/Delval.

Perret, J.-F., Perret-Clermont, A.-N., & Golay Schilter, D. (1998). Penser et réaliser un usinage à l'ordinateur: approche socio-cognitive d'une situation de formation professionnelle. *Didaskalia. Recherches sur la communication et l'apprentissage des sciences et des techniques* (13), 9–32.

Perret, J.-F., & Runtz-Christian, E. (Eds.). (1993). *Les manuels font-ils école?* Cousset: Del Val/Neuchâtel, IRDP.

Perret-Clermont, A.-N. (1980). *Social interaction and cognitive development in children.* London: Academic Press. Available at: http://doc.rero.ch/record/12854?ln=fr.

Perret-Clermont, A.-N. (1992). Transmitting knowledge : implicit negociations in the teacher-student relationship. In F.-K. Oser, A. Dick, & J.-L. Patry (Eds.), *Effective and responsible teaching* (pp. 329–341). San Francisco: Jossey-Bass.

Perret-Clermont, A.-N. (2004). Thinking Spaces of the Young. In A.-N. Perret-Clermont, C. Pontecorvo, L. B. Resnick, T. Zittoun, & B. Burge (Eds.), *Joining society. Social interaction and learning in adolescence and youth* (pp. 3–10). Cambridge, UK: Cambridge University Press.

Perret-Clermont, A.-N., Carugati, F., & Oates, J. (2004). A socio-cognitive perspective on learning and cognitive development. In J. Oates & A. Grayson (Eds.), *Cognitive and language development in children* (pp. 303–332). London: Blackwell.

Perret-Clermont, A. N., & Perret, J.-F. (2006). Apprendre quand le métier change. *Education Permanente, 2,* 11–13.

Perret-Clermont, A. N., Perret, J. F., & Bell, N. (1991). The social construction of meaning and cognitive activity in elementary school children. In L. B. Resnick, J. M. Levine, & S. D. Teasley (Eds.), *Perspectives on socially shared cognition* (pp. 41–62). Washington, DC: American Psychological Association.

Perret-Clermont, A.-N., & Nicolet, M. (2001). *Interagir et connaître. Enjeux et régulations sociales dans le développement cognitif.* Paris: L'Harmattan.